RUGS

*"Themistocles replied that a man's discourse was
like unto a rich Persian carpet, the beautiful
figures and patterns of which can be shown only
by spreading and extending it out . . ."*
PLUTARCH, Lives

RUGS

DESIGNS • PATTERNS • PROJECTS

MARY ELIZABETH JOHNSON

in collaboration with

MARY JO SHERRILL

SONDRA ALBERT

CINDA SILER

Oxmoor House, Inc. Birmingham

Copyright © 1979 by Oxmoor House, Inc.
Book Division of the Progressive Farmer Company
Publisher of *Southern Living*®, *Progressive Farmer*®, and *Decorating and Craft Ideas*® magazines.
P.O. Box 2463, Birmingham, Alabama 35202

Eugene Butler	*Chairman of the Board*
Emory Cunningham	*President and Publisher*
Vernon Owens, Jr.	*Senior Executive Vice President*
Roger McGuire	*Executive Vice President*

Conceived, edited and published by Oxmoor House, Inc., under the direction of:

Don Logan	*Vice President and General Manager*
Gary McCalla	*Editor, Southern Living*®
John Logue	*Editor-in-Chief*
Mary Elizabeth Johnson	*Senior Editor, Crafts*
Mary Jo Sherrill	*Associate Editor, Crafts*
Jerry Higdon	*Production Manager*
Mary Jean Haddin	*Copy Chief*

Rugs: Designs, Patterns, Projects

Designers: Viola Andrycich, Steve Logan, June Shrum
Photographers: Bill Hawkins, David Matthews, Steve Logan
Illustrator: Don K. Smith
Consultants: Annabel Hollingsworth, Hooking; Charlotte Hagood, Stenciling and Weaving; Louise Madden, Crochet, Knitting, Needlepoint; George Courson, Bordered Rugs
Interiors designed by: Andrea Carmichael, Sandra Hood, William Dry, Elaine Kartus, Ann Schuler Aird
Project designers: Charlotte Hagood, Lawrence Rives, Susan Witt, Peyton Carmichael, Carol Tipton, Jane Lorendo, Annabel Hollingsworth, Barbara Christopher, Jo Kittinger, Charlotte Foley, Margaret Masters, George Ollsen, Susan Harris, Rebecca S. Andrews, Eva Roy, Zuelia Ann Hurt
Locations provided by: Mrs. Robert H. Adams, Mr. and Mrs. R. Glenn Carmicheal, Dr. and Mrs. Joseph M. Donald, Jr., Mr. and Mrs. Allen E. Willey, Mr. and Mrs. Hobart McWhorter, Mrs. Inez Jackson, Mr. and Mrs. Louis A. Prosch, Jr., Mr. and Mrs. David H. Gilchrist, Mr. and Mrs. P.M. Waldrop, Dr. and Mrs. Rick Becker, Dr. and Mrs. Patrick Mills
Special help provided by: Betty Taylor, Linda Bagwell, Richard S. Riley, Jane Joyner, Sarah Jane Ball, Kay Savage, Virginia Turnbull, Dr. and Mrs. Alvaro Ronderos, Tom Hagood

Photographic credits: Pages 19, 23, 132, 149—Transworld; Page 24—The Bettman Archive, Inc.

Library of Congress Catalog Number: 78-59616
ISBN: 0-8487-0490-8

Manufactured in the United States of America
First printing

CONTENTS

LIVING WITH RUGS

There was once a beautiful woman named Arachne, who lived in Lydia, in what is now modern Turkey. Arachne was famous for her skill at weaving exquisite rugs and tapestries. She eventually became so enamored of her own prowess that she challenged Minerva, the goddess of arts and needlecrafts, to a contest. The work of the goddess was fine but Arachne's was enchanting. The girl had the misfortune to win the contest. This made Minerva so jealous that she threw her spindle at Arachne, and punished her presumption by turning her into a spider. (This, of course, is why spiders, weavers as they are, are "arachnids.")

This Graeco-Roman myth parallels a similar story of Egyptian origin, establishing rug making as one of the most ancient crafts in the world. Today when textiles made by machines threaten to overwhelm society with conformity, rug making has again assumed a favored place among the crafts which provide the satisfaction of working with one's hands. As ancients created rugs both for warmth and beauty, so we today create rugs not just to fill a space but to lend a touch of individuality amid a host of mass-produced items.

Fortunately for modern rug makers, the craft has been streamlined dramatically. Manufactured backing can be bought by the yard, ready for tufting, hooking or stitching. Ready-made yarns, felts and woolen strips supplement the leftovers from sewing baskets and castoffs from wardrobe closets which were traditional sources for materials. Speedhooks, braiding aids, metal crochet hooks and powerful sewing machines help the contemporary rug maker. And, the techniques of rug making are simple crafts which can be mastered in just a few hours. The availability of materials and tools from craft shops and catalogs open a world of creativity to anyone who cares to try.

This dramatic rug fools the eye by making the room appear larger than it is. The glass-topped dining table provides an uninterrupted view of this classic Dhurrie rug.

RUGS AS INSULATION

No one knows for sure, but the first rugs were probably invented by nomadic tent dwellers in Asia Minor to provide insulation from the cold. They anchored tufts of wool or fur in a fabric backing to create a flexible, long-wearing alternative to animal skins—practical in another way because it was readily obtainable without killing the animal. When used to cover the earthen floor of their tents, the rugs provided warmth and comfort underfoot. At bedtime the whole family could roll up in them, tufted-side-in, for protection against the chill of the night. The rugs were easily bundled up when the tribe moved, and opened quickly in the new campsite. They were also hung on the walls of the tent to furnish protection from the slicing winds of the desert.

The insulating features of rugs are not lost on the present-day ecologist. Like fur, the tufts of fabric or yarn trap small pockets of air to create a protective layer identical to nature's own heat-retentive devices. With the recent public urgings to protect the dwindling supply of natural fuels have come recommendations for using rugs to prevent drafty floors. And nothing is more inviting than a thick cozy rug on a cold day. Modern interior designers recommend beautiful rugs as wall hangings on cold north walls, as a decorative way of trapping an insulating layer of air for protection against winter's direct blasts.

An added insulating feature of rugs is the protection from noise. City dwellers have long been aware that rugs or carpets on floors insure against complaints about noise from neighbors in the apartment below them. However, in single family houses, the noise-insulating properties of rugs are just as effective for second floor (particularly children's) rooms.

Rugs can insulate not only the senses but the feelings. Since a home should be designed to afford protection and retreat from the pressures

of affairs outside, rugs and carpets can play a significant role. Modern homes built with hard surfaces and furnished with metal, plastics and glass may look angular and cold and can reflect sound, without the cushion of carpets underfoot. Texture and color as well as the luxury of the muffled step provide a feeling of warmth and refuge. The eye perceives colorful designs and soft texture as cheery and inviting, even luxurious. If a man's home is his castle, rugs contribute to that perception of ease more readily than any other single furnishing.

RUGS DEFINE SPACE

Considerations of practicality and comfort can be combined with the overall design scheme to gain another important benefit—that of defining the space. This is not only an advantage in the barn-like rooms of older houses, but also in modern multi-use rooms such as combined dining rooms, studio apartments, and the newly popular loft dwellings in converted industrial buildings. The rug used for definition can provide a sense of order and emphasis that makes an unwieldy space look comfortable and inviting.

With the current trend toward modularity, carpets and rugs have actually come into use for seating as in earlier times. Banquettes covered in the same carpet as the floor and decorated with pillows combine clean good looks with softly understated luxury. The conversation pit, one of the most dramatic innovations among modern design schemes, is achieved by lowering the floor level of a banquette arrangement. Reversing the floor level to create a covered platform with coordinated seating can be equally effective, particularly if there is a view to be seen. And nothing could be more inviting than a window seat or an alcove with seating and walls covered in soft carpet and sprinkled with cushions.

Sleeping areas reap many benefits from the delineating rug as well. Everyone is familiar with the bedside rug to greet the feet on a frosty morning. But now modern furnishings have

Two rugs that are very similar, yet not identical, solve decorating problems in a large room. The rugs define seating areas, leaving an uncovered area that leads to an adjoining sunroom.

gone a step further with the narrow carpet-covered platform that surrounds the bed, rising up around it to provide shelf space for books or television set, and a handy backrest from any angle. The platform frames the bed, setting it apart as a place in which to relax and spend one's quiet hours. A similar feeling can be achieved with a sleeping alcove by continuing the carpet right up the wall and even over the ceiling. The result is a cave-like haven, an inviting spot for retreat.

Another variation which is practical for a small bedroom is carpeting the walls, preferably with liberal padding underneath. The inevitable scuffed-and-scratched painted wall, caused by traffic in the crowded space, is totally eliminated. It is a good solution for a child's bedroom that serves as a playroom as well.

Throwing a rug over the bed provides an attractive way to preserve a delicate or valuable rug, and if the rug is flexible it can act as a cover, providing extra warmth as well. A dramatic effect might be achieved by making a rug to cover the bed, and a coordinated one to hang on the wall behind it to form a comfortable backrest-headboard combination. A very inexpensive custom headboard can be achieved by covering a plywood slab with a remnant of the floor carpet and fastening it to the wall at the head of the bed.

Finding a way to break up space with rugs doesn't have to be all practicality. Perhaps the most fun in decorating is deciding what features of the house or what furniture are favorites, and emphasizing them. Naturally a fireplace is going to be a focal point both visually and psychologically. It deserves the accent of a beautiful rug before it to invite family and friends within its circle of warmth. Likewise a wide entry hall can be a gracious reception area with the correct choice in floor covering. And if a family heirloom is attractive, don't put it in a dark corner. Design a room around it and put an elegant rug in front so no one will overlook it.

Accenting with rugs can help overcome difficulties in the design of a house. If a passageway looks well-traveled and inviting, traffic naturally follows. Steering the traffic through the house is simplified with a carefully planned pattern of rugs on the floor. Make sure no one goes down the back hall past the paint closet by omitting the rug there, or using a quiet pattern in dark tones. Stop the rug well before the entrance from dining room to kitchen if guests are encouraged to keep their distance from the cook.

CARPETS AND/OR RUGS

Historically, the words "rug" and "carpet" have not been defined exclusively. "Carpet" has in the past referred to large pieces, especially those used on the floor. The word "rug" generally referred to smaller items used for purposes other than floor coverings, but made with similar techniques, although this differentiation was not hard and fast. For instance, small rugs were used as coverings on tables, beds or walls, as portieres, for coverings similar to afghans—lap rugs, carriage rugs, and upholstery. In discussing Orientals, the two words have been used interchangeably.

In modern usage "carpet" has come to signify more generally the seamless wall-to-wall covering, but can also refer to very large pieces which cover the greater part of the floor space in a room. The term "rug," which was not common until the Ninteenth Century, has come to signify smaller pieces for specific areas, but it is also acceptable as a general term for any floor covering.

The decision, in a modern home, between carpets and rugs is dependent on many factors, to which one's personal preferences must be added. Naturally, one of the first considerations is the condition of the flooring. If it is beautifully finished and care does not pose a major problem, then any consideration of wall-to-wall carpeting should be dropped. If, on the other hand, either the floors are not particularly attractive or the family schedule does not allow for extensive upkeep of hardwood finishes, then wall-to-wall carpeting can provide an excellent solution.

The cherished Kerman color and pattern of this contemporary copy are the perfect accent for fine antique mahogany furniture. Quiet dining is insured with the thick pile that muffles the sounds of chair movement. In a dining room, be sure to choose a rug size that is generous enough to prevent chair legs from hooking the edge when the chair is slipped away from the table.

If the life-style of the family is more formal in winter and more relaxed in the summer, it is preferable that the look of a room change with the seasons. A large rug that covers most of the floor space can be used in winter, with a summer replacement made of informal materials such as rush or sisal. Changing floor coverings with the seasons can prolong the life of a rug, and is definitely recommended if the piece is particularly valuable. A sturdy rug can be used for the season when the family schedule is more active, and it can be replaced with a more delicate rug when traffic is lighter.

PLAN YOUR FLOOR COVERING FIRST

Unfortunately, the floor covering is usually the last article considered in planning a room. Since it is the setting for the rest of the decor, it should really be first on the list of elements that will go to make up the overall design. Be aware of the following considerations when planning a floor treatment.

Function

The first thing to do when choosing a floor covering is to decide on the purpose of it. Must the room look larger? Should separate areas of the room be used for separate activities? Does one particular feature need emphasis or de-emphasis? What is the historical theme, if any, of the house and its furnishings? Will the floor covering need to contribute color, warmth, intricacy or texture to the total picture? These questions must all be answered before the design of the rug or carpet can be approached.

Once decisions are made about the function a rug is expected to perform in a room, it is time to look at ways to accomplish that objective. Each element the rug must contribute should be examined to be certain that it will be done properly, and in proportion with the rest of the features of the room.

If a small room needs to look more spacious, a relatively light color, plain or muted pattern, and large size will be needed. A larger room can accommodate deep, rich colors, complicated textures or designs, or several smaller rugs. If certain features should be defined, decide whether color or texture or an elaborate design will focus attention most successfully. Be careful that the rug does not overpower the point to be defined: a brilliant Oriental pattern in front of an exquisite antique breakfront may overshadow it. Traffic patterns leading in all directions, or accents that fight for attention make the room look unsettled.

On the other hand, rugs may be a focal point themselves. Don't be afraid to use them to make bold strokes in a simple room, or to liven up a quiet color scheme. But remember, rugs make very big statements. It is necessary to plan carefully the accent they will give so that they won't be fighting with other parts of the design.

If a rug must lend the room warmth, look into the warm colors of the spectrum—shades of red or yellow. Texture should be longish or even fluffy. An impression of warmth can also be achieved with an intricate design. On the other hand, if the warm elements of the design will come from some other features in the room, or if a cool overall look is desired, seek out flat surfaces, colors in the green and blue families, and little or no pattern. But if the floor covering must simply provide a cohesive background for the rest of the room, it can be achieved with subtle textures, small repeated patterns, and neutral colors just slightly darker in tone than the major colors of large expanses in the room, such as wall and drapery color.

Design

Once objectives and ways to achieve them have been considered, think about the designs for the rugs themselves. Start by searching in the local library for books on home decorating, historical homes, and Oriental rugs. Magazines on the home, both American and European, are also good sources. Look for ways in which the objectives have been achieved by other people. If the rug is to be handmade, ideas for the design can come from books on such subjects as art collections, quilts, stamps, flags and stained glass. Even paintings and sculpture can be reproduced in rug designs very successfully, particularly for wall hangings.

Another souce for design ideas is the family itself. Think about the daily activities that might lend themselves to designs, such as children's drawings, sports motifs, pets, hobbies, household implements, collections, even family history. An interesting line can be stolen from any object, repeated, and turned into an abstract design. The fanciful designs of Oriental rugs reflect an interest in the daily lives of the people and their activities. They picture soldiers, houses, castles, birds, flowers—whatever the gaze of the rug maker happened to fall upon

The stunning diagonal design of this cut pile rug unifies an intimate conversation nook.

when looking up from the loom.

Of course, nature is one of the richest design sources. Plants, birds, and animals have appeared in rug designs throughout the centuries. Abstract designs can be copied from the tracing a shadow makes, or water droplets, the texture of wood or stone, leaves, grass stems, tree branches, even the patterns that rain makes in the earth. Take a good look around to see what appeals to the eye. No finely developed artistic talent is needed to make up a design. Just recognizing a line or shape that catches the eye is enough. Everyone admires the beauty of nature. Designing from it simply means looking a little closer and picking out one or two interesting elements.

The elements of any rug design are color, texture and size. If the purpose the rug is to serve has been well thought out, then these elements will already have begun to fall in place. Reconsider them as you study the pattern you have chosen and decide how they can be used most effectively to execute the pattern.

COLOR

Color is the most important element. Neutral colors are classic and will be livable over a long period of time. Bright colors can be used sparingly, because they make strong statements. In arranging the colors in the pattern, bear in mind the usual effect on the eye. Cool shades enlarge, soothe, recede. Bright colors will stimulate, warm, dominate. Dark colors give shade, depth and quiet.

Since color is a function of light, consider the kind of light in the room and adjust the design accordingly. It was once traditional for interior decorators to use warm colors in north rooms and cool colors in rooms with southern exposures. Now, with so many families absent from their homes during most of the day, it may be more appropriate to check colors in the type of electric lighting that will be used in a room. When in doubt, a classic combination of colors, such as those found in Oriental rugs, will stand the test of time. They coordinate with many changing decors over the years, continuing to ornament the room as it changes.

"Wave length" is the appropriate title given an unforgettable rug designed by Edward Fields. Neutral walls and furnishings in this large open room provide a perfect backdrop for the electrifying colors and design. In addition to defining spaces, area rugs add flair to, and can even be the focal point of, a decorating scheme. The deep pile, softens the starkness of the wood flooring, glass walls, and vast spaces.

TEXTURE

The next element to consider is texture. A pattern will be more highly defined on a flat texture, so that if the rug is decorated with a large, bright pattern, it may outweigh the normally spacious, cool effect of the flat texture. It is always a good idea to give some texture to a flat rug, such as hooking the loops in a hooked rug in several different directions. This provides a relatively flat surface with subtle dynamics.

Soft, fluffy surfaces tend to blur the edges of a design, so do not plan intricate patterns with this texture. A shadowy, impressionistic look will be much more successful. The longer the pile of the rug, the more intense the feeling of closeness in a room; therefore, proceed carefully if the room is small.

Try using pile in just portions of the design. Raise some areas higher than others—this technique is called "carving." This is particularly good for wall hangings, where the pile won't be flattened. Or use unusual materials, such as uneven yarns, bits of rope, metallics, even small stones or other objects. The ancients used threads of gold and silver to decorate their rugs for royalty, or sometimes pearls and fine gems. Many modern artists use combined techniques and unusual materials to give their creations added textural interest.

In the case of hooked rugs, cut the loops in some parts of the design to create a plush effect. Since this will make the color more intense, plan the color scheme of the design accordingly. An interesting informal effect is the addition of pile to hooked rugs by leaving the tails of the wool strips on the top so that they form an uneven shaggy effect.

Both of the rugs on these two pages are off-white—it is the texture of each that makes it distinctive, and that makes them entirely different from one another. The formality of the setting at the left is reinforced with an elegant, velvety-surface rug that has a carved floral design around the outer edges. The small study at the right is brightened with a home-spun, coarse-grain Irish woven rug. The rhythmic plain weave of the large fibers helps to create a richly informal, but not at all casual, environment.

SIZE

The size *of the pattern* on the rug will expand or diminish the space. The function of the pattern depends on the role the rug plays in the total design of the room. If it is to perform as a neutral background, the rug should have little or no pattern. If it should add depth or dimension, a medium-sized intricate pattern will solve the problem. But if the rug will be the brilliant emphasis of a room, make the design a big one.

The best way to decide *how large* a rug should be is by marking out the dimensions on the floor with tape, heavy string, or some wide strips of paper. If the rug is to be rather small, make a pattern in brown wrapping paper and tape that to the floor. Then stand back and visualize how that area will look when it is covered. Walk around the room and view it from all angles. Check doors to see if they must be trimmed at the bottom to clear a high pile. Slide chairs away from tables to make certain they will not hook the edges of the rug when people rise from the table. Decide where the dominant pattern will fall by drawing it on the brown paper, or cutting out the shape of the pattern and centering it. The effect will be lost entirely if it falls under a table or sofa.

Make adjustments in the size and then measure the markings carefully. In the case of purchased rugs, approximate the standard sizes available, and then rearrange the room to see if the rug can be accomodated. For hand-made rugs, use the measurements as an aid to ordering the materials.

When is a rug not a rug? When it's a painted floor cloth! The advantage of a floor cloth is that you can have exactly the design you want at much less expense than with a custom-woven rug. And, as illustrated, floor cloths are not limited to an informal decorating scheme. The graceful formal pattern of the floor cloth illustrated was adapted from the fabric on the sofa.

MAKING YOUR OWN RUG

To insure that your rug project will be a rewarding experience, take time to do some clear-headed advance thinking. Remember, for example, that the larger the rug planned, the longer the project will be. Personal experience and the level of skill must be taken into account. Small projects are recommended for beginners. First, try making something in the same technique to be used for the rug, such as a pillow, a small wall hanging, a book bag or a handbag. Next try a small area rug. Leaping into a large project without knowing if the skill involved will be satisfying to you personally can be an easy road to discouragement.

It is also important to consider the expense. Rugs can be big investments, depending on the size and the kind of materials that will be used. A project left incomplete for lack of funds can be very disconcerting. Be realistic, and avoid disappointment.

The size of the rug will determine the portability of the project. If a frame will be needed, then your life-style must allow you to be sedentary for several hours at a time. If a portable project is more suited to your daily activities, consider making the rug in small pieces and then joining it together. Otherwise, a small rug should be considered. However, even small rugs get heavier as they near completion, meaning that the very last portion of the rug will probably need to be finished at home.

Next it is time to consider the kind of techniques to use for a rug project. Personal preference will dictate to some extent the particular technique chosen. If you are already accomplished in one technique, don't be afraid to try another. All are relatively easy, and success in handwork of one sort can be transferred easily to another without trouble.

Think about pattern definition. If the pattern will be intricate, the length of the pile must be short enough to give it the delineation needed. Also consider the durability that will be required in the area where the rug will be used. One solution is combining techniques, using the more fragile technique for the center design, and a sturdier technique for the border where the wear will be heaviest.

In the case of the actual design of the rug, again consider personal skill and the pattern definition. But most important, don't match the design of curtains or slipcovers, unless the project is a small, fast one. With good care, rugs last far longer than other furnishings. Choose a pattern that will survive several changes of decor.

Once the size, technique and design have been determined, look for the proper materials. It is important to spend some time on this and get the best quality and color range possible. Rugs are big investments. A choice of color that is not quite right will be regretted over the years. Write away for catalogs, research special dyes that may be available, and test the materials. It is a good idea to make a swatch using samples of the materials. In this way the technique and color can be checked for pattern definition and coordination with the rest of the room. A test swatch is also an excellent way to estimate the amount of materials that will be needed. Measure the swatch and then measure the amount

The rugs shown on these two pages are made from carpeting, pieced together to form borders around a central field.

The room at the left is large enough to handle easily the saturation of color provided by a huge rug that matches the wall coloring. Note the use of two accent colors in the three borders, repeated by the woodwork, the sofa fabric, and the plants.

The room above works on a different principle— the border of the rug, rather than the field, matches the soft yellow wall color. The floral fabric of the wing chair has accents of the same coral used for the rug field. It is a gently elegant, under-stated look, but full of impact.

of material used to make it. By multiplying according to the size of the rug, and adding a bit more for spoilage and overage, the exact amount of materials that will be needed can be gauged. This is particularly important if the materials at hand must be dyed or if they will be ordered. The same materials may not be available later, so order a sufficient amount at the start.

Check the colorfast properties and shrinkage factors of materials. This is especially important for those that will be used in rugs which will get heavy wear, but it is a good idea to check for all projects, just so that the aging of the materials will not be a surprise. Some fading is desirable because the look becomes softer and richer. But if several of the materials age well while others, perhaps man-made fibers, do not, the color balance of the design may be ruined.

A hand-dyed rug, which is apt to run, would not be suitable in an entryway where moisture is present. Likewise, rugs that will be used over carpets should be constructed with colorfast materials to avoid spotting the carpet in damp weather. Colors that run should not be used next to lighter shades in a design, or the definition of the design will blur.

Save unusual materials for special effects. It's fun to make a small rug out of something like gift-ribbons, for instance, but use it for a Christmas Tree skirt rather than on the floor of the children's room. Imaginative hooked rugs using fur and leather bits, cotton tufts, metallic yarn or even paper will have a longer life as wall hangings than in front of the fireplace.

When working on a rug project, keep the materials in plastic bags. It's easy to see the colors needed, and they will be convenient to store.

After the project is complete, keep leftovers for a repair kit. If possible, keep a larger quantity of the materials used in the edges of the rug, since the edges will be the first to wear out.

Blocking is very important to make the finished rug settle evenly. The most convenient way is having it blocked by a professional, particularly if the piece is large. Specify that the piece is to be steamed only, not pressed down. Mothproofing and stain repellant can also be added by professional cleaners, or the rug can be treated at home with sprays from the hardware store. Follow directions carefully; the sprays can be toxic.

Padding is an inexpensive way to prolong the life of a rug, and prevent slipping. For small rugs a rubberized backing may be more convenient; it can be applied in liquid form with little trouble. But if the rubberized backing is used, it will have to be replaced after each drycleaning because it separates in the cleaning process.

Backing a rug that is made with yarn can prolong the life of the rug. Use sturdy burlap or canvas, but check the weight first. If it is too thick, the hem will distort the edges.

A wall hanging can be hung from a dowel which is slipped through the top hem, then suspended on the wall with nylon fishing line. If the edges tend to curl, mount the wall hanging on a wooden frame like a painting.

When rugs and carpets are new, a settling period is needed to allow them to adjust to their new environment. Treat them gently for a week or so, until they have relaxed. If they have pile, brush it carefully every few days to prevent it from being pressed down too early. When the rug has settled, a light vacuuming once a week should be sufficient care. A stiff broom may be used. Don't forget to vacuum wall hangings occasionally. A dust-repellant spray will help keep their colors bright.

Grass rugs provide an inexpensive way to cover a floor, and the textural interest they provide is worth far more than their purchase price. This rug soundproofs and insulates this stone-floored sitting room while blending perfectly with the wicker, wood, and marble used for the furnishings.

CARING FOR RUGS

Whatever the method used for cleaning, treat all hand-made pieces tenderly. Vacuums with beater attachments should never be used on handmade rugs. Shaking and hand-beating are not recommended, unless the rug has become extremely gritty. Small rugs with pile can be fluffed in a dryer with the heat turned off, but leave them in only a few minutes. Two-faced pieces such as woven and braided rugs benefit from an occasional turning, which not only allows them to wear evenly, but also helps to dislodge dirt embedded on the underside.

An overall cleaning once every year or two is advisable for every floor covering. One method for home cleaning is to use a soap-and-water solution to shampoo rugs. But unfortunately, home methods can be disastrous. It is hard to achieve the expertise of a professional without some trial and error, and cleaning mistakes cannot always be taken out and done over. Cleaning is also very time-consuming and requires a large space to allow the rug to dry undisturbed. Since rugs and carpets represent a big investment in time and money, it is best to trust them to professionals for expert cleaning.

For small rugs made from garment fibers, a regular garment cleaner is often the best choice. Larger rugs and carpets should be cleaned by a firm specializing in floor coverings. When choosing a cleaning specialist for a handmade rug, be sure to specify gentle care. Inquire about how the rug will be cleaned. If the firm uses harsh soaps and mechanical brushes, look for another firm.

After cleanup, mothproofing and stain-repellant treatments will need to be repeated because they will be cleaned out of the fibers along with the soil. Rubberized backings may need to be re-applied, because cleaning solvents tent to separate them from the fabric.

It is advisable to remove backings from rugs for cleaning. The backing will act as a trap and prevent the dirt from being thoroughly removed.

If materials were chosen carefully, whatever fading may occur from the cleaning process should not ruin the rug. Of course some fading is desirable, to soften the tones and give the piece of the patina of age. Decorators often deliberately choose natural fibers because they fade well, lending character to the piece.

Stains

Nothing which is underfoot constantly will remain free from stains. Accidents will happen, and it is a poor hostess who cannot accept that fact gracefully. However, stains are best treated when they are fresh, so give them some attention as quickly as possible after the mishap.

Generally, stains are divided into two distinct categories: greasy and non-greasy. Two distinct methods of treating them are required. It is advisable to try out both methods on the test swatch used in planning a handmade rug, or in an unobtrusive spot of a purchased rug, to insure against nasty surprises. If the rug does not react well to either method, the only recourse is consulting a professional cleaner. In all cases, exercise caution. Read all directions carefully before beginning. Stain-removal agents can be abrasive to the skin. Adequate ventilation is usually recommended for cleaning fluids.

Generally speaking, rugs made from sisal, rushes or other grasses may be treated for stains in the same way as regular rugs. Many of them have an added advantage, because for normal cleaning they can be wetted completely. When buying the rug, check to find out for sure if wetting is recommended.

Moving

Moving day presents no special problems for rugs, as the nomadic tent dwellers who invented them could easily attest. Rugs can simply be rolled and tied securely to be ready for transport. It is best to roll them with the face out, to prevent strain on the backing. A covering of plastic or canvas will be sufficient to keep them clean. Never fold rugs or use them to pad other household objects, unless the investment they represent is no longer important.

Storing

Rugs should be prepared for storage in the same manner as for moving. If the rug is soiled, cleaning is recommended before storing, because dirt and grime left in the fibers for a long time can cause deterioration. However, mothproofing will need to be repeated after cleaning, for protection during storage. Mothproofing treatments are effective for about five years.

Curling edges occur from moving, storage, and changes in temperature or humidity. If the problem is not serious, use double-faced tape to anchor the edge or corner until the rug has a chance to settle. If the problem continues, steaming can be helpful. A hot steam iron can be held just above the rug (do not press it) and moved back and forth over the area. Use double-faced tape to anchor the edges in place until the rug has time to dry completely. A word of caution: steam can ruin the finish on wood floors. If the rug cannot be moved to an area without wood flooring under it, cover the floor with a thick layer of newspapers while steaming.

Repairs

No matter how carefully rugs are treated, everyday wear and tear will eventually produce frayed edges, and in handmade rugs, occasional snags can leave holes. Minor repairs are very easily made in handmade rugs if, when the piece is finished, a repair kit of leftover yarns or fabrics is assembled to cope with any future problems. When repairs need to be made, the replacement fabrics should be faded slightly to match the area surrounding the repair. Wash the fabric several times in cool water and allow to dry naturally. If further fading is required, try a very mild bleach (oxygen bleach, not chlorine, for woolens and other fine fibers).

If the repair entails a loss of color, water colors or crayons may be used in small areas. They even work for purchased rugs such as Orientals. But don't try to revive a large area which has lost its color in this manner. The results are not consistent or durable.

If the rug is damaged beyond repair, consider re-designing the rug completely. Areas which are still fresh-looking may become part of an altogether new look. For example, a hooked rug with an intact central motif may be trimmed and rebordered with new materials. Or a geometric design may be cut apart in strips and used to border a new pattern. Braided rugs might be disassembled and the braided strands cut to eliminate the damaged areas. Then the strips can be rejoined to create an entirely new shape or pattern. In the case of extensive damage, cut the rug into small pieces for area rugs or stair treads.

Wall-to-wall carpeting can be salvaged if you move, provided it still has areas in good condition. Smaller rooms, halls and entryways are likely spots for reuse. Bind the trimmed edges with wide rug tape, then turn the tape back as a hem and attach to the underside with a hemming stitch or with rug adhesive. Oriental rugs can be trimmed easily because the knots are tied separately and will not ravel, but following a pattern line will make them look more attractive. A blanket stitch along the cut edges will hold the warp and weft in place.

Attaching a border can be as simple as sewing on fringe. But there are other more elaborate methods which can have very beautiful effects. Hooked or braided borders made from complementary colors look lovely on hooked rugs, for instance. It is wise to make a sample swatch of the new border, to match the height of the pile with the rug to be trimmed and to check the color coordination.

When planning a border or trimming a rug, it is helpful to determine first the proportions of the finished product. A simple method of doing this is to cut wide strips of brown paper and lay them over the rug so that only the trimmed portion will show. Squint so that the design is correctly placed and the proportions of the rug are pleasing. Then mark the cutting line with tailor's chalk. To test a border, use brown paper strips to simulate the exact width and even the color, if possible. As in the original design of a rug, planning is of the utmost importance. The time it takes will be repaid many times over in satisfaction with the results.

THE FIRST RUGS

Archeological findings indicate the existence of rugs in Persia centuries before the birth of Christ. The earliest rug to be found intact was discovered frozen in ice in a tomb uncovered in Outer Mongolia. It appears to have been made in Persia in 300 or 400 B.C., and indicates that the craft of making rugs was already highly developed. Rugs in the Oriental sense refer to either floor coverings or wall coverings, and they were usually made in similar ways. For example, the "curtains" referred to as part of the Hebrew Holy Tabernacle described in the Book of Exodus were quite probably examples of Oriental rugs.

Floor coverings varied widely with materials available, weather and degree of sophistication. In tropical regions, grass mats developed. Shepherds made rugs from wool. In warm regions, rugs without pile were dominant, while in cooler areas rugs with pile were more common. Isolated rural areas produced utilitarian rugs with very simple designs. More complex aesthetic requirements arose in villages where people had more leisure to enjoy them, and the division of labor allowed the development of elaborate craftsmanship.

As nomadic tribes wandered and trade routes developed, advanced examples of the rug-making craft spread east and west from Persia and found acceptance wherever they were affordable—in public areas, royal dwellings and homes of the well-to-do. The craft spread as well, accounting for the development of similar rug-making traditions in India, China and Central Asia to the East, and Turkey, Egypt and the Greek Islands to the West. Each area adapted the designs to its own traditions and needs, producing a multiplicity of methods, uses, and materials in the overall category of the "Oriental" carpet.

While rugs and carpets were reserved as decorations and comforts for the very wealthy classes, poorer people used different materials to cover their floors. Sand and straw were strewn on the floors of even middle-class homes to absorb the residue from boots mud-died on unpaved streets and in farmwork. In the Middle Ages even royalty used straw mixed with sweet-smelling herbs on the floors in the summer to offset the increase of odors from infrequently washed bodies and clothing.

Another popular device was the floor cloth, used throughout the Eighteenth Century and well into the Nineteenth in Europe and America. Originally designed as an imitation of an imported carpet or expensive marble entryway, the floor cloth, a carefully painted canvas, came to be popular for its own sake. The best of floor cloths repelled water and stains, providing protection and easy cleaning. They were used over carpets in summer, or to replace them entirely. In winter, floor cloths were often left on the floor under carpets as added insulation.

The floor cloth was popular because of its adaptability to every pocketbook. Plain cloths with little or no design were inexpensive while more elaborate cloths with stenciled or free-hand designs could cost as much as a carpet. Inventories of household goods from the period indicate that floor cloths were considered as important as rugs in a well-run household because of their special qualities: durability, practicality, and adaptability in size, cost and design.

In Scandinavia, a separate evolution apparently occurred beginning with tufted cloaks which replaced animal skins. The tufting techniques came to be used for bed covers, again probably replacing animal skins. As folkways changed, a cloak bed-cover came to have a ritualistic importance in the marriage festivities. At one point it was laid tufted-side down on the marriage bed. The tufting originally was made of long yarns in neutral shades of grey and beige, perhaps the natural colors of the wool. It became a tradition to decorate the untufted side with bright-colored needlework, which then evolved into a short pile. As the work became more elaborate, the non-decorative pile underneath was eventually dropped entirely, and the tradition of brilliant rya rugs and wall hangings came into being.

Ritual had its place not only in the evolution of

the craft, but in the very methods by which the rugs were made. For example, the Navaho Indians (who learned weaving from the Spanish via the Pueblo tribes) developed elaborate regulations associated with the techniques. A woman could not begin to string her loom unless the work could be finished in the same day, and she traditionally sent her family away because it was most properly done alone. Once the weaving was begun the weaver kept the shuttle in her hand at all times; if she once laid it down, the weaving stopped for the day. No doubt rituals such as these, like all traditions, were associated with very practical beginnings related to unbroken concentration on the work at hand, but they came to be practiced as ends in themselves, a distinct part of the craft, setting it apart from the rest of the work of the community.

In our ecology-minded society, we can achieve the look of fur rugs by using rich wool yarns and latch hook or rya knot techniques. The warm, intimate feeling of the room is reinforced by the snuggly texture of the deep pile.

Rugs in colonial America had a glamorous introduction. Supposedly the first Oriental rug was brought to these shores by Captain Kidd in 1700. Before the Revolution in America almost all the carpets were imported, and therefore highly prized. Ordinary people covered their floors, depending on their means, with sand, straw mats, floor cloths, or painted designs. All of these were used in combination with each other and according to the pocketbook of the house owner.

Of course homemade rugs were used as well, probably beginning with the woven rugs similar to our rag rugs. Made with strips of fabric—wool and cotton mostly—they were often used like straw mats and baize to cover imported pile carpets in areas of wear. Strips of them were sewn together for wall-to-wall carpeting and stair treads.

Hooking and braiding seem to have been brought to America from England around the beginning of the Nineteenth Century. Both techniques grew quite popular, especially during wartime, for they were easily produced at home, required no complicated design, and used materials that were readily available. Even the hooking device could be put together from a bent nail affixed to a piece of broom handle.

Rug hooking became popular among men as well as women. In New England the sailors took it up as a pastime on voyages and during the long winters when weather kept them in port. Ready-made printed designs were developed by a Yankee peddler named Frost who, because of ill health, was forced to develop a new business. Soon he found the demand so great that he had to hire a crew of assistants. After a few years he was able to sell his business quite profitably and move to California to enjoy the fruits of his initiative.

The availability of jute helped along the trend toward tufted or pile rugs. Manufacturers were anxious to use this less expensive replacement for the wool or flax used as backing in the European manufacturing industry, and pile hid the coarser grain produced by jute backing. Carpets could be made with less expense and with less regard for the availability of wool, giving the fledgling industry a leg up in the growing world market.

The carpet industry has become one of the giants of American business because of the innovative development of machinery in this country. Simple woven carpets were quickly replaced by several tufting techniques. At the end of the Nineteenth Century with the development of the broad loom (hence the name broadloom carpet), carpeting could be made in large seamless pieces. Modern technology put unlimited design capabilities in the hands of the manufacturers. The result is a fascinating display of possibilities in the decorative arts, resulting in carpets for every taste and pocketbook.

Today rugs and carpets are not only utilitarian objects within financial reach of most American homes, but also a burgeoning medium for artisans and craftspeople throughout the country. The relative simplicity of techniques and their incredible versatility together with the rise of nostalgia for the past and the old ways of doing things have accounted for the growing popularity of rug making. Modern rug makers enjoy the simple pleasures of making rugs which are not only utilitarian and beautiful, but also reflect our pioneering heritage.

The ultimate rug . . . Douglas Fairbanks Sr. and Julianne Johnston fly over Bagdad on a magic carpet in "The Thief of Bagdad." Photo from the Bettman Archive.

**PORTFOLIO OF
RUG TECHNIQUES**

HOOKING

Hooking is a technique of drawing loops of cloth or yarn through a fabric backing to form a thick pile, which can be sheared or left uncut.

There are two basic techniques for hooking a rug. Hand hooking, which is the traditional method, is worked from the right side of the backing (or foundation) fabric, and the loops are pulled up to the surface from underneath. Strips cut from "rags" (meaning used fabric, not literally rags) are the classic materials used in hand hooking, but new fabric or yarn may be used as well. Traditionally, the looped pile was left uncut, but nowadays the pile—particularly in the case of yarn—is often sheared.

Punch hooking is the second, and newer, form of rug hooking. It is worked from the wrong side of the foundation fabric and requires that the design be marked as a mirror image. Several types of hooks may be used, all of which punch the hooking material— almost always yarn—through the backing fabric, automatically forming loops of a predetermined and uniform height on the underside of the backing. Punch hooking is even simpler to master than hand hooking, and speedier as well. Since all punch hooks work best with yarn (and some work only with yarn), however, a punch-hooked rug is likely to be more expensive to make than one that is hand hooked with strips of cloth cut from used clothing, blankets, yard-goods remnants or mill ends. Whichever method you select, both are very enjoyable and easily mastered techniques for creating rugs of lasting beauty.

Equipment

To hook a rug, the basic tool you will need to buy is one of the various types of specialized hooks made for this purpose. In most cases, you will also need a frame, which can be purchased or homemade. In addition, a pair of sharp scissors or other type of cutting tool is essential, and you will need various ordinary sewing basket items such as needles and thread.

HOOKS

Two different types of hooks can be used for rug hooking, the simple traditional hand hook and the speedier punch hook, of which there are several different varieties.

HAND HOOKS. The hand hook, which looks like a metal crochet hook with either a straight or curved shank, set into a wooden or plastic handle, is the simpler and more

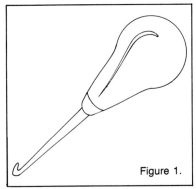

Figure 1.

traditional tool (Figure 1). It is usually used for hooking with fabric strips, although it can be used with yarn as well. Requiring no threading, it can be used with very short as well as long strips or strands. Hand hooks come in a number of lengths and hook sizes. Choose one that feels comfortable in your hand, and that has a hook large enough to accommodate the yarn or fabric you will be using, but that

slips easily through your foundation fabric. Although hooking with a hand hook is slower than working with one of the punch hooks, and somewhat harder because you must learn to regulate the height of the loops yourself, it allows for a greater latitude in the choice of materials. Interesting textures can be achieved by mixing yarn or fabric strips. With a hand hook, the rug is worked from the right side of the backing fabric, and while a frame is not essential, most people prefer stretching the backing on a frame.

SPEED HOOKS. The punch needle and other speed hooks are modern refinements of the older hand hook. They are actually needles, not hooks, and are used primarily for hooking with yarn, although some will also accommodate very narrow fabric strips. These hooks simplify and speed the process of hooking, and automatically produce loops of uniform height. There are three different varieties of speed hooks: the punch needle, the egg-beater hook and the shuttle hook. Most can be adjusted to produce loops of different heights. The punch needle is the simplest and cheapest of the speed hooks and is operated with one hand. Depending on the particular manufacturer, these tubular needles make loops of one basic height or can be adjusted to produce loops of from two to ten different heights. Some come in different sizes for different weights of yarn, while others have several interchangeable points for use with yarns of different weights. Punch needles are usually used only with yarn, although some of the larger sizes will take very narrowly cut cloth

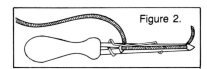
Figure 2.

strips (Figure 2). Shuttle hooks, on the other hand, can be used to hook both yarn and fabric strips, and come with two needle points so they can be used with materials of different weights. They are very fast, move automatically from one stitch position to the next, and usually can be adjusted to make loops of several heights, but they do require two hands

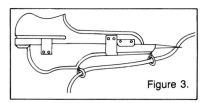
Figure 3.

to operate (Figure 3). Speediest of all is the "eggbeater" hook (so named because it looks like and is operated in much the same way as a manual eggbeater) which can form up to 500 low, medium, or high loops per minute (Figure 4). It is somewhat tricky to

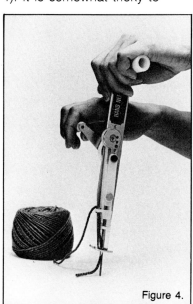
Figure 4.

thread, and so fast that it takes practice to learn to control it. But it is certainly effective if you want to work up a large project in a hurry. One major drawback, however, is that the eggbeater hook cannot be used with fabric strips, nor even with rug yarn, since it will take yarn no thicker than a four-ply knitting worsted.

All punch hooks come with manufacturer's instructions for assembling, threading and operating. When using any of these speed tools, the work is done from the wrong side of the backing fabric, and since the backing must be kept taut, the work must be mounted on a frame.

FRAMES

Although hand hooking can be done with the work resting unframed on a table or in your lap, stretching the foundation fabric on some sort of frame is strongly recommended. When hooking is done with any of the punch needles or other speed hooks, the work MUST be stretched taut on a frame.

If you are working on a large project, or enjoy the craft enough to wish to make more than one hooked rug, a large adjustable easel-type frame or hoop—either a floor-standing or a table model—is a good investment. (Figure 5.) These frames can be tilted to any angle, raised and lowered, and many collapse for storage. Some of the rectangular models are fitted with adjustable rollers at the top and bottom of the frame, which simplifies the task of moving the finished part of the rug out of the way when you want to work on a new section of the backing. For small projects, a large embroidery hoop with a thumbscrew will do just as

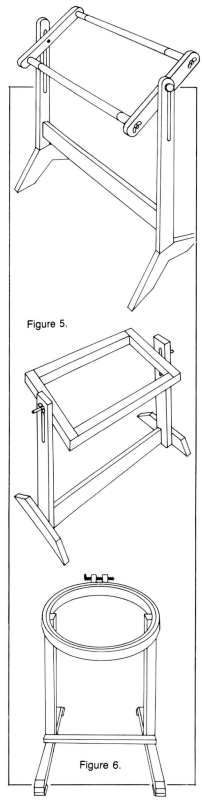
Figure 5.

Figure 6.

well, however. (Figure 6.)

To work, you can clamp a small frame over a table edge with G-clamps, or hold it in your lap, tilting it up so that the top rests against a table.

Larger frames can be rested on the backs of chairs or a pair of sawhorses. Or you can buy inexpensive screw-on legs sold in hardware or unpainted-furniture stores and make your frame self-supporting. Use very short legs—4 to 6 inches—for small frames, and set the frame on a table. Large frames should be floor-standing, with legs high enough so that you can sit comfortably in a chair next to the frame.

The size of your frame, whether purchased or home-made, will depend somewhat on the size of your project, but need not be as large as the project. When using a small frame for a large rug, you simply move the work from section to section, reattaching it to the frame when you want to work on a new portion. A frame smaller than about 18 inches square, however, isn't very practical, except for small mats or samplers. On the other hand, frames that will be propped up in your lap or rested on a table top, are hard to manage if they are larger than about 2 feet square. Floor standing frames can be much larger, as can any frame that will rest against a wall.

CUTTING TOOLS

If you don't want to spend extra money on equipment, you can do all the cutting chores involved in making a hooked rug with a good pair of sharp scissors or bent-handled dressmaker's shears. For a "rag" rug, however—particularly a large one—you may want to consider a pair of electric scissors, which are less tiring to work with than ordinary shears, or a fabric-cutting machine. Fabric strip cutters, though rather expensive, are handy gadgets that automatically cut lengths of fabric into strips of uniform width, and can appreciably reduce the time you will have to spend in slicing up large amounts of material. Depending on the model, the rotary blades can be adjusted or interchanged to cut several different widths from 3/32 inch to 2 inches (which means you can also cut the strip widths used for braided rugs). Some models can cut six strips at a time (Figure 7).

If you are going to hook your rug with yarn and plan to cut the loops and then shear and bevel them for a sculpted look, you may want to buy a pair of special rug shears. While you can use ordinary scissors, rug shears are specially shaped so your fingers are out of the way and so the flat of the blades can rest against the surface of the pile as you cut, allowing you to bevel and sculpt with greater precision.

Materials

A backing fabric and either yarn or fabric strips are the primary materials you will need to assemble to make a hooked rug. Hand hooking is usually done with fabric strips, though you can use yarn if you prefer. If, on the other hand, you are going to work with a punch needle or one of the other speed hooks, you will probably have to hook with yarn, because most speed hooks will not accommodate fabric strips. To finish your rug, you will also need rug binding, a long needle and strong carpet thread. A rubberized backing, applied to the rug to protect it and keep the loops from pulling out of the backing, or a sturdy lining material, are also strongly recommended. (See Finishing and Trimming.)

BACKING FABRIC

Rug hooking has undergone such a resurgence of popularity in recent years that backing fabrics with a great variety of pre-marked designs are readily available. Kits can be purchased complete with backing, yarn and instructions, or you can buy the marked backing fabric alone and select your own yarn or fabric strips. But a great deal of the fun and satisfaction of making a hooked rug comes from creating and marking your own design as well as doing the hooking.

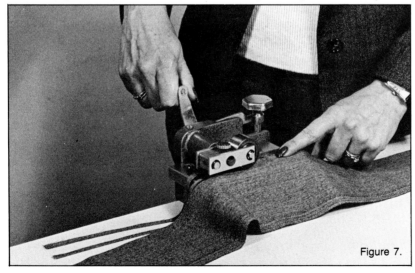

Figure 7.

Any firm and sturdy, even-weave fabric can be used as a backing for a hooked rug, as long as it is not too dense for a hand hook or punch needle to penetrate (an average of 12 to 15 threads per running inch is good). But fabrics especially made for hooking can be found in many craft, needlework, and yard goods shops.

The highest quality backing fabrics are made of cotton, or occasionally of a combination of cotton and linen. Monk's cloth and various canvas-like backing fabrics are excellent examples. These are somewhat open, but very strong and stable, even-weave fabrics, and are generally made of 100 percent cotton. Monk's cloth, which is a basket-weave fabric, is comparatively soft and comes in various weights and thread counts. Dura-Back is a heavier and stiffer type of fabric, and is extremely durable; a plain weave material, it has approximately 14 threads per running inch. Knot-In, a very coarse, plain-weave cotton rug backing is also excellent; although it is woven with only 8 threads per running inch, the threads are so heavy that it can be used for hooking with all but very fine yarns. Osnaburg, another strong, coarse, plain-weave cotton, is also good.

Heavy even-weave burlap is the traditional backing fabric for hooked rugs, and many of the beautiful colonial rugs now hanging in museums were hooked into backings pieced together from used-burlap flour and feed sacks. Although it is not as durable as some of the other rug backing fabrics now available, burlap is easy to hook through and comparatively inexpensive. If you choose burlap, however, use a 12- or 14-ounce fabric, not the 10-ounce variety, which is not as firm or durable. There are also a number of other even-weave jute-fiber backing fabrics aside from burlap. They come in a number of weights and make serviceable foundations for rug hooking.

All these rug backings are sold by the yard and, depending on the particular type of fabric and the manufacturer, come in widths ranging from 40 to approximately 200 inches. Some are available with evenly spaced horizontal and/or vertical guide lines woven in a contrasting color, which can be very helpful when you transfer your design to the backing or if you need to count stitches. If you are planning to use particularly heavy rug yarns or wide fabric strips, choose one of the slightly more openly woven backings; for finer yarns and fabric strips, the more tightly woven backings are more appropriate. Whatever type of backing fabric you select, however, be sure it is of high quality—woven on grain, with no thin spots or excessive knots. Remember: your rug will be only as durable as the backing.

DETERMINING AMOUNTS AND PREPARING THE BACKING. Whatever the final shape of your rug, the backing fabric must always be cut in square or rectangular shapes in order to be able to stretch it on the frame. Allow 4-inch margins on each side of the fabric beyond the measurements of the pattern area—you will need this margin for attaching the backing to the frame and, later, for hemming. If, however, you plan to finish your rug by raveling the threads of the backing fabric itself and knotting them into a fringe, you will need to leave wider margins along the edges to be fringed—up to 10 inches, depending on the length of the fringe and the type of knotting design desired. (See Finishing and Trimming.) When cutting your fabric, follow the line of the lengthwise and crosswise threads; if you find it difficult to see where you are cutting, you can pull out a thread to give you a better guideline.

Sections of backing fabric can be joined if you are unable to obtain a width appropriate for your needs, or if you prefer to work a large rug in smaller, more manageable pieces. Be sure to buy all your fabric at one time and from the same bolt, however, because the weave may vary slightly from one bolt to the next. Allow 4-inch margins on all sides of each section, and cut the pieces so that when you join them, the warp (vertical) threads in each section and weft (horizontal) threads in each section will match at the seam. Joining the sections may be done before you begin to hook the rug, or after most or even all the work has been completed, whichever approach best suits your own particular needs. Several alternative methods can be used to join the pieces. These are discussed later in the section.

To finish preparing your backing fabric, turn under the edges ½ inch and machine stitch, or bind them with masking tape on both the front and back sides of the material. This will keep the edges from raveling as you work. Mark center lines lengthwise and widthwise on the fabric, drawing the lines along a lengthwise and crosswise thread.

Then, measuring out from the center, outline the edges of the design area, drawing these lines along lengthwise and crosswise threads of the fabric as well. Marking can be done with charcoal, tailor's chalk, or an indelible fine-tipped felt marker. Remember that, if you are going to hook your rug with a hand hook, these lines must be drawn on the right, or finished, side of the fabric; whereas if you are planning to punch hook the rug, the lines must be drawn in mirror-image on the worng side of the fabric. To enlarge or reduce an original design and mark it on your fabric backing, follow the directions given in the Appendix (again remembering to mark designs for hand hooking on the right side, and designs for punch hooking on the wrong side (mirror-image) of the fabric).

MOUNTING THE BACKING ON A FRAME. The backing fabric can be tacked, laced, or sewed to the frame, or a combination of methods may be required. The technique you select will depend on the size of your backing fabric as well as the size and type of frame you plan to use. In all cases, however, the fabric should be attached with the design side facing up, and the design edges at least 1 to 2 inches inside the inner edges of the frame. (Without this clearance you won't be able to hook the edges of your rug properly.) In addition, the fabric edges to be attached to the frame should be folded under once or even twice so that the fabric will not pull away from the frame.

To mount the backing fabric on a rectangular roller frame, center the folded top edge of the fabric over the cloth tape

attached to the top roller— making sure to keep the fabric perfectly straight—and whip or backstitch it to the tape (Figure 8). Then whip or back-

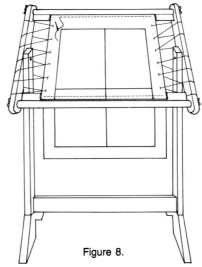

Figure 8.

stitch the folded lower edge of the fabric to the tape attached to the bottom roller in the same way, again making sure that the fabric is centered and straight. Allow excess fabric to hang free behind lower roller. Give the top roller another turn or two until the backing is taut and tighten the roller screws. Then lace the side edges of the backing to the side bars of the frame, using household twine or several strands of strong carpet thread.

If you are using a simple frame without rollers, the backing can be tacked or laced. To tack, center the fabric, design side up, on the frame. If the design is appreciably larger than the frame, let the excess hang down over the back or sides, and remember to make a fold where the tacks will be inserted so the fabric will not pull apart. Then hammer in a long thumbtack, carpet tack or pushpin (or use a staple gun, if you prefer) at the center point along each

edge, pulling the fabric taut and keeping it straight as you work. Continue tacking outward from the center points, alternating sides every few tacks and pulling the fabric taut, until you reach the corners.

Lacing is an excellent method to use if your backing fabric is smaller than the size of your frame. Use a large tapestry needle and household twine or several strands of strong carpet thread. Stitch through the folded edges of the fabric and wrap the lacing around the frame or thread it through holes drilled in the wood. If your fabric is smaller than the frame in only one direction, tack two or even three sides and then lace the remaining edge. A piece of backing fabric that is smaller than the frame in both length and width may be laced around all sides, or tacked on two and laced on the other two edges.

If you are using an embroidery hoop rather than a frame, simply place the backing fabric, design side up, over the smaller hoop, then slide the larger hoop over the fabric and tighten the thumbscrew.

YARN

Yarn is a very satisfactory material for hooking rugs and does not require all the time-consuming preparations necessary when hooking with fabric strips. A yarn rug, however, is usually much more expensive to make than one hooked from fabric strips, especially if "rags" are used.

Depending on the effects you wish to achieve and the use to which you will put your rug—whether it will be a wall hanging or a floor rug that will be subjected to greater wear, for example—just about any yarn that can be drawn up by a hand hook or that will slide smoothly through the mechanism of a punch needle or other speed hook can be used for hooking. Some types are better than others, however, and rug yarns are the best of all. This is a broad category covering a variety of yarns of different weights, thicknesses, fiber content, and number of ply. What they have in common is the fact that they are spun of long fibers or filaments and usually have a harder finish than other types of yarns so that they will be able to withstand harder wear. Rug yarns are available in a rainbow of colors, and in light, medium and heavy weights. There are wool, cotton, and synthetic rug yarns, as well as blends, and they range from two to six ply. In some cases you can separate the ply, in others you cannot; some of the yarns have a pronounced twist, others are smooth. In general, the lightweight yarns are the thinnest, and the heavy yarns, the thickest; but there are some very bulky yarns available that are comparatively light in weight, making them particularly appropriate for use in hangings.

In addition to the rug yarns, tapestry and Persian yarns, which are long-fibered, hard-finished, durable yarns commonly used for needlepoint, are also appropriate for rug hooking. Available in a great variety of colors, they can be used as single strands or doubled if a heavier yarn is desired.

Appropriate yarns can be purchased at most needlework shops and in the home sewing sections of large department stores as well as dime stores.

There are also manufacturers and suppliers from whom yarn can be ordered by mail. (Upon request, these houses will generally make available sample cards and price lists for a nominal handling charge. Refer to the list of suppliers given in the Appendix.) Whatever your source, be sure to estimate the amounts you will need generously. Colors vary from one dye lot to another and will be difficult to match if you run out; and, of course, remnants and close-outs can never be matched. Unused extra skeins can often be returned, so you probably won't be wasting money by buying too much.

Only the vaguest kind of general estimates of yarn requirements can be made, since so many factors are involved—the bulk and weight of the yarn, the type of backing used, the height of the loops. But, very broadly, 8 to 10 ounces of rug yarn will probably be needed to cover 1 square foot of a hooked rug. The best way to judge your own particular yarn requirements is to hook a few square inches as a sample, using the same or an equivalent yarn and backing.

New yarn requires little or no preparation. Mill remnants, however, may be dirty and, if so, should be washed. Wind the yarn in long skeins, tie the skeins loosely in several places with cord of a different color (preferably white, which will not run), and swish in cool water and a mild soap. Rinse thoroughly and hang to drip dry. Since the yarn must be able to feed smoothly, wind any that does not come in a pull skein into a ball. Short lengths of yarn may be used for hand hooking, but all types of punch hooks require long strands.

FABRIC

"Rags" that have been cut into narrow strips—that is, old material salvaged from used garments, blankets, and household linen—are the traditional filling materials for hooked rugs. But nowadays, new yard goods are also commonly used, and precut strips can be purchased by the pound from a number of mail order suppliers. Hooking with fabric strips is generally done with a hand hook, although some shuttle hooks and punch needles can accommodate very finely cut strips.

Firm, smooth-surfaced, closely woven (woven—not knit) fabrics are the best types to use for hooking. They may be solid colors, prints, plaids, even some tweeds, but if your rug will receive hard wear, all the fabrics you select should be similar in weight, thickness, and fiber content.

Heavy, woven woolen goods—such as coating, suiting, blanket, and flannel material—have been the most prized filling materials for hooked rugs. They remain the best choice for any rug that will receive hard wear because they are very durable and don't show soil as badly as do other types of fabric.

ESTIMATING AMOUNTS. It is difficult to make exact estimates of the amount of material you will need for a given project, since this will depend greatly on a combination of many factors—the width and weight of the fabric strips, the closeness with which they will be hooked into the backing, as well as the height of the loops. Various authorities estimate that roughly ½ to ¾ pound of cut fabric strips will cover one square foot of backing fabric; or you can figure 1½ to 2 square yards of woolen goods or 2 square yards of cotton fabric will provide enough strips for 1 square foot of hooking. The best gauge, however, is to actually hook a square inch yourself, using the same (or equivalent) backing and strips cut to the width and hooked to the height you plan to use for your project. Then remove the filling and weigh or measure it. Multiply this figure by the total number of square inches in your project. To figure how much you will need of each color in your rug, estimate the proportion of each color by eye, and divide the total amount needed by each of these figures.

Whether you are using new or recycled fabric, be sure you have enough of each color you will need—and particularly of the background color—before you begin hooking your rug.

PREPARING THE FABRIC. All fabrics to be used for hooking should be clean and, with the exception of real and imitation leathers, they should also be preshrunk and treated to ensure that they will be colorfast. This should be done before the material is cut into strips. Fortunately, all these tasks can be accomplished in one operation. If you are going to use old garments as your hooking material, dismantle them first: remove linings, pockets, collars, cuffs; open all seams and darts; and remove buttons, snaps, zippers, and other fasteners. Then separate the colors and wash each one separately in warm water and borax or, if the fabric is particularly soiled, with a mild soap.

Rinse until the water is completely clear and hang to drip dry without wringing. Don't worry if your woolens shrink; this will simply make the weave even tighter and less likely to ravel; and any bleeding of colors that occurs will simply add an interesting mottled effect that won't show up badly in your finished rug. If you are going to dye any of your fabric, do it after washing.

Cut—*Never* tear—your fabric into strips of uniform width, cutting with the lengthwise grain of the fabric. For hand hooking, strips can be any length, from several inches to several yards. If you are going to use a punch hook, cut the strips as long as possible to avoid the necessity of constantly re-threading the needle. The width that you cut the strips is determined partly by the weight and weave of the fabric and partly by your own personal preference. Heavy, firmly woven woolens, for example, can be cut as narrow as 3/32 to ¼ inch wide; lighter and more loosely woven woolens can be anywhere from 3/16 to 5/16 inch wide. Lightweight cottons are usually cut in ¼- to ½-inch-wide strips, but if the fabric is particularly thin you may want to cut the strips twice the width and double them over. Wider strips work up more quickly and are particularly good for backgrounds or if you want a rug with a coarser, more informal look; narrower strips are useful for details and for delicate designs. These are simply guide lines, however. Experiment with a sample before you cut all your strips, trying different widths until you achieve the effect you want.

You can cut your strips one at a time by hand, using a

sharp-bladed dressmaker's shears or an electric scissors. Another method is to roll up a length of fabric and slice through the roll with a single-edged razor blade or a utility (mat) knife. You can also buy a strip-cutting machine, which will make this tedious chore considerably easier.

Separate the different colors as you cut the strips, and store them in plastic bags to keep them clean until you are ready to use them. It isn't necessary to have all the fabric cut into strips before you begin to hook your rug, but do prepare a batch of each color you will need.

Techniques of Rug Hooking

Hooking a rug, whether with a hand hook or one of the speedier punch hooks, is a very simple procedure that takes only a short time to learn. Before actually beginning to work on your rug, however, it is a good idea to practice a bit in the margin outside your design area. This will give you a chance to develop an even and regular rhythm of working and will, in addition, allow you to experiment with various loop heights and stitch spacings until you find the ones most appropriate for the weave of your backing and thickness of your yarn or fabric strips, and for the nature of your design as well.

USING A HAND HOOK

Hold the hook in your right hand on top of the backing fabric, supporting the handle in your palm or, if you find this uncomfortable, holding it as you would a pencil. Hold one end of a fabric strip or strand of yarn underneath the backing fabric with your left hand, grasping it between your thumb and index finger. If you are left-handed, simply reverse hands, holding the hook on top of the backing in your left hand and the strip underneath in your right hand.

To begin hooking, point the tip (barb) of the hook in the direction in which you wish to hook and insert it into the backing between the threads of the fabric, pushing the shaft about half-way down. Catch the end of the fabric (or yarn) with the tip of the hook, guiding it onto the barb with your

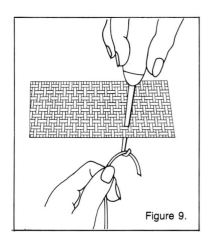

Figure 9.

left hand (Figure 9). Then draw the end of the strip through to the right side of the backing fabric and pull it up about 1 inch. Skip one or two threads and insert the hook again between the threads of the backing fabric. Using the hand underneath to keep the strip (or strand) untwisted, draw up a loop and give the hook a slight clockwise turn (counterclockwise, for left-handers) as you pull the loop through. Adjust the loop to the desired height and then—not before—withdraw the hook from the loop (Figure 10). If you have pulled the loop up higher than you want it to be, you can use

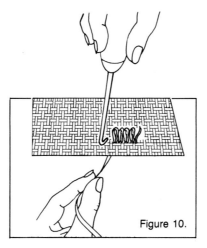

Figure 10.

your left hand to pull it down to the desired height from underneath—or pull it out completely and start again.

Continue to draw up loops in this fashion, taking care to make them all the same height (Figure 11). When you reach the end of your fabric strip or

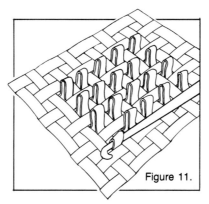

Figure 11.

yarn strand, or when you are ready to start a new color of your design, draw the strip end through to the right side of the work. To start a new strip in the same row, insert the hook and draw the end through to the right side of the work in the same hole through which you pulled the end of the last strip (Figure 12). When

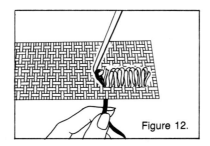

Figure 12.

starting or finishing a strip of fabric or strand of yarn, always draw the end through to the right side of the work and leave the ends unclipped until you have completed the rug. This will ensure that the ends won't be accidentally pulled out as you continue to work.

Adjusting the height of the loops so they are all uniform takes a little practice, but you'll find that you will develop the knack very quickly. If, at first, each loop you make seems to undo the one before it, try making the loops slightly higher. Loops are generally made ¼ to ⅜ inch high, but finely cut fabric strips may be as low as ⅛ inch, while loops that will be cut should be somewhat higher than ⅜ inch. Height, however, is really a matter of personal preference. You can make the loops any height you wish, and vary the height to create unusual effects—just keep in mind that loops made too high can easily be snagged on the heels of shoes.

USING A PUNCH NEEDLE

Before you can begin to hook with a punch needle, the tool must be threaded and, if it is adjustable, you must set it for the loop height you wish to make. The specifics of threading and adjusting loop height vary from model to model, but the principles are the same for all of them.

Loop height is determined by the length of the needle shaft that will be inserted into the backing fabric: the shorter the portion of the shaft inserted, the lower the loops will be, and vice versa. Some needles can be adjusted for as many as ten different loop heights, ranging from ¼ to ¾ inch; this is usually done by sliding the entire needle shaft back or forward in the handle and then locking it in place at the desired setting. The simpler (and usually less expensive) needles do not have movable shafts and make only one basic loop height, generally about ½ inch. Some of them, however, come with a wire loop that can be slipped over the needle shaft to make lower loops, usually about ¼ inch high. If your needle is not equipped with this little accessory, you can make one yourself very easily with a bit of flexible aluminum household wire.

To thread a punch needle, turn it so the slotted side of the needle is facing you, and insert the end of the yarn from the outside through the hole or ring at the base of the needle. Pull a length of yarn through and thread the end from the inside through the hole at the point of the needle. To force it through the slot and into the channel of the needle, grasp the yarn beyond the threaded points with both hands and pull tight; draw the yarn back and forth, if necessary, until it slips into the channel.

Pull the yarn end so it extends about 2 inches beyond the tip of the needle, and unwind some of the skein or ball so that the yarn will be able to move freely through the needle as you work. Hold the needle in your right hand (reverse hands if you are left-handed), grasping the handle between your thumb and index finger and supporting it with the middle finger, much as you would hold a pencil. Place the yarn from the skein over the back of your hand.

Position the needle so that it is perpendicular to the tautly stretched backing fabric, with

the open slot facing in the direction in which you plan to stitch, and push it through the fabric as far as it will go (Figure 13). Pull the yarn end

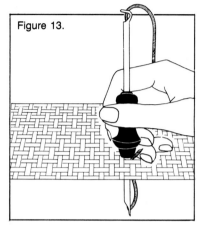

Figure 13.

through to the underside (the finished side) of the work and hold it there with your left hand. Then, keeping the needle in a perpendicular position, withdraw it from the fabric, lifting it just far enough for the very tip of the point to touch the upper surface (the wrong side) of the backing. Without ever raising the needle above the fabric, slide it over the surface to the position where the next loop is to be punched. Plunge the needle through the

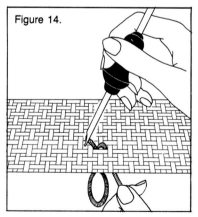

Figure 14.

fabric as far as it will go (Figure 14), and withdraw it as before. You can now release your left hand from yarn end.

Continue working in this manner, turning the needle when necessary so that the slot always faces in the direction you are hooking, and keeping the yarn from the skein loose so that it feeds over the back of your hand

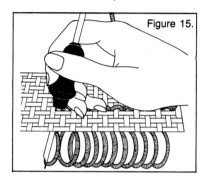

Figure 15.

(Figure 15). Take care not to raise the needle above the surface of the backing fabric or you will disturb the loops you have just made, pulling them out entirely or at least causing them to form unevenly. Also be sure to keep your needle in a perpendicular position, or it will become entangled in the completed loops as it enters the fabric. A good way to avoid this problem is to position your left hand underneath the frame, and shield the worked loops with your fingers.

To make the last stitch in a particular area, or to change colors, plunge the needle through to the underside, leave it there, tilt the frame, and cut the yarn halfway up the needle (Figure 16). Then withdraw the

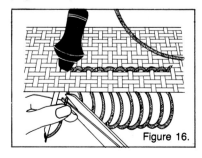

Figure 16.

needle, leaving the cut yarn end on the underside. Do not trim these ends until the entire rug has been completed.

USING SHUTTLE AND EGGBEATER HOOKS

Shuttle hooks can be adjusted to make loops of several different heights from ¼ inch to nearly 1 inch; and they usually come with two needle points, one for heavy yarns and fabric strips and the other for finer materials. Insert the needle point you wish to use and set the loop height adjustment as directed by the manufacturer of your particular hook. To thread a shuttle needle, simply push one end of your yarn or fabric strip downward (in the direction of the needle point) through the metal guide loop located on one side of the tool. Then draw the yarn through the eye in the point of the needle, leaving an end several inches long. To operate the shuttle, you will need to use both hands, positioning one on each of the movable sections of the wooden mechanism

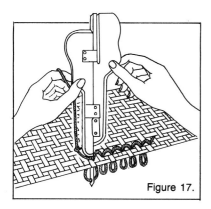

Figure 17.

(Figure 17). When you push down on the right section, the needle will be plunged through the backing fabric. As you raise the right section, the left

will automatically be lowered, securing the loop. The shuttle then moves automatically to the next position where, by repeating the procedure, you can create your next loop. Learning to guide the shuttle from position to position so that it goes where you want it to go takes some practice, but once you get the rhythm, hooking with a shuttle is very easy and the loops work up quickly.

SPACING OF STITCHES

Whether you are hand hooking or using a punch hook, you must space your stitches so that they are close enough to cover the backing well, filling it fully so the loops are held firmly in the fabric, but not so close that the rug will buckle. No exact formula can be given for the number of stitches and rows per inch that you will need to make to meet these requirements, because this will depend on the weave and weight of your backing fabric and the weight and thickness of the yarns or fabric strips you are using. In many cases, stitches and rows will be properly spaced if you make them every other horizontal and vertical thread of the backing, but in some instances you will need to space them further apart or to hook a loop between each thread of the backing. A general rule of thumb, however, is that finer yarns and fabric strips and shorter loops need to be spaced more closely than do heavier yarns (or strips) and longer loops. A heavy rug yarn, for example, worked on a 13-thread-per-inch monk's cloth backing, will require about 24 stitches per square inch (6 rows of 4 stitches each) when making ½-inch-

high loops, whereas about 30 stitches per square inch (6 rows of 5 stitches each) will be required if the loops are only ¼ inch high. This is just an example, however, for one specific yarn and backing, and the most accurate way to find the best stitch density for your own particular backing fabric and hooking materials is to work a sample swatch in a corner of your backing or, better yet, in the margin outside the design area. Whatever number of stitches and rows per inch you determine to be most satisfactory, try to work your stitches evenly over the entire backing so that you don't leave large open spaces in some spots and crowd the loops in other places.

The edges of the rug, and sometimes design outlines and fine detail as well, are exceptions to the general pattern of stitch spacing. Because the outer edges usually get the hardest wear of any part of a rug, you should protect them by making the outer two or three stitches and rows of loops much closer together than the spacing you will use for the rest of your rug. In addition, never begin or end a row directly along an edge, because this will weaken the edge; instead, start and end several stitches in from the edge.

Some people like to space the stitches along design outlines or fine lines of detail more closely than the general spacing used for filling in an area. This helps to define the lines more clearly, but you must be careful not to pack the stitches so densely that the rug will buckle. A row of loops, worked next to the outline, can also be used to clarify lines and shapes.

DIRECTION OF STITCHING

There are no hard and fast rules governing the direction of stitching. Hooking is usually done in rows, but these may be made horizontally or vertically, they may be curved to follow the contours of a portion of the design, or they may be directional—spirals, scallops, zigzags, diagonal lines, and the like, invented to achieve unusual effects, usually of texture but sometimes of color as well. One of the few things that you should not do is to cross over rows of stitching to get to some other spot. When you want to move elsewhere, draw your yarn or fabric strip through to the finished side, clip it, and then start afresh in the new location.

Stitching design outlines following their natural contours, and then working the rest of the rug in simple straight horizontal and/or vertical rows is probably the easiest and fastest method. Just remember never to weaken your rug by beginning or ending a row directly along an outer edge. Vertical rows can be worked with equal ease from bottom to top or top to bottom. Right-handers, however, usually find horizontal rows easier to stitch when worked from right to left, and if you are left-handed, you will probably find that working from left to right is more convenient. If you are going to clip the loops of your rug for a velvety pile, working in horizontal or vertical rows is the most practical approach. Since the direction in which you made the stitches will not be apparent once the loops have been cut, using any more involved method of stitching would be wasted.

VARIATIONS ON BASIC METHODS: BLENDING

When you need to work two or more adjoining areas independently, but wish to de-emphasize the separation between them, simply zigzag the ends of the rows along the common edge so that they intermesh instead of meeting in a straight line. This is an effective way to blend several tones if you wish to shade portions of your design so that the color change appears to be a

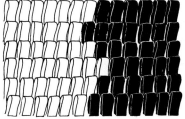

Figure 18.

gradual one (Figure 18). It is also useful if you are hooking a large area of either the design or the background and wish it to appear rather uniform in color but need to use yarns or fabric strips that aren't all of exactly the same shade.

In addition, this method of zigzagging and intermeshing the ends of rows should always be used if you are making a rug that is larger than your frame. When you reposition your fabric and begin working the new section, the loops of the two sections will intermesh and appear to have been hooked in one continuing line, if the inner edes of one section are zig-zagged. But if the two sections meet in a straight line, the pile will tend to separate slightly and you will have a visible line in your finished rug.

DEFINING LINES

Sometimes rather than making the separation between two portions of your design indistinct, you may want the joint edge to be clearly defined. A good way to do this is to hook one row of very low loops between the two areas. This row, being lower than the surrounding ones, will not be visible in the finished rug, but will separate the loops on either side and prevent them from becoming intermeshed and blurring the outline. If you are using a hand hook, you will have to gauge the height of the separating row by eye; with a punch hook, simply change the setting to a lower one. In either case, make the separating row about half the height of the surrounding rows, or even slightly lower than that.

VARYING THE TEXTURE

Often, a busy or intricate design will be most effective when hooked in simple rows and loops of uniform height. But many designs can be enhanced by an imaginative use of texture; and, as a medium, hooking allows great scope for textural contrasts. Combining different hooking materials will immediately create a play of textures, as will contour and directional stitching. But there are additional ways to vary the surface texture of a hooked rug as well: the loops themselves can be hooked to different heights, or the pile can be cut and also sculpted—and all these techniques can be variously combined to multiply the design possibilities enormously.

CUTTING AND SCULPTING PILE. If you want a rug with a lush, velvety surface, you can cut the looped pile or, with some designs, the scissors can be used even more imaginatively to shear and bevel selected areas for a three-dimensional, sculpted look. These techniques are most often used on rugs hooked with yarn, but if you hook fabric strips high enough, they, too, can be cut and also sculpted. Don't clip a single loop, however, before you have completely finished and rubberized your rug. Sizing with liquid rubber or white glue is essential to prevent the cut strands from being pulled out of the backing.

Once the rubber or glue sizing has dried, place the rug on the floor and study it for a while before you actually begin to cut. Decide whether you want to clip the entire rug or only selected portions. Very interesting textural contrasts can be achieved by cutting the pile in some areas and leaving other parts uncut; and since clipping changes the way light reflects from the surface of the rug, it affects color as well as texture. Loops always appear to be lighter in color than cut pile. Be quite sure of exactly what you want to do before you start cutting—because your can't change your mind once you have begun.

Cutting should be done systematically. If you are going to clip the entire rug, work row by row from bottom to top or top to bottom, whichever direction you find most comfortable. If only selected areas are to be cut, complete each individual area, working row by row, before going on to the next one. To cut, use a very sharp scissors or shears, preferably one with long, narrow blades. Slide a blade of the scissors through several loops. Gently pull upward on the blade so all the loops are cen-

tered and taut, and then cut (Figure 19). Continue along the

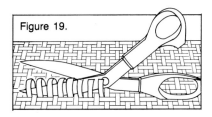

Figure 19.

row as far as you need to go, cutting as many loops at a time as you can comfortably slip onto your scissors blade and slice cleanly.

When you have finished all the cutting you plan to do, you can correct any unevenness, if you wish to, by shearing the surface of the pile. The technique used for shearing is slightly different from that used for cutting the loops. The scissors must be held with the flat sides of the blades parallel to and resting lightly on the surface of the pile, so you can lop off the very tops of the overly-high strands much as if you were trimming a hedge

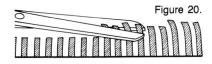

Figure 20.

(Figure 20). This is most easily accomplished with a pair of rug shears, which are specially designed for just this purpose, but you can work with an ordinary scissors—it will simply be a little more awkward.

Shearing, along with the closely related technique of beveling (shearing at an angle), can be used to sculpt the pile as well as to correct minor unevenness. Sculpting means shearing and shaping the pile so that some areas are higher than others, and can be used to create many

different looks depending on exactly where and how the pile is shaped. An entire background, for example, can be sheared to make it lower than the design; beveling can be used to incise lines in the pile or angle the edges of a raised area; or a raised component— such as a flower—can actually be shaped into a rounded form by a combination of beveling and shearing. All of this must be done very carefully, and you can eliminate a great deal of work by planning any sculpting you wish to do in advance. If, to begin with, you hook higher loops in the areas that you want to be raised, for example, you won't have to shear a large expanse of background so deeply, but will only need to go over it lightly and correct any unevenness, and then bevel the edges of the raised area of the design.

JOINING RUG SECTIONS

Should you want to make a very large rug, but can't find backing fabric wide enough for your needs, you can join narrower panels and then hook the rug all in one piece. Or, if you prefer, you can make your rug in two or more small, individual sections and join them after you have completed most or even all of the hooking. Several methods can be used to join rug sections. The lapped join is the most satisfactory technique, since it leaves no visible traces—and it can be used either before or after you start to hook. If you prefer to finish all the hooking before tackling the job of joining, the sections can be seamed by hand. A simple backstitched seam is probably the easiest method of all, but since it is more difficult to match the sections exactly, this join will usually be at least slightly visible. You can also finish and hem each section separately, and then whip them together. If the pieces are all the same size and the nature of the design doesn't require careful matching, this is an easy and satisfactory method to use.

LAPPED JOIN. If you intend to use this method after you hook the sections of your rug, be sure to plan and transfer your pattern to the backing so that the horizontal and vertical threads of the fabric run in the same direction on each section, and so that the design segments will match when the sections are overlapped. And don't forget to leave 4-inch margins around all edges of each section. It is also a good idea to draw or baste a line 2 inches inside and parallel to each of the edges that will be joined. Since this is where you will lap the sections, do not hook past the markings.

Work each section of your rug, zigzagging the ends of your rows along the 2-inch marking. (See Blending, Figure 18.) Then trim one of the sections to be joined along the edge of the design area; trim the other section in the margin, 2 inches outside the edge of the design area. Lap the section cut directly along the design edge over the other section, matching the two parts of the design and aligning the fabric threads as closely as possible. Pin the layers together and, using heavy-duty sewing or carpet thread, make three lines of stitching inside each of the overlapped edges and the third down the center. Use small diagonal or regular basting stitches, or machine stitch if the rug is not too unwieldy

to place in your sewing machine. Then hook the unworked strip through both layers of the backing.

When joining panels of backing fabric before hooking your rug, trim selvages if they are woven too closely to be able to insert your hand hook or punch needle. Then overlap the edges 2 inches, carefully aligning the fabric threads, and stitch. Once this has been done, you can turn under or tape the outer edges and transfer your design to the fabric.

BACKSTITCHED SEAM. Finish hooking each section to be joined. Then place them right sides together, aligning the outer rows of hooking and matching the design. Pin and backstitch the seam with carpet thread as close as possible to the hooking—or machine stitch if the rug is not too bulky to slide under the presser foot of your machine. Trim the seam allowances to 2 inches, open them flat and whip to the backing—but wait to complete these steps until you are ready to turn and stitch the hems.

WHIPPED SEAM. If the sections of your rug are exactly the same size and the various segments of the design do not need to be closely matched, you can sew them together

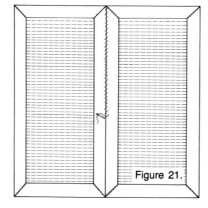

Figure 21.

after they have been completely finished and hemmed. Simply place the sections right sides down, line up the edges, and whip or blindstitch them together with strong carpet thread (Figure 21).

Order of Work

PREPARATIONS. Before beginning to hook, assemble ALL the yarns or fabrics you will need for hooking as well as your rug backing and frame. Wash yarns that are soiled and roll any not packaged in pull skeins into balls. Preshrink all fabrics; test some strips to determine the widths you will need to cut. (If you will be hand hooking simply hold a small sample of your backing in your hands to make the test. For punch hooking, you can use a small embroidery hoop or secure a swatch of backing with cord or rubber bands over an open widemouthed can or jar.) Cut all your fabric into strips, or at least prepare enough strips of each color to begin working.

Cut your backing fabric, if necessary overlapping and basting sections together for a large rug to be made in one piece. Turn under or tape the edges to prevent raveling, and then mark center lines and outline the edges of the area to be hooked. Enlarge or reduce your design, as required, and transfer it to the backing fabric, remembering to mark designs for hand hooking on the right (finished) side and those for punch hooking on the wrong side. Then mount your backing, design side up, on a frame and begin to hook your rug.

STITCHING. As with many other aspects of making a hooked rug, the order in which you choose to work is basically a matter of personal preference—though some approaches are more popular than others. You can, if you wish, hook your rug row by row, changing colors as required along each row and completing an entire section before going on to the next one. If you are a beginner, you may find this way of working less confusing than jumping around.

Once you gain a little confidence, however, try working different components of your rug pattern selectively—you'll find it allows more scope for creativity. If you take this approach, start with the center of the design, then do the border (if your rug has one), and finish by working the background. To stitch the design, work fine lines and small details first, small areas of the pattern next, and then the large ones. Try to leave light colors for last wherever you can. As you come to an area, outline it first, then fill it in. After you complete the design, start on the border. Work a row of stitches along the outline separating the border from the background, and complete the two or three rows of closely spaced stitches along the outer edge of the rug first, then fill in the border. To work a patterned border, follow the same plan of stitching used for working the main design; if it is a solid color area, you can stitch in straight rows or directionally, as you prefer. Finally, fill in the background. Begin by hooking one or two rows around the edges of the design, following its contours, and another row or two along the edge of the border. Then fill in the rest, working in simple horizontal or vertical rows,

or using the contour or directional methods, whichever is best suited for the effect you wish to achieve.

When hooking a rug that is larger than your frame, one section should be completed before you undo the tacks or laces and reattach the backing fabric to work a new section. You can stitch each section row by row, or work one component—design, border, background—at a time, as you prefer. But in either case, stagger the ends of your rows along the inner edge of the section so that, when you start the new portion of the backing, the two sections will mesh without creating hard artificial lines.

FINISHING. Before you remove your rug from the frame, check to be sure that you haven't missed any large spots, and fill in loops where necessary. Should you find any really glaring mistakes—don't worry about minor ones—you can carefully pull out the loops and rework the area if you wish. Minor unevenness in height can often be corrected merely by slipping a knitting needle through the loops in question and gently pulling upward. Once you have completed these chores, you can take the rug off the frame.

The next step in finishing a hooked rug is usually to size the back by painting it with a solution of liquid rubber—which also provides a nonskid surface—or of diluted white glue. (See Finishing and Trimming, for directions.) If you have decided to cut, shear, or bevel any portion of the looped pile, this procedure is an absolute must: clipped yarn or fabric strips tend to wander right out of the backing if not

held securely in place by the sizing. Sizing is also recommended for rugs with uncut loops, but if you prefer to skip it, the rug should be lined instead (lining rugs that have been sized with glue is also a good idea). A word of caution about applying the sizing: if instead of hemming, you plan to finish the edges of your rug by adding a yarn fringe or by knotting the threads of the backing fabric into a fringe, be very careful not to spread the sizing beyond the last row of hooking, or you won't be able to insert the yarn or unravel the backing threads to make fringe.

Once the sizing has dried (or if you haven't applied any), trim all long yarn or strip ends to the same height as the surrounding loops, and cut and sculpt the pile if you wish to do so. Then finish the edges of your rug by unraveling and fringing the threads of the hem allowances or by turning them under and hemming. Instead of a self-fringe, you can also cut and hook a yarn fringe into the backing fabric—either before or after the hem has been stitched. Hooked rugs do not require blocking, but steaming will freshen up the pile and help the rug to lie flat.

BRAIDING

Braided rugs have been popular in this country ever since the first sailing ship discharged its hardy passengers upon these shores. When the rag bag was full enough, colonial housewives cut long strips from the worn but still valuable remains of clothing and blankets and fashioned thick and sturdy rugs for their hearthsides and bedsides.

The simple round and oval shapes, and the generally muted tones of traditional braided rugs fit well in almost any room, so you need not hesitate to make one if your home is not furnished in colonial style. But a braided rug doesn't have to look traditional at all. Use color vividly and boldly if you wish. And you don't have to wait patiently until your rag bag is overflowing: new fabric, though more expensive of course, is readily available and is usually a much quicker way to assemble all the material you'll need and in exactly the colors you want. And, polyester knit scraps are perfect for braided rugs. In addition, there are now a variety of gadgets that you can buy to speed the process of preparing your strips for braiding. Once you have started braiding, you will probably find your entire family demanding to participate in the process of making the rug, as the progress is so easily marked.

Equipment

All you really need is a good pair of sharp scissors or bent-handled dressmaker's shears; a long, curved, blunt-tipped sack or rug lacing needle, along with a tapestry needle and an ordinary large-eyed sewing needle; a supply of straight pins and large safety pins, tailor's chalk, a ruler and a tape measure or a yardstick. You may also want to consider supplementing this basic list with a few of the helpful and time-saving gadgets or homemade improvisations described below, most of which are very inexpensive.

CUTTING, MEASURING, AND MARKING AIDS. All the cutting chores involved in making a braided rug can be done with a pair of ordinary scissors or bent-handled dressmaker's shears. But if you are planning to make a large rug, you may want to consider buying a strip cutting machine or a pair of electric scissors, which are much less tiring to use. Fabric strip cutters, though rather expensive, can also greatly reduce the time you will have to spend preparing the fabric strips for braiding. These handy gadgets automatically cut lengths of fabric into strips of uniform width.

Braiding strips to be cut by hand can be measured and marked with a ruler and straight pins or tailor's chalk, but most yard goods and home sewing stores carry several inexpensive measuring aids that can help streamline these procedures. One such device is a type of hem gauge that combines an adjustable ruler and chalk marker, allowing you to measure and mark at the same time. Another, even simpler, gadget is a small gauge that slides right onto your scissors, permitting you to cut even strips without measuring or marking at all.

BRAIDING, SEWING, AND LACING AIDS. Fabric strips must be folded for braiding. You can do this by hand but it is much easier to buy a set of braid aids to do the job for you. These are small cone-shaped metal devices that slip onto the ends of your braiding strips and, when pushed down the strips as you braid, turn the edges of the fabric inward. Braiding cones, available from mail order suppliers, come in several sizes for strips of different weights and widths. You can get simple cones or a fancier type that has a holder onto which a length of fabric strip may be rolled.

To anchor the fabric strips for braiding, you can purchase a special vise-like clamp. (A nail hammered into a board, wall, or door will serve the same purpose.) Any time you must release your hold on the finished portion of a braid, you will have to secure it so it won't come apart. Large safety pins are good for this purpose, or clamp the braid with an ordinary spring-type clothespin. When lacing and sewing, you may want to protect your middle finger with a thimble; keep a crochet hook handy, as well—you will find it helpful for tucking in braid ends.

Materials

The only materials you will need in order to make your braided rug are a quantity of fabric—either "rags" or new yard goods—to cut into the strips that you will braid, and two kinds of thread. To stitch the fabric strips together for braiding, use a heavy-duty mercerized cotton or cotton-wrapped polyester sewing thread in a color matching that of the fabric. Lacing the braids together to form the rug should be done with special lacing cord made for this purpose, or with extra strong carpet thread.

FABRIC

Buying yard goods or pre-cut strips is a quicker and

easier way to assemble all the fabric you'll need, in precisely the colors you want, than collecting "rags"—and preparing them is less time consuming as well. On the other hand, you can make just as lovely and practical a rug out of old blankets, coats, suits, skirts, trousers, and the like, as you can with brand new yard goods—and, what is more, it will be far less expensive. Filling your rag bag may take a little more time but, if you go through your closets and storage chests, you'll be surprised how many appropriate garments you will find that you know you'll never wear again but are "too good to throw away."

Firmly woven, medium- to heavy-weight woolen goods—durable, soil resistent, and easy to work with have always been considered to be the most suitable fabrics for rug braiding, particularly for large rugs that will receive considerable traffic. Lighter weight woolens, as long as they are closely woven, generally wear reasonably well, however, and are quite satisfactory for smaller rugs or those that will not be constantly trod upon—and you can compensate for the flatness of these materials by lining them with a padding as you fold them for braiding.

Most other types of materials—cottons, silks, synthetics, blends, and the like—don't wear as well as wool, but you can braid all sorts of interesting rugs with them as long as you aren't overly concerned about long-term durability, or if you plan to place your rug where it won't get unusually heavy wear. Some of the sturdier canvas-like cottons—such as the ducks, denims and sailcloths—can be used for fairly large rugs, and are especially

attractive if the strips are padded before being braided. Knits can be used, as can the thinner woven cottons and synthetics, for very small rugs—kitchen and bathroom mats and the like—where washability is an asset.

A braided rug need not be made of fabric at all. Rope, twine, heavy rug yarn and the various macrame cords—used singly or in multiple strands, depending on their bulk—can also be braided and then laced into a rug.

Whatever type of material you select for your braided rug—whether it is fabric or one of the other "braidables," and in the case of fabric, whether it is new or recycled—your rug will look smoother and more even, and it will last much longer if you don't combine materials of different fiber contents or of appreciably different weights. This is particuarly important when working with fairly heavy-weight woolen fabrics—which will work up into an extremely durable rug if used alone, but will be considerably weakened if combined with lighter weight wools or other types of fabrics.

There are no such crucial restrictions, however, where color is concerned. The colors you choose for your braided rug are strictly a matter of your own personal preference: combine any or as many as suit your fancy. Solid colors are basic, but don't ignore checks, plaids, and prints of all sorts—and tweeds, as well, if the weave is tight enough and the surface quite smooth. All can be used to create interesting effects. Before you reject any readily available fabrics—whether solid color or patterned—because they don't look well together when large pieces are placed side by

side, cut a few test strips and make some sample braids, combining colors and patterns in various ways. Patterned fabrics take on a very different appearance when cut into narrow strips and braided, and you may also be very surprised how well some seemingly outlandish color combinations work and blend together when braided.

ESTIMATING FABRIC REQUIREMENTS. The amount of fabric you will need to assemble will, of course, depend first of all on the overall size of the rug you are planning to make. But beyond this basic consideration, fabric requirements may vary appreciably depending on the weight and thickness of the fabric, the width of the strips you intend to use and, to some extent, how tightly you braid and how you will assemble your rug. Depending on the "hand" of the braider, for example, anywhere from one-fourth to one-half the original length of the fabric strips will be taken up in the braiding process itself. All these variables make exact recommendations difficult, but a good rule of thumb to follow is that, if you are using woolen goods of medium weight and thickness, and cutting strips about 2 inches wide, you will need about ¾ pound (or one yard) of fabric to complete enough braid to make one square foot of your rug. For a particularly heavy woolen fabric, you may need a pound or more to braid a square foot of your rug; and lighter weight fabrics may require somewhat less than ¾ pound—unless you plan to fold the braiding strips an unusual number of times in order to make a thicker braid.

If you have already assembled a portion of your fabric or

have on hand some scraps of an equivalent type that you can use for a test, you can make more accurate overall calculations by cutting a measured (or weighed) amount of the fabric into strips of the width you intend to use, and making a braid long enough to coil into a one-square-foot sample. Then multiply the total number of square feet in your rug by the weight or yardage you used to make the one-square-foot sample. To be sure you will have enough fabric, always add a reasonable amount of extra goods beyond the basic figure you have determined you will need.

Don't try to figure out to the inch how much of each color you will need. For a completely random hit-or-miss rug, simply decide what colors you wish to use and make sure you have the total amount of fabric you will need. Or, if you prefer a hit-or-miss rug that has an overall sense of uniformity, choose a single color or series of closely matched tones—light or dark, subdued or bright, depending on the effect you want—and use one strip of this color and two random strips in each braid; in this case, figure that one-third of the total fabric you will need should be in that particular color, and the rest may be in any combination of other colors.

Preparing Fabric For Braiding

INITIAL PREPARATIONS

All fabric for braiding should be clean and preshrunk and treated to make if colorfast. These tasks should be completed before you cut the material into strips. *(See Hooking.)*

CUTTING THE STRIPS

Before you begin any large-scale cutting, experiment with several strips, cutting, folding, and braiding them to see whether they work up into a satisfactory braid. Consider the weight and thickness (or bulk) of the fabric when deciding how wide to make the strips, and remember that a finished three-strand braid will be about half the cut width of one strip. Very thick, heavy fabric can be cut into strips as wide as 2½ or even 3 inches, and will work up into plump 1¼- to 2-inch-wide braids, excellent for large rugs. Fabrics of medium weight and thickness should be cut into 2- to 2½-inch wide strips and will make braids that are 1 to 1¼ inches wide. Lightweight fabrics work best in narrow braids, ½ to ¾ inches wide (for these widths, cut strips 1 to 1½ inches in width). You can add bulk to braids made from lightweight fabrics by cutting the strips twice as wide as usual and folding them in half before beginning the usual folding procedures; or, you can cut padding material, such as felt or even quilt batting, into strips half the width of the fabric strips and fold the outer fabric over the padding.

When you make an experimental braid, it is a good idea to start by cutting the strips a little wider than you think they will need to be, and then work up the braid. If the strips turn out to be too wide, you can trim the edges slightly (cutting away the same amount on each strip) and braid again. Then take the braid apart, measure the strip width, and cut the rest of your fabric to that measurement. While you are experimenting with strip widths, you can test different

color combinations at the same time. This will help you in planning the design of your rug and in estimating your fabric requirements as well.

Although some fabrics can be torn into strips without damage, cutting is always the preferred method: it is less likely to disturb the weave and is a much more reliable way to ensure strips of uniform width.

Electric scissors are a great convenience if you are going to cut by hand, but ordinary scissors or shears will do just as well, as long as they are sharp. Bent-handled dressmaker's shears, with blades as long as you can handle comfortably, are easier to work with than straight scissors, because you can rest them on a flat surface, sliding the blades along as you cut.

Wherever possible, cut your strips along the lengthwise grain of the fabric. They will be strongest and least likely to stretch when cut in this direction and, in addition, will usually be longer than if you cut them crosswise. Don't, in any case, cut on the bias. If you are using yard goods, all you need to do is to trim away the selvages, cutting along a lengthwise thread, and unravel one or two threads from the cut edges until you can pull a single thread the entire length of the goods. The easiest way to find the lengthwise grain on pieces of old garments is to hold your hands on opposite sides of the fabric and pull from various points along the edges until you find the direction of least stretch (Figure 1). Then mark this line with pins or chalk and, measuring outward, mark a line parallel to it as close to one edge of the piece of fabric as is practical. Trim along the outer line and

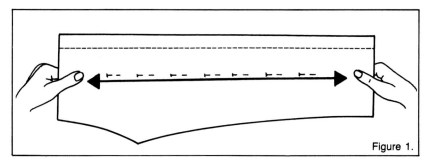

Figure 1.

cut all strips parallel to this edge.

Measuring and marking off strip widths on the fabric are not necessary if you will be using a mechanical cutter or have a special gauge that you can fasten to your scissors.

If you plan to cut your strips by hand without a gauge, you will have to mark the fabric first. You can do this with a line of pins, spacing them 2 to 3 inches apart; but if tailor's chalk will show up on your material, you will usually find this is a faster way to mark, and a chalk marker is even quicker. If your fabric is not too heavy and your shears are very sharp, you can also save time by placing two sections of fabric together, or folding a large piece in half, pinning the layers so they will not slip, and cutting through both layers.

JOINING THE STRIPS

Unless you have cut your strips from fabric several yards long, you will need to join a number of shorter strips in order to make lengths that are appropriate for braiding. Braiding strips should be long enough so you don't have to stop constantly to join new pieces, though not so long that working with them becomes unwieldy. Ten to fifteen feet is generally convenient, but there is no reason why you can't tailor the length you use to your own specific needs. If

you have a definite color plan for your rug, be sure to match colors closely when joining the strips.

Braiding strips should always be sewed together on the bias. To do this, place the ends of two strips—right sides together—at right angles to each other, and stitch diagonally. Use heavy-duty mercerized cotton-wrapped polyester thread in a color that matches your fabric, and either backstitch the seam by hand or, preferably, make two lines of machine stitching, one directly over the other. Trim the seam ¼ inch beyond the stitches (Figure 2), and then

Figure 2.

press open the seam allowances. Join additional strips in the same manner until the strip is as long as you need it, making certain that each succeeding seam is on the same side of the fabric as the others. As you finish each strip, roll it up into a flat reel (not a ball) with the seam allowances toward the inside, and place a rubber band loosely around it.

FOLDING THE STRIPS

Before the pieced strips can be braided, they must be

folded to conceal the long raw edges. While it is possible to fold them by hand, this is so tedious that use of inexpensive braiding cones is recommended. You will need one cone for each strip in your braid. Braiding cones can be purchased from mail order suppliers; they come in different sizes for strips of different widths and weights, so be sure to buy a size appropriate for the strips you plan to use. Before starting the braid, thread a braiding cone onto the end of each strip. To do this, slip the end of each strip (wrong side up), from outside to inside, through the long horizontal slit at the base of the cone (Figure 3), and pull

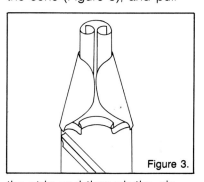

Figure 3.

the strip end through the circular opening at the tip of the device (Figure 4). Then, as you push the cones down the strips, they will turn under the raw edges and fold the strips automatically.

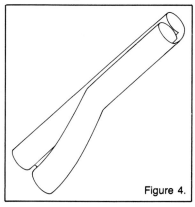

Figure 4.

Making a Three-Strand Braid

STARTING

Select three strips for braiding and, if they have been pieced, check to be sure that the seams will not fall in the same spot, because this will cause the braid to bulge unattractively. To avoid this problem, unroll the strips and try starting one or more of them from the opposite end, but if this doesn't work, cut and rejoin strips as necessary so no two seams meet. If you are making the starting braid for a rug that is to be worked in one continuous spiral round, also make sure that your three strips are not the same length, so that when you add new strips the seams will not occur in the same place. Reroll each strip, leaving about one yard loose to start the braid, and re-pin to secure the rolls. Slip your braiding cones onto the ends of the strips and push them down several inches.

There are several ways to start a braid. The T-start is the preferred method for beginning the center (or starting) round of most rugs, or whenever it is desirable to enclose the raw ends at the beginning of a braid. Open the folded ends of two of the strips, and join them with a bias seam in exactly the same way you pieced the individual strips together. Then refold the long raw edges toward the center. Keeping the open (double-folded) edge facing toward the left, center the end of the folded third strip over the seam joining the other two strips, forming a T, and stitch it securely in place by hand or by machine (Figure 5). Fold down the strips forming the top bar of the T (strips #1 and #2), matching the

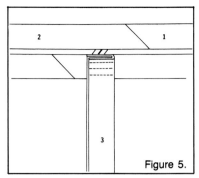

Figure 5.

open folded edges and enclosing the end of the vertical strip. Press lightly or restitch the opened portion of the folded edge. Then, to position the strips so that all the open double-folded edges face in the same direction—toward the left—flip the top left strip of the T (strip #2) down and over the center strip (strip #3), so the underside is up (Figure 6). The strips are now ready to be anchored and braided.

In order to create the tension necessary for making a

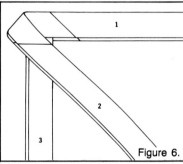

Figure 6.

firm, tight braid, the strips must be anchored to something that you can pull against as you braid. You can clamp them to the edge of a table with a vise—special braiding clamps can be purchased from mail order suppliers, or use a general purpose C-clamp, available at most hardware stores (Figure 7); pin them to a strip of fabric that has been wrapped around a chair back or door knob; or attach them to a wall, door, or board with a hook or nail. The arrangement need not be fancy or elaborate, just something that will not give way as you pull against it.

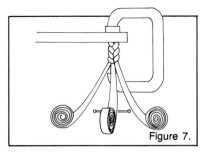

Figure 7.

BRAIDING

Hold the right strand (strand #1) between your right thumb and index finger, with the thumb up and the index finger underneath and bring it over the center strand (strand #2), (Figure 8). As you bring the strand over, be sure to keep the thumb on top (do not turn your wrist) and the strand flat, so that the same side of the strand always faces up. Then hold the left strand (strand #3)

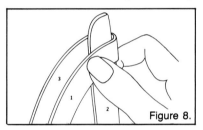

Figure 8.

between your left thumb and index finger, and, keeping the thumb on top and the strand flat, bring it over the center strand (strand #1), (Figure 9).

To continue braiding, repeat the process, bringing the right strand over the center one, then left over the center, and so forth. Hold the strands taut to maintain a firm, even ten-

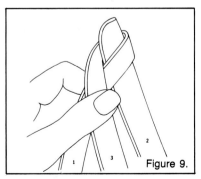

Figure 9.

sion, and always keep the open edges of the strands to the left (if you remember to keep your thumbs facing up, this will happen automatically).

Whenever you have to stop braiding for any reason, keep the work from becoming loose by clamping it with a spring-type clothespin, or by weaving a large safety pin through all the strands. As you braid, the unworked portion of the strands will probably become tangled, impeding your progress. To minimize this, keep only about a yard of each strand unwound from the roll, and stop regularly to untangle the loose strands. If you undo one strand from the tangle, the remaining two will be released at the same time. If new strips must be attached to complete the desired length of braid, add them one at a time to avoid unsightly bulges in the braid. Join all strips with bias seams (Figure 2), checking to make sure that all the seam allowances will be on the inside when the strips are folded.

DOUBLE AND TRIPLE LOOPING

Double and triple looping are techniques that are used to shape the braid as it is being made so that it will lie flat around curves and corners when the rug is laced. Double loops (sometimes called round turns), for example, are often used for shaping the first few rounds of round rugs, as well as for the center round of oval rugs. Triple loops, or square turns, are used to shape the right angle corners required for square and oblong rugs. Depending on the particular shape desired, one or the other—or both—of these techniques can also be used when

forming the braid into various angles, corners, and turns for more unusual braid arrangements. Right-hand double and triple loops, which shape the braid so that it turns to the left, are the most frequently used types.

DOUBLE LOOPING. To make a right-hand double loop, or round turn, bring the right strand of the braid (strand #1) over the center strand (strand #2). Bring the right strand (strand #2) over the center strand (strand #1) once more (Figure 10). Then

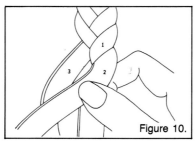

Figure 10.

bring the left strand (strand #3) over the center one (strand #2) and pull it tight (Figure 11). Continue braiding

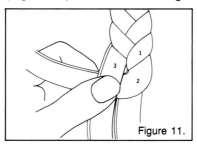

Figure 11.

in the normal way, or repeat the steps shown in Figures 10 and 11 to make as many additional double loops as necessary.

Left-hand double loops are made by bringing the left strand of the braid over the center strand, left over center again, and then right over center. Repeat the process if additional turns are necessary, then continue braiding in the regular way.

TRIPLE LOOPING. To make a right-hand triple loop, or square turn, bring the right strand of the braid (strand #1) over the center strand (strand #2), and bring the right strand (strand #2) over the center strand (strand #1) again, as you would for a double turn. Next, bring the right strand (strand #1) over the center strand (strand #2) once more. Then bring the left strand (strand #3) over the center strand (strand #1) and pull it tight (Figure 12). Continue braiding in the regular manner,

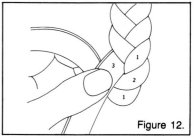

Figure 12.

or repeat the steps to make as many additional triple loops as necessary.

Left-hand triple loops are made by bringing the left strand of the braid over the center one, left over center again, and left over center a third time. Then bring the right strand over the center strand and pull tight. Repeat the process if additional turns are necessary, then continue braiding in the ordinary way.

Lacing

Although many old-time braided rugs were held together by stitching on the underside with an ordinary sewing needle and thread, lacing is a much better way to join the braids. Not only is lacing faster than sewing, it is easier (you can assemble and lace with the finished side of the rug facing you), stronger, less visible, and allows for a smoother and better meshed rug surface as well. A special blunt and curved-tipped lacing needle (available at most dime stores) should be used, along with a heavy cord-like carpet thread or, if you can find it, lacing cord made especially for braided rugs.

Always work on a flat surface and place the braid finished side up, arranging it with the loops to be laced together intermeshing rather than side by side. If you plan to lace the braid in a continuous spiral or in butted rounds, the double-folded edge of the braid should face inward.

The lacing itself is done by slipping the needle and cord through the loops of the braids without ever actually penetrating into the fabric. When a piece of lacing cord is used up, a new piece is spliced to it, enabling you to lace a large portion and sometimes the entire rug with what is, in effect, a continuous length of cord.

THREADING AND SPLICING

Two basically different methods are used to thread and splice lacing cord, one appropriate for ordinary solid core threads and cords, such as heavy carpet thread, and the other used with hollow core braid lacing cord. Either can be used with both single- and double-eyed needles.

SOLID CORE THREADS AND CORDS. Cut a 5- to 6-foot length of thread. Double it and knot the cut end. Thread the looped end of the double strand through the needle eye and pull a little more than a needle length of thread through. If you are using a lacing needle with two eyes, first thread through the eye closest

to the end of the needle and then thread back through the other eye. Next, open the thread loop a bit and bring the tip of the needle through it (Figure 13). Then pull the

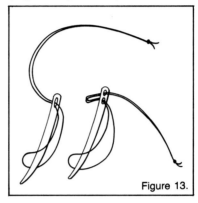

Figure 13.

thread tight, closing loop around needle eye(s).

When you have laced until only about 1½ needle lengths of your thread or cord remain, a new length of cord should be spliced to the old one. To do this, loosen the slipknot around the eye of the needle, draw the loop up and over the tip of the needle and pull the needle off the thread end. Next, cut a new 5- to 6-foot length of thread and thread the needle with it. Then tie the new and old threads in a square knot, as follows: place the knotted end of the new thread over the looped end of the old thread. Slip the tip of the needle into the overlapped loops (Figure 14). Draw the

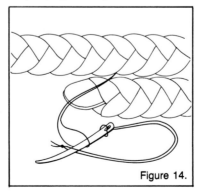

Figure 14.

needle and thread through, and pull the knot tight. Then continue lacing and, when you get to the knot, conceal it under the nearest loop of the braid. Repeat the procedure to splice additional lengths of lacing cord as needed.

HOLLOW CORE LACING CORDS. Cut a 2½- to 3-foot length of cord. Thread a lacing needle with a single eye in the same way you would an ordinary sewing needle. If you are using a lacing needle with two eyes, first thread the cord through the eye closest to the end of the needle and then thread back through the other eye.

Lace until only about 6 inches or so of the cord remain. Remove the lacing needle and re-thread it onto a new 2½- to 3-foot length of cord. Then, to begin splicing the two cords, thread a blunt-tipped tapestry needle onto the other end of the new lacing cord and insert the tip of the needle into the hollow end of the old cord (Figure 15).

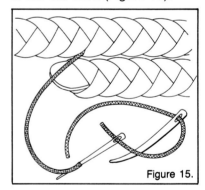

Figure 15.

Push the tapestry needle through the center of the old cord for about 4 inches, and then bring it out, pull the end of the new cord through, and remove the needle. Tug gently on the spliced portion to straighten out the cords, but allow a short end of the new cord to remain protruding from the old cord. Continue lacing, and when you reach the spliced portion of the cord, tuck the protruding end under the nearest loop of the braid. Repeat the procedure to splice additional lengths of lacing cord as needed.

ANCHORING THE LACING CORD

To anchor a doubled strand of a lacing cord such as carpet thread, insert the threaded lacing needle from the underside through the braid loop in which you wish to begin lacing. Draw the needle and cord through the braid loop, leaving the knotted end of the cord extending about an inch beyond the edge of the braid. Then insert the needle between the two strands of the lacing cord just above the knot and pull it through (Figure 16),

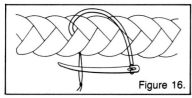

Figure 16.

forming a loose knot around the loop of the braid. Push the cord knot toward one end of the braid loop so it will be concealed under the next braid loop, and then tighten it.

If you are going to lace with a single strand of a heavy, hollow core lacing cord, make a small slipknot near the end of the cord and insert the threaded lacing needle through the braid loop in which you wish to begin lacing. Draw the needle and cord through the braid loop, leaving the slipknot extending beyond the edge of the braid, and insert the needle into the slipknot. Then tighten the slipknot and pull the needle and cord through, forming a loose knot

around the loop of the braid. Push the cord knot toward one end of the braid loop so it will be concealed under the next braid loop, and tighten it.

LACING ALONG STRAIGHT EDGES

Working on a flat surface, arrange the braid(s) finished side up, with the loops to be laced together intermeshing. Insert the lacing needle through a loop of one braid, sliding it under the loop from the center toward the edge of the braid (Figure 17); draw the

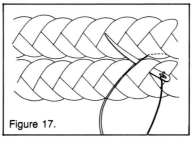

Figure 17.

cord through and pull it tight. Next, insert the needle through the nearest loop of the adjacent braid, again sliding it under the loop from the center of the braid toward the edge (Figure 18); draw the cord

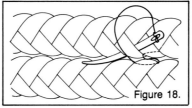

Figure 18.

through and pull it tight. Then return to the first braid and lace through the next loop in the same way. Continue lacing in this manner, alternating one loop on each braid. Do not skip loops or lace more than one loop at a time as long as the braids being joined are arranged in a straight line; and remember to conceal the lacing cord, by pulling it tight through each loop.

LACING AROUND CURVES

When lacing braids together around a convex (outward) curve—as, for example, when making a round or oval rug—a technique known as "increasing" must be used along the outer braid (the one being laced to the rug) in order to make it full enough to lie flat around the inner braid (the one already joined to the rug). Increasing is done whenever the loops of the outer braid do not mesh one for one with those of the inner braid. It is accomplished by lacing through one loop of the inner braid in the ordinary way, then lacing through two consecutive loops of the outer braid (Figure 19), and again through

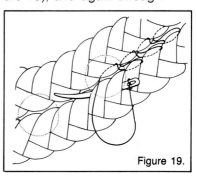

Figure 19.

one loop of the inner braid. If your rug buckles, you have not made sufficient increases: unlace the buckled portion and re-lace, making additional increases. On the other hand, if your rug is frilled around the edges, you have made too many increases: unlace this portion and re-lace with fewer increases. Remember that increasing should be done *only* on the outer braid and *only* around a curve—never on the inner braid or along the straight portion of an edge.

LACING SQUARE CORNERS

Unlike curves, the right-angle corners required for

square and oblong rugs cannot be properly shaped by lacing alone, but must be formed as the braid itself is made. To lace successive rounds of braid at these square turnings, work through one loop of the outer braid and one of the inner braid alternately, as you would for an ordinary straight edge, until you reach the very corner. Then increase once (insert the lacing needle through two loops) to turn the corner of the outer braid (Figure 20), and continue along

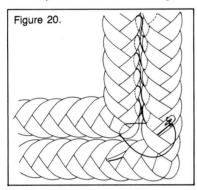

Figure 20.

the next edge by alternately lacing one loop on each braid. Increase along the outer braid in the same manner at each ensuing corner.

Finishing Braid Ends

The end of a braid can be finished off in several different ways, the method you choose depending largely on how you are assembling your rug.

Tapering the end of the braid is the appropriate way to finish off a round or oval rug made in a single continuous spiral, and can also be used for square or oblong rugs. The technique used for finishing two braid ends that will be joined can also be used to finish off single braid ends, and is often substituted for tapering to complete the end of a square or oblong rug made in a continuous spiral.

TAPERING

Lace your rug to a point about 6 inches before you wish to end the braid. This can be anywhere along the circumference of a round rug, but on an oval rug should be at or just past the beginning of a curved shoulder, and on a square or oblong rug should be about 6 inches from a corner.

Cut off the braid about 12 inches beyond the point where you have stopped lacing, unravel the strands until you are about a loop away from the laced portion, and clamp the braid at that point so it doesn't loosen up. Now trim the unbraided strand ends again so they are 12 inches long. Then unfold them and, cutting an equal amount from each edge, taper each strand from the clamp down to half the original width at the end. Refold each strand, slipstitching the double-folded edges if you find it difficult to keep them from opening up (Figure 21).

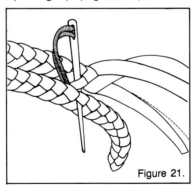

Figure 21.

Remove the clamp and rebraid the tapered strands until the ends are only about 6 inches long, ending by bringing the right, or outer, strand (strand #1) over the center one (strand #2). Clamp the braid again at this point. Then continue lacing up to the very last braided loop. Do not remove the clamp from the braid. On square-cornered

rugs, however, lace until only three loops remain along the rug edge before the corner, braiding a few more loops or unraveling a few, as necessary. Turn the rug wrong side up and lace back for about 8 inches to secure the cord, trim close to the surface, and turn the rug right side up again.

To begin weaving the strand ends into the edge of the rug, push a crochet hook from the wrong side to the right side through the next loop along the rug edge beyond the last one that has been laced (Figure 22). Once you have done

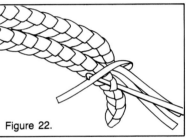

Figure 22.

this remove the clamp on the braid. Then bring the center strand (strand #1) under the inner strand (strand #3), catch it with the tip of the crochet hook and pull it through to the wrong side of the rug.

Now, insert the crochet hook in the same manner as before through the next loop along the edge of the rug. Take the outer strand of the remaining two strands of the braid (strand #2), bring it over the inner strand (strand #3), catch it with the hook and pull through to the wrong side of the rug. Repeat the process to pull the remaining strand of the braid through the next loop of the rug. Then adjust the three loops you have just woven into the edge of the rug so that all the double-folded edges face inward and the loops look even in relation to the rest of the edge. Once you have done this, turn the rug wrong side up and, using the crochet hook, weave each strand for several inches through the loops on the back of the rug—taking care that they don't show through on the finished side—and trim any remaining ends closely.

BUTTING

If both ends of the braid are to be finished so they can be joined to form a complete round, allow for butting at the start of the braid by securing the strands with a safety pin 6 inches from the ends (don't bother with a T-start). At the other end, secure the completed braid with a safety pin at the point where you wish to butt it, unbraid the strand ends beyond this point and trim them to 6 inches. Finish each of the ends in the following way: slipstitch or whip the strands together on the wrong side of the braid along the last few overlapping edges. Then taper each strand end diagonally, cutting along the double-folded edges (Figure 23). Fold

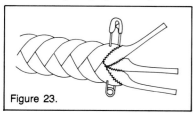

Figure 23.

the tapered strands to the wrong side of the braid, squaring the ends and aligning the center strand down the middle of the braid (Figure 24). Then,

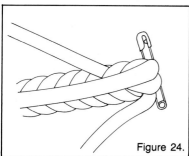

Figure 24.

using a crochet hook to help pull the strands through, weave the two outer strand ends through the back of the braid for several inches, crisscrossing them over the center strand, which is lying flat on the surface of the braid. Take care to keep the braid as flat as possible and avoid having the strands you are weaving show through on the right (finished) side of the braid. After you have woven the strand ends back into the braid for several inches, trim them off and tack to the back of the braid. As you lace the round of braid to the rug, align the two finished braid ends and stitch them together securely (Figure 25).

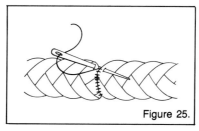

Figure 25.

Assembling a Braided Rug

Making and assembling your rug in a single continuous braid is one of the simplest of all methods and can be used for a rug of any of the basic shapes, though it is especially popular for round and oval rugs. The braid is started with a T-start and is then coiled into a spiral that winds continuously from a small center round into increasingly larger rounds until it is finished off by tapering the end to give the outer edge a smooth line. The usual circular or oval configuration of the spiral can be varied to create rugs of all sorts of different shapes.

If you are arranging your

colors in hit-or-miss fashion, you can finish as much of the braiding as you wish, even all of it, before you stop and begin to coil the braid and lace it in place. Just add additional strips to your braid as necessary, changing colors at random. Don't forget to stagger the new strips, however, so that you won't have more than one seam in a given spot.

You will need to calculate with greater care where to end one color and begin the next if you are making a rug with a definite color plan. On round and oval rugs, colors are usually changed one at a time so that the change appears as a gradual blending rather than as an abrupt switch. Changing colors on a round rug can be done at any point along the circumference, but for ovals, new colors should only be added along the curved portion of the edge (sometimes called the shoulder), preferably near the beginning or end of the curve.

If you are making a round or oval rug with a fairly simple arrangement of colors and prefer to complete a great deal of your braiding before you stop to coil and lace, you can make a very rough approximation of where you will need to change colors by figuring that each succeeding spiral round will be about 8 to 10 inches longer than the previous one. This approach is far from exact, however, and alternating braiding with coiling and lacing is a much more foolproof way to ensure that your colors will appear exactly where you want them to be.

NEEDLEPOINT

Exquisitely elegant and at the same time extremely durable, needlepoint is the acknowledged aristocrat of the decorative needle arts. A form of counted thread embroidery, it is worked over and completely covers a grid formed by the evenly woven threads of a canvas backing. Time consuming and expensive (though far less so now than it once was), for centuries needlepoint was the exclusive property of the upper classes. Prototypes of needlepoint stitchery adorned the garments of ancient rulers from Egypt all the way to China, and later embellished the robes of Church and State, the tapestries and heraldic banners of medieval Europe.

Kings have sponsored its production, and queens have practiced the art themselves. The English embroidery industry, for example, took root under the protection of Henry VIII, and blossomed under that of Elizabeth, his daughter, herself an accomplished needlewoman. Bess was particularly partial to "canvas work," as needlepoint has always been called in Europe, and the workmanship of her own rugs and tapestries was unequalled—except perhaps by those of her cousin Mary, the hapless Queen of Scots.

Some needlepoint of this type was done in the early days of this country as well. The shell motifs that Martha Washington stitched for her drawing room chairs can still be seen at Mount Vernon, but less expensive and less time-consuming forms of embroidery were more popular. As for rug making, crafts like braiding and hooking that could utilize recycled strips of precious yarn and fabric, were far more practical in a new

land hacking its existence out of a wilderness.

It remained for nineteenth century industrial ingenuity—the mass production of vividly-colored aniline-dyed yarns, of cheaply printed paper design patterns, and of the inexpensive large-mesh canvases we are familiar with today—to turn needlepoint into the modern, broadly popular craft it has since become. Called Berlin Work, after the city where it was introduced, this new kind of needlepoint became the rage of the bourgeois Victorian era, both in Europe and America. It revolutionized canvas embroidery, wresting it from the hands of the aristocracy and placing it comfortably in the laps of the middle classes, where it has remained.

Thus, needlepoint remains an aristocrat, but one that all of us can enjoy. For the rug maker, it is a medium that offers a broader range of creative alternatives than is possible with any of the other rug crafts, except perhaps weaving—and unlike weaving, it requires little by way of tools and equipment. A needlepoint rug can be any size and shape you wish to make. It can be flat or have a shaggy pile stitched into it; it can be smooth-surfaced or textured. The simple, classic Tent Stitch continues to be a mainstay, but is only one of dozens of stitches that may be worked. Color can be used with bold simplicity, or with the subtlest gradations of shading. Needle and yarn can be used with equal facility to create a naturalistic scene or an abstract pattern, to render complex detail or simple shapes. The choice is up to you.

Equipment

NEEDLES

Needlepoint work is always done with tapestry needles, which are longish, blunt-tipped needles with large oval eyes. The blunt tip is important in order to avoid splitting the yarn or the threads of the backing, so don't substitute sharp-tipped needles. Tapestry needles come in a dozen different numbered sizes, ranging from size 13 for the largest and longest ones, to size 24 for the shortest and most slender. The needle should be able to slip through the canvas mesh easily, without distorting it, but at the same time must have a large enough eye so the yarn can be threaded without fraying. Thus, the size you will need will depend on the mesh size of the canvas you plan to use and the thickness of the yarn. The larger, or lower numbered needle will be used with the larger (lower numbered) mesh canvases and heavier yarns, while the relatively finer, higher numbered needles are appropriate for the higher numbered, smaller mesh canvases and thinner yarns. Fine petit point, for example, worked on a 24-mesh-to-the-inch canvas, requires size 24 needles; 10-mesh canvas is usually worked with size 18 needles, 7-mesh canvas with sizes 16 to 18 needles, and the 3- to 5-mesh canvases with jumbo size 13 needles. Since needlepoint rugs for floor use are usually made on the larger mesh canvases, unless you are making a rug for a very unusual purpose—a doll house miniature, for instance—you will generally use only the larger needles (sizes 13 through 18) for rug making.

FRAMES

It is not essential to stretch the canvas mesh backing used to needlepoint on a frame. Many people prefer to work with the canvas in the hands. Frames reduce the portability of your needlepoint work, but they do keep the canvas from pulling out of shape and, if you don't care about being able to carry your needlepoint around with you, you may want to consider mounting your canvas on a frame. Appropriate frames, which can be purchased or homemade, are discussed in the section on Hooking.

MISCELLANEOUS ACCESSORIES

You will need two different pairs of sharp scissors at various stages of your needlepoint project: long dressmaker's shears for cutting canvas and skeins of yarn, and small embroidery scissors with narrow blades and sharp points for trimming yarn and making repairs as you work. If you find your fingers getting sore from constantly pushing the needle through the canvas, try using a thimble. A small emery bag, such as is usually attached to a pincushion, is also handy for cleaning needles.

Materials

Canvas, or another kind of foundation fabric, and yarn are the basic materials used for making any kind of needlepoint, including rugs. To finish your rug, rug binding or a sturdy lining fabric (or both) are also recommended.

BACKING MATERIALS

The type of backing most commonly used for needlepoint is an open-weave canvas, generally made of cotton and highly stiffened with sizing; but other rug foundation fabrics, as well as plastic mesh "canvas," can also be used. For rug making, only the sturdiest, most durable canvases and fabrics should be considered.

There are three different kinds of needlepoint canvas (not including the plastic variety), all suitable for rug making. Sold by the yard, they are made in a number of different sizes and widths, and usually in two colors—white and ecru. Size is determined by the number of mesh, or threads, per running inch. The fewer the number of threads, the larger are the holes between them, and thus the heavier will be the yarns used to cover the canvas. The various mesh sizes are generally divided into three categories: the finest mesh canvases, 16 or more mesh per inch, are used for petit point work; the middle range, from about 8 to 15 mesh per inch, are called gros point; and the largest mesh, from 3 to 7 threads per inch, are known as quick point. Rugs are most often worked on the larger mesh canvases, from 3 to 10 mesh per inch. Simple designs work well on canvas of any mesh size, but if the design you plan to use for your rug has a lot of fine detail, choose a 10-mesh canvas.

Mono canvas consists of single vertical (warp) threads crossing single horizontal (weft) threads. It is an evenly woven, sturdy, all-purpose canvas, but since the threads are not interlocked, it tends to pull out of shape when worked and may require repeated blocking. The size most suitable for rug making is 10 mesh per inch, but mono canvas also comes in various finer sizes from 12 to 24 mesh per inch. Available widths range from 36 to 60 inches.

Penelope canvas is woven with pairs of vertical and horizontal threads, the vertical ones spaced closely together and the horizontal ones slightly further apart. The threads of penelope canvas are usually somewhat finer and flatter than those of a similar size mono canvas, but penelope has the advantage that stitches can be worked over pairs of threads, or the threads may be separated and finer detail can be stitched over individual threads. The size of penelope canvas is usually indicated by a set of two numbers, the first indicating the number of stitches per inch that can be made when working over pairs of threads, the second referring to the number of stitches per inch that can be made if the canvas threads are separated and stitches are worked over individual threads. Penelope canvas is made in 40- and 60-inch widths and in sizes as fine as 14/28 mesh; but for rug making, 5/10, 7/14, 9/18, and 10/20 are the most appropriate mesh sizes.

Rug canvas looks and is worked as though it were made of single vertical threads crossing single horizontal threads. But it is actually a type of leno weave, in which double warp (vertical) threads are twisted around double weft (horizontal) threads. Because of the twist, the threads cannot be separated like those of penelope canvas. A very sturdy and stable canvas, it comes in 40- and 60-inch widths and is made in the largest mesh sizes—3, 3½, 4, 5, and 7 mesh per inch—and is excellent for rugs worked with the heavy rug yarns or multiple strands of the thinner yarns.

Other backings that can be used for needlepoint rugs include monk's cloth, Dura-Back, Knot-On, or any heavy-duty even-weave cotton or cotton and linen rug-warp cloth. Those made with 6- to 8-threads per inch work well with the heavy rug yarns, while 12- to 14-thread per inch fabrics can be used with finer yarns. Since all these fabrics are softer than canvas, they must be stretched taut on frames.

Plastic mesh "canvas" is also a suitable backing for needlepoint. One virtue of stitching on a plastic mesh foundation is that it will never shift out of shape and thus will never require blocking. It is somewhat thicker than ordinary cotton canvas and comes in fewer sizes, but 5- and 10-mesh sizes, which are appropriate for rugs, are available by the yard in 36 inch widths; and a 7-mesh size is made in 10½ by 13½ inch sheets that can be pieced together to make a rug of any size.

DETERMINING AMOUNTS AND PREPARING THE BACKING.

Whatever actual shape your rug may be, always cut the canvas in a square or rectangle. (This is necessary in order to be able to block the finished work properly.) Margins of at least 3 inches should be allowed on each side of the design area, so buy a piece of canvas at least 6 inches longer and wider than the desired finished length and width of your rug. Since canvas (and all other backings except plastic) has a definite direction and should be worked lengthwise, don't try to skimp on canvas by planning to arrange the longer sides of your rug

widthwise across the canvas. Always measure length in the same direction as the vertical (warp) threads of the canvas—that is, parallel to the selvages; and measure width in the direction of the horizontal (weft) threads—across the canvas from selvage to selvage. If you are going to cut away the selvages—before doing so—it is a good idea to mark one crosswise edge as "top" (use an arrow or any other symbol you wish) so that you will be able to tell which direction the threads should run when marking and working your design.

Sections of canvas or other backings can be joined if you wish to make a rug that is wider than the widths available, or if you prefer to work a large rug in smaller, more manageable and portable sections. But be sure to buy all your canvas at the same time and from the same roll, because mesh size occasionally varies from roll to roll. Leave 3-inch margins on all sides of each section and cut them so that, when matched, the threads will run in the same direction. Joining the sections may be done before you begin to work the rug or after most of the stitching has been done, whichever approach best suits your own particular needs. Several alternative methods (discussed later) can be used.

To prepare your canvas, bind all cut edges (selvages need not be bound) with masking tape on both the back and front sides of the canvas. This will keep the edges from raveling as you work. Fabric backings may be prepared in the same way, or you can run a line of machine zigzag stitching ¼ inch inside the edges if you prefer. Mark

center lines lengthwise and widthwise on the canvas or fabric, using a soft pencil or a

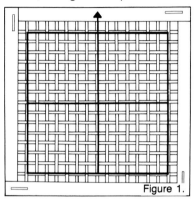

Figure 1.

fine-tipped indelible felt marker; then outline the edges of the design area, carefully counting out from the center the exact number of mesh required to complete the design (Figure 1). To make and enlarge an original design, and to mark it directly on the canvas, follow the directions given in the Appendix. Then, if you are planning to use one, mount your canvas or fabric backing on a frame. (See Hooking).

YARNS

Yarns for needlepoint rugs must be especially durable. Not only will they receive hard wear once the rug has been completed, but they also must be able to withstand the abrasion and the pulling and tugging of being repeatedly drawn through the canvas. The best yarns for this purpose are made of wool (though there are some suitable synthetics), have long, tough fibers, and are tightly spun—all of which gives them the hard finish and resiliency needed for the rough treatment they will receive. In addition, needlepoint yarns should be colorfast and moth-proofed. There are several yarns that meet these requirements admirably, notably the

Persian, tapestry, rya, and rug yarns. They differ in weight and thickness, in number of ply and type of twist, and in the range of colors available—and your choice will be based on these factors. All can be found in needlework stores or ordered by mail from many different suppliers.

Crewel yarns and Nantucket twist, along with various cotton, silk, rayon, and metallic embroidery flosses are also used for many types of needlepoint projects, but they are not good for rug making because they are either too fragile or too fine (or both) for the canvas mesh sizes best suited for rugs. Knitting yarns, both wool and synthetic, also should never be used to make a needlepoint rug: they are too soft and springy, and will fuzz up and fray when pulled through the canvas (or later, when walked upon).

Persian yarn. A wool yarn with a lustrous sheen, Persian is one of the highest quality and most popular of all the needlepoint yarns. Each full strand is made of three loosely-twisted individual two-ply strands that can be worked as one or separated and used individually. A full strand (three individual strands together, that is) will cover 10-mesh canvas well, and two full strands work satisfactorily on 7-mesh canvas. Three or more full strands can be used together on the 3- to 5-mesh canvases, but on these sizes the heavier rya and rug yarns are easier to work with. Persian yarns come in an almost bewildering array of vibrant colors. (Paternayan, for example, dyes their fine line of Persian yarns in 343 different shades.) They are sold in skeins of different sizes from little 8 or 9 yard packets to large 8-ounce skeins. Some stores even cut large skeins and will sell quantities as small as a single 30-inch strand.

Tapestry yarn. A tightly twisted four-ply wool yarn, tapestry yarn is slightly heavier than a full strand of Persian yarn. The two are often used interchangeably, though the ply of tapestry yarn cannot be separated into individual strands and the range of colors available is somewhat more limited. One strand works well on 10-mesh canvas and two strands will cover a 7-mesh canvas. Tapestry yarns are readily available in small 8 to 9 yard skeins and in larger 30 to 40 yard skeins; some manufacturers also package 100 yard skeins, though these are harder to find.

Rug yarn. The heaviest of the needlepoint yarns, these are often called "quick point" yarns because they are used with the largest mesh canvases and work up very quickly. Rug yarn is actually a group of different yarns made by many manufacturers. The finest, and most expensive, rug yarns are made of wool; but there are others made of cotton, polyester, acrylic, rayon, and various blends—and some needlepointers find these wear quite well. Rug yarns range from two- to six-ply, and come in different types of twists from quite smooth to rather ropelike. Some are just a bit thicker than tapestry yarn and work well on a 7-mesh canvas, while others are extremely bulky and will fill the 3- to 5-mesh canvases beautifully. The range of colors available varies with the particular manufacturer and line of yarn—some are made in 40 or 50 colors, while others come in more than 200 different shades. With such a great combination of choices available, however, you should have no difficulty finding a rug yarn that will fit your needs exactly.

Determining Yarn Requirments. Yarns are dyed in batches, called dye lots, and the same color often varies from one dye lot to another (except for tapestry yarn, which is dyed very uniformly and always seems to match). With the other yarns, however, it is important to buy all you will need of each color—and a little extra for good measure—at the same time. And always check to make sure that all the skeins of each color are marked with the same dye lot number. Don't be afraid to buy too much yarn: unused full skeins can often be returned, and you can always use the leftovers for small details in other projects.

To figure out how much yarn your rug will require, you must first decide on the mesh size of the canvas, the type of yarn, and the various needlepoint stitches you will use. Then work up a 1-inch-square swatch in each different stitch, using a measured amount of yarn, and make a note of how much yarn each stitch uses up. Next, determine the total number of square inches in your rug by multiplying the length by the width, and roughly apportion the total among the different stitch/color combinations you plan to use. Multiply each of these figures by the amount of yarn used per square inch for that particular stitch, and then add up the totals for each different color. If your figures are in inches, remember to convert them into yards (divide by 36).

Preparing the Yarn. All you have to do to prepare yarns for use is to cut the skeins into strands about 30 inches long. For ordinary skeins, simply untwist the coil. If the ring of yarn is small, cut it through once, at the point where the two yarn ends are tied. Cut larger rings twice, once where the yarn ends are knotted, and again at the opposite end. Some yarns are packaged in pull skeins, in which case just pull out, measure, and cut a batch of 30-inch lengths. (You don't have to cut the entire skein at once.) To keep the different colors from getting mixed up, make a loose knot in the middle of each batch.

Planning a Needle-point Rug

To make a needlepoint rug, you can buy a prepackaged kit, which will contain all the materials you'll need, including either a painted canvas or a blank one and separate design graph. You can follow the instructions to the letter or, if you're feeling adventuresome, substitute some different stitches or even exchange some of the yarns supplied for ones of your own choice. Another alternative is to purchase a painted canvas in any design that appeals to you, and choose your own yarns and stitches. Needlework stores carry all sorts of prepared canvas in various mesh sizes; any size from 3- to 10-mesh per inch is appropriate for a rug, and you can do quick point on any canvas that was actually meant for latch hooking because the mesh sizes are the same for both crafts.

Kits and prepared canvases are very expensive, however, especially if (as is advisable) you buy high quality ones. Designing your own rug is far cheaper, and allows you unlimited choices of materials, patterns, and sizes. What is more,

it is very satisfying and you need not be an accomplished artist to do it. Practically any design, from the most intricately detailed scenes and patterns to the simplest and boldest ones, can be translated into needlepoint.

Before you become confused by the abundance of possibilities, decide how large a rug you want to make, and whether you prefer to work it in sections that you can tote around or all in one piece. Consider whether you want to be able to finish your rug very quickly, or whether you don't really care how long it takes. Once you make these choices, all the others—designs, canvases, yarns, and even colors and stitches—will be easier, because some combinations work better than others. Designs with intricate detail, for instance, are best suited to the smaller-mesh needlepoint canvases, such as the 10-mesh per inch size; and these, having many more stitches per inch than the larger-mesh canvases, take appreciably longer to work. If you want a rug that will work up very rapidly, choose the larger 3- to 7-mesh canvases. You'll have to make only 1/10 to ½ the number of stitches that you would for an equal-size 10-mesh canvas; but if this is your preference, eliminate the complicated, detailed designs in favor of the simpler ones, since they are better suited to the large-mesh quick point canvases.

Whether you select the speed of quick point or the detail possible with finer-mesh canvases, if you want to make your rug in small portable sections, consider eliminating large pictorial scenes or continuous patterns. While you can break such a design into pieces if you really want to, the joinings will often be hard

to conceal completely. Smaller individual designs that are repeated a number of times, or a series of related designs—a dozen different flowers or fruits traced from a seed catalog or botanical journal, for instance—are much better suited. You can make the pieces one at a time and join them later, separating each or surrounding them all (or both) with borders if you wish. Patterns for needlepoint pillows, which appear in numerous books and magazines, can be used in the same way: simply repeat them as many times as you wish and then stitch the squares together.

Once you have selected the canvas and design you're going to use, your choice of yarns will be automatically narrowed to those that combine the characteristics of weight and bulk sufficient to cover your canvas well, with a texture and a selection of colors appropriate to the design and to your overall decorating scheme. With so many different yarns available, you should have no trouble finding the right one.

Then study your design and select the stitches you wish to use. There are many to choose from in addition to the basic tent stitch—flat and smooth stitches as well as textured ones of various sorts, some simple and others more complex (though none are very hard to make). When deciding which stitches, and how many of them, to use, there are several helpful guidelines to keep in mind. An abstract design with large areas of color can be given added depth and dimension by the use of several different stitches of contrasting textures. Or set off flat tent-stitched components of a rug made in sections with solid-color borders worked in textured stitches. And if you wish to make texture the primary design element you can combine many different stitches. But choose your stitches judiciously; don't clutter up a design that is already strong or very busy in terms of color or pattern with too many textured stitches—they will just confuse the eye and divert it from the natural focus of attention.

Structurally, some stitches are better for rug making than others. Stitches used for rugs should distort the canvas as little as possible and this is especially important if you are not planning to work with your canvas stretched taut on a frame. Blocking will restore a rug to its proper shape in most cases, but even repeated blocking will not be able to completely true-up a badly distorted canvas or keep it in the desired shape once it is on the floor. If you use any stitches that tend to pull the canvas out of shape—even the basic Continental Stitch, for example—work them very carefully and somewhat loosely, and use them only over small areas. In addition, choose stitches that cover the canvas completely so that no bare threads will show through; or if you find that some of your favorite stitches are not covering the backing very well (Half Cross Stitch and some of the vertical stitches sometimes exhibit this characteristic) use additional strands of yarn, or use the tramé technique to pad the canvas. Long stitches, where the yarn crosses over more than four mesh of the canvas, should also be avoided, particularly on the 3- to 7-mesh per inch quick point canvases, because long strands of yarn lying atop the canvas are easily snagged by the heels of shoes. Many of the popular Bargello (or

Florentine) patterns are of this type, but they can often be adapted very easily by breaking each long stitch into several short components (Figure

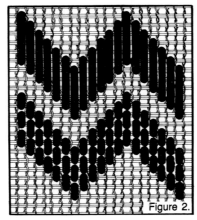
Figure 2.

2). If you are in doubt about the appropriateness of any stitch, test it first by making a swatch.

Fundamental Techniques of Needlepoint

THREADING THE NEEDLE

Before you even start to thread your needle, you should be aware that most yarns, but especially Persians, have a definite direction, much like the nap of a fabric. Run your fingers up and then down a strand of yarn and you will see that the fibers lie flat and the yarn feels smooth when you move one way, but that the yarn becomes fuzzy and feels slightly rough when you move in the opposite directiion. Always thread your yarn so that the fibers are running away from the needle—that is, in the direction of the "nap"—and if you are using multiple strands, be sure to arrange them with the fibers all going in the same direction. If you do this, the yarn will get less roughened as you pull it through the mesh of the canvas. Never

double over a strand of yarn to avoid using two separate strands: one-half of the strand will always be going in the wrong direction.

Sometimes trying to thread the ends of heavy yarns through the slender eye of a needle can be an exasperating chore. There are several tricks you can use, however, to easily overcome this obstacle.

Method 1. Fold the end of the yarn over the needle and pinch the fold tightly between your thumb and index finger (Figure 3). Slide the needle out

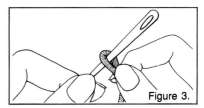
Figure 3.

and push the eye over the folded yarn, using a sawing motion to help it slide over the yarn (Figure 4). Then pull the

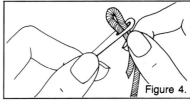
Figure 4.

yarn through with your fingers until you have disengaged the looped end.

Method 2. Cut a strip of paper slightly narrower in width than the size of the needle eye. Fold the paper in half and slip the yarn end into the fold. Insert the narrow cut ends of the paper strip into the needle eye, and then pull the paper and yarn through the eye (Figure 5).

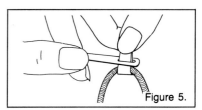
Figure 5.

METHODS OF STITCHING

To stitch your needlepoint rug, you can work with the canvas resting on a table top or in your lap—or, of course, with the canvas mounted on a frame. The canvas is usually worked with the selvages at the sides, that is, with the vertical (warp) threads of the canvas running straight away from you; but it is frequently rotated 180 degrees (turned so the bottom becomes the top and the top becomes the bottom) to work alternating rows of stitches. Occasionally, the canvas may be worked with the horizontal (weft) threads running straight away from you, but this is done much less often, and generally only with some of the more unusual stitch patterns.

If your canvas is a large one, you can roll up the end you aren't working on and secure it with a few safety pins to keep it out of your way. Pin in the margins, however, so that you will not distort the canvas mesh within the design area or snag any stitches you may have already completed.

There are two different ways to insert the needle into the canvas to form any given needlepoint stitch. Many needlepointers prefer the faster and more ryhthmic single motion of the "needle-through" technique as a general purpose method of stitching, reserving the slower, two-motion "punch-and-stab" technique for special circumstances—as when working with the canvas stretched on a frame, when the direction in which the needle must be pointed to form a particular stitch is an awkward one or one that will push the canvas threads out of line. There are no hard and fast rules that must be followed in selecting one or the other method—just the advice that you should feel comfortable stitching, and that your stitches should be plump and even and should distort the canvas as little as possible. With both methods, a uniform tension should be maintained, one that is not so tight that the canvas will become misshapen or so loose that the stitches themselves will be malformed and uneven. This is not difficult; it simply takes a bit of practice. After making several stitches, you will usually find that the yarn has become twisted: if you drop the needle and let the yarn dangle, it will untwist by itself. Don't forget to do this; stitching with twisted yarn will detract from the look.

NEEDLE-THROUGH METHOD. In this method, one stitch is completed and the next one begun in a single operation. To begin, bring the needle up from the wrong side of the canvas in the hole where you wish to start your first stitch (this is usually referred to as the base of the stitch), and pull the yarn through. Then, in one continuous motion, simply insert the needle from front to back (that is, from the right side to the wrong side) into the canvas at the top of the first stitch, slide the needle along the underside of the canvas and bring it out in the hole that will form the base of the next stitch, drawing the yarn all the way through as you pull the needle out (Figure 6). This will tighten

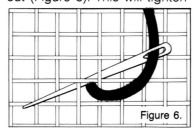

Figure 6.

the first stitch and begin a new one at the same time. Repeat the procedure to make each succeeding stitch, inserting the needle into the canvas in the top of the stitch, bringing it out in the base of the next stitch you wish to make, drawing the yarn through, etc.

PUNCH-AND-STAB METHOD. In this method, the needle is inserted into the canvas and then brought out again in two distinctly separate motions. Holding the needle perpendicular to the canvas, punch it through from underneath (Figure 7), then switch

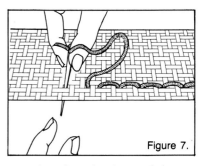

Figure 7.

your hand to the front of the canvas and pull the needle through, drawing the yarn all the way through. Then stab the needle straight down into the canvas in the next hole appropriate for the stitch you are making, switch your hand to the underside of the canvas, and pull needle and yarn all the way through. Repeat the two operations for all succeeding stitches.

If you are working with your canvas stretched on a standing frame, you can use both hands for stitching. This will allow you to develop a more regular rhythm of stitching and increase your speed. Keep one hand on top of the canvas and the other one underneath. Stab the needle down into the canvas with the top hand, and draw the needle and yarn through to the underside with the other hand. Then punch the needle through from underneath with the lower hand, pull it and the yarn through to the front of the canvas with the top hand (Figure 8).

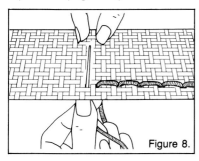

Figure 8.

STARTING AND ENDING

STARTING A NEW STRAND OF YARN. Yarn can be anchored in several ways. Choose whichever method you find most comfortable. After you have finished the first strand, try to stagger the beginnings and endings so that they don't fall at the same spot on each row.

Method 1. This method can be used to start the first strand or to begin new strands once the work is in progress. Bring the yarn up from the back of the canvas in the first hole of your stitch pattern, leaving an end about 1 inch long on the wrong side of the canvas. Point this end in the direction in which you will be stitching and hold it flat against the canvas with one hand. Then work your stitches over the yarn end, fastening it securely against the back of the canvas (Figure 9).

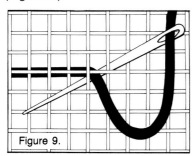

Figure 9.

Method 2. This method can also be used to anchor the first strand of yarn or new strands once the work is in progress. Knot the end of the yarn and insert the needle through the canvas from front to back (right side to wrong side) about 1 inch away in the direction you will be working from the first hole of your stitch pattern. Then bring the needle up from the back in the first hole of your stitch and work the stitches over the yarn end. When you approach the knot, trim it away and push the short end to the back of the work. Knots are *never* left in a finished piece of needlepoint, so do not stitch over them or forget to trim them away.

ENDING A STRAND OF YARN. When only 3 or 4 inches of the strand you are working with remain, or when you need to end one color and begin another, bring the needle through to the wrong side of the work and weave the yarn for about 1 inch through the backs of the adjacent stitches. Then trim the excess yarn close to the canvas. Avoid weaving dark color yarns through light ones wherever possible (Figure 10).

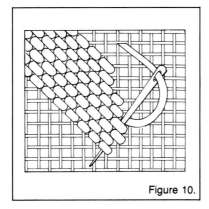

Figure 10.

CARRYING YARN ACROSS THE CANVAS. To avoid having to end a strand of yarn and

start it again in a nearby area, you can carry yarn across the back of the canvas to begin working in a new spot. But if the area you are finishing and the one you are about to start are more than ½ inch apart, weave the yarn through the back of the work in the intervening space to avert potential snags.

FOLLOWING A STITCH DIAGRAM

Instructions for working needlepoint stitches are usually presented in diagram form. The canvas backing is shown as a grid or graph, with each vertical and horizontal line representing one vertical or horizontal mesh (thread) of the canvas, and the blank squares themselves representing the holes between the canvas mesh. Heavy lines or bars, representing the stitches, are arranged on the grid in exactly the same way they are to be worked on the canvas.

The order in which the needle is to go in and out of the canvas is usually indicated by a series of consecutive numbers, one of which appears at each end of every stitch. The odd numbers indicate the beginning (or base) of the stitch and the even numbers signify the end (or top) of the stitch. To follow any stitch diagram, bring the needle up from the back (that is, the wrong side) of canvas at the point marked "1," insert it into the canvas from front to back at "2," bring it up again at "3," reinsert it from front to back at "4," and so forth. The needle is always brought up from underneath on odd numbers (1, 3, 5, etc.), and inserted from front to back (right side to wrong side) on even numbers (2, 4, 6, etc.) When the numbers along a row of stitches are printed upside down, it means that in order to work the stitches along that particular row, the canvas is to be rotated 180 degrees, so that the top edge is at the bottom and the bottom edge is at the top. When a pattern stitch may be worked with a combination of different colored yarns, the bars representing the stitches in the diagram will often be printed in different colors, or marked in some other way to indicate each color to be used.

COMPENSATING STITCHES

When making needlepoint stitches that cover more than one vertical and horizontal mesh of the canvas, you will often find that blank spots remain around the edges of the area being stitched. To fill in these spaces, shortened versions of the same stitch (called compensating stitches) are used (Figure 11).

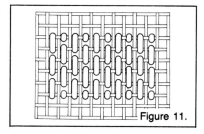
Figure 11.

STITCHING DETAILS ON PENELOPE CANVAS

The double mesh of penelope canvas may be separated and finer stitches worked over individual threads of the canvas. This is an excellent solution if you want to combine detailed design areas with a fast-working background.

Stitching over the individual mesh of the canvas will be easier if you separate them first. Just poke your needle between the threads and push them apart until they are

evenly spaced. The fine work is usually done first, using fewer strands, or a finer yarn, than the one you will use to work the larger stitches. Continental (tent) stitch is appropriate for small areas of detail, and the basket weave (diagonal tent) stitch is often used for larger sections. When you are ready to fill in the gros point or quick point stitches of the background, work over the double mesh of the canvas as close as you can get to the areas of detail. If any single open spaces remain between the larger and the smaller stitches, fill them in with small stitches, worked in fine strands of the background color (Figure 12).

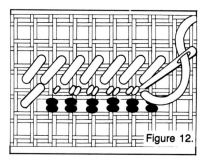
Figure 12.

TRAMÉ

Tramé is a method of stitching long horizontal threads of yarn across the front of the canvas to serve as an underpadding for various needlepoint stitches, which are then worked right over the "grounding." It can be used for purely decorative reasons, but is also very useful for filling out stitches that don't completely cover the canvas by themselves. The tramé stitching is usually done in the same color yarn that will be used for the stitches made over it, but for unusual effects the ground may also be laid in a contrasting color. Tramé works best on penelope canvas, but can also be used on mono and rug

canvases.

To lay the grounding, bring the needle up from underneath between a pair of horizontal threads of penelope canvas (or between two individual horizontal threads of other canvases) at one edge of the area to be covered. Then make long running stitches of irregular length across the paired canvas threads, going under only one vertical thread of the canvas between stitches. If you plan to lay the grounding over more than one row of horizontal canvas threads, avoid ridges by staggering the stitches so that they don't go in and out of the canvas at the same points. (Figure 13).

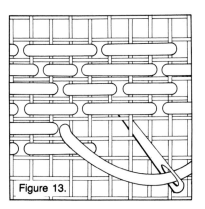
Figure 13.

PATCHING CANVAS

Should you accidentally cut into the canvas while removing stitches, the damage can be fixed with a patch. Or, if your canvas has a bulky knot here and there—and it is often hard to find a large piece of canvas completely devoid of knots— you can avoid the unsightly bumps that will result from stitching over them by cutting off the knots and patching the canvas. Cut a 3-inch square from some extra canvas of the same mesh size (Figure 14). Place the patch against the wrong side of your canvas, centering it over the damaged

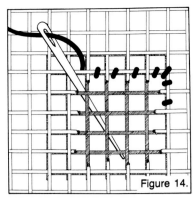

Figure 14.

area and matching the vertical and horizontal threads. Hold the patch with one hand, or tape the edges temporarily, if you prefer. Work a square inch or so of stitches through both layers of canvas, then trim away the excess portion of the patch.

JOINING SECTIONS OF CANVAS

Sections of a needlepoint rug may be joined in a number of different ways, depending on whether you want the join to be unobtrusive or decorative, and also on how much time you are prepared to spend at the chore. Canvas may be joined before you begin to work the needlepoint (as when available widths are not sufficiently large to make the size rug you wish), but it is usually done after most or all of the stitching has been completed.

BACKSTITCHED SEAM. This is the easiest and fastest method of joining sections of worked canvas and is often used to piece rugs made in long strips, though it is appropriate for small sections as well. The join is not invisible, but is can be quite unobtrusive, particularly if it is made in a background area or along a long, straight line of the design. The individual sections should be blocked before you join them.

Before seaming, work one or two extra rows of needlepoint stitches in the seam allowance beyond each edge to be joined. Then place the two sections right sides together,

matching the canvas mesh and the worked stitches very carefully. Using heavy carpet thread, backstitch the seam just inside the extra row (or rows) of needlepoint stitches, or machine stitch if you prefer. Trim the seam allowances to about 1½ inches, open them flat, and whip the edges of the raw canvas to the back of the completed work.

WHIPPED SEAM. A nearly invisible join, this method can be used before working the canvas, but is usually done after the needlepointing has been finished and the sections blocked. Fold the unworked canvas seam allowances to the wrong side one canvas thread beyond the needlepointed area. Place the two sections right side up and align the two edges to be joined, matching mesh for mesh. Thread your tapestry needle with strong carpet thread and whip with the two unworked mesh of the canvas together. Then make a single line of continental, half cross, or cross stitches—whichever is most appropriate—over the whipped canvas threads, using yarn of a color that matches the surrounding needlepoint work (Figure 15). Trim the

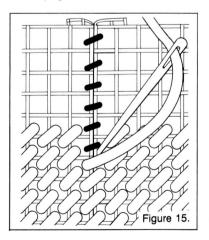

Figure 15.

seam allowances to about 1½ inches, open them flat, and

whip the raw edges of the canvas to the back of the completed work.

BINDING STITCH SEAM. If a decorative join is appropriate to the overall design of your rug, the strong and durable Binding stitch (see Dictionary of Needlepoint Stitches) is an excellent way to seam the sections. It is done after the needlepoint work itself has been completed and the individual sections have been blocked.

Fold under the unworked canvas seam allowances of each edge to be joined one canvas thread beyond the needlepointed area. Place the two sections together right sides out and align the edges to be joined, matching mesh for mesh. Then work the Binding stitch through both the folded edges. Trim the seam allowances to approximately 1½ inches, open them flat, and whip the raw edges of the canvas to the back of the completed work.

LAPPED JOIN. This is the method to use if you want a practically invisible join. It is appropriate for all rugs made in sections, and is particularly recommended for joining sections of an intricate design, which would be difficult to match using other seaming techniques. You can piece the canvas sections before you begin needlepointing, or after most of the work has been done. Block the rug after the sections have been joined and the needlepoint stitching completed.

If you are going to needlepoint the individual sections before joining them, work all but the last two inches inside the edges to be joined. Then trim the canvas on one section along the edge of the design area; trim the other section two inches beyond the edge of the

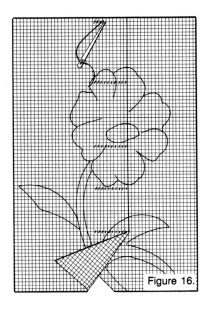

Figure 16.

design area (Figure 16).

To keep the canvas from raveling, apply a drop of white glue along the cut edges at every intersection of the vertical and horizontal mesh. When the glue has dried thoroughly, lap the section that was cut along the design edge over the other section, matching the two parts of the design and aligning the vertical and horizontal mesh of the canvas. Whip the layers together with sewing thread along the top and bottom ends, and at intervals along the length of the overlap. Then complete your needlepoint work, stitching through the two layers of canvas as though they were one.

Order of Work

PREPARING. Once you have cut and bound the edges of your canvas, and marked the center lines and design outline, you can transfer your design to the canvas or prepare your pattern graph. Then, if you cut your yarn into 30-inch strands and thread a few needles, you'll be ready to start needlepointing.

STITCHING. There are no absolute rules about how you must go about stitching your rug. Every design is differernt and the order of work will vary with the nature of the design. There are some guide lines, however, that experienced needlepointers have found to be helpful. Generally the design area is worked first, then the background and borders, if any. Within the design itself, start by completing all the fine lines and details; you won't be able to find them if you stitch in the areas around them first. Some people like to stitch any areas with subtly graded shading next, because once too many colors have been worked into the canvas it becomes difficult to distinguish the closely related shades. Thereafter, you can complete small segments of the design and then go on to the larger ones, or work color by color, as you prefer. In either case, however, it is wise to work the dark tones first and leave the lighter colors for last. Your rug will stay cleaner longer this way.

Usually the background is worked next, and then the outer borders, if there are any. But if your background is to be done in light-colored yarn and the border is appreciably darker, you might do the border first. When you get to the background, you may be stitching vertically, horizontally or diagonally, depending on the particular stitch or stitches you are using. But whatever the specific direction of stitching, work complete rows wherever possible. Don't jump around because, if you work little blocks of background here and there, you will find that there will be faint but unsightly lines and ridges where the blocks come together. If the design interrupts the background for many rows, work the solid portion of the background all the way down one side and then all the way down the other until the end of the interrupted area; then begin working across the entire row again.

The actual direction in which you should stitch any given portion of your rug will vary with the stitch you are using. Some stitches are easiest to make when worked from left to right, and others from right to left; some are worked vertically from the top of the canvas downward, others from the bottom upward, and still others diagonally in one or another direction. The most practical direction for working each specific stitch is indicated in the Dictionary of Needlepoint Stitches that follows.

FINISHING. When you have finished needlepointing your rug, check to make sure that you haven't missed any stitches. You can tell this quite easily by holding the rug up to the light. If you spot any missed stitches, fill them in if you can do so unobtrusively. After you have done this, weave any remaining loose yarn ends into the back of the work for an inch or so and trim away the excess.

If you are making your rug in sections and plan to join them by lapping the edges of the canvas, remember to stop stitching two inches away from the edges to be joined. Then join the pieces following the directions for the Lapped Join (Figure 16), complete the needlepoint stitching, and block the rug in one large piece. To join sections of canvas by any of the other methods—backstitched, whipped or binding stitch seams—complete the needlepoint work first, block the individual sections, and then join them, following the instructions for the particular method you have chosen.

Blocking is absolutely essential. Even a rug worked on a frame can pull slightly out of shape and require light blocking. Some rugs may even need repeated blocking to pull them back into proper shape, and rugs made in sections sometimes need to be blocked both before and after the pieces are joined. Complete instructions for blocking are given in the section on Finishing and Trimming. Directions for hemming, stitching on carpet tape, and lining your rug are given in this section as well. Hemming and taping are required for finishing the edges of your rug, and lining, although not mandatory, is recommended: it will provide added protection and extend the life of your rug.

Before hemming, however, decide whether you wish to fringe or decoratively bind the edges of your rug. Either of these edge finishes can be worked around the entire rug, or you can fringe the ends and bind the side edges, if you prefer. To fringe, one or two (or even several) rows of Turkey Knot stitches (Figure 48) or Surrey stitches (Figure 50) can be worked around the edges, or you can cut yarn and tie in the fringes with a crochet or a latch hook (see the Finishing and Trimming section). Do this before turning and completing your hem. Alternatively, you may prefer to work the decorative and protective Binding stitch (Figure 52) around the edges of your rug. Although this procedure is done after the hem has been turned and stitched, you must prepare for it by turning under the hem allowance of unworked canvas one or two mesh beyond the needlepointed area, the number of mesh depending on how deep you want to make the binding.

A Dictionary of Needlepoint Stitches For Rug Making

BASIC NEEDLEPOINT STITCHES:

The fundamental stitches of needlepoint are actually a family group know as the tent stitches, and include the continental stitch, which is also known as the tent stitch; the basket weave, or diagonal tent, stitch; and the half cross stitch. From the front of the canvas they all look alike: small, flat, slanted, and closely woven stitches, each one crossing only a single intersection of vertical and horizontal canvas threads, and all slanting in the same direction. But each is made in a slightly different way, looks different on the underside of the canvas, and can be used for different purposes.

CONTINENTAL (OR TENT) STITCH

The continental stitch can be worked in either horizontal or vertical rows, and covers the back as well as the front of the canvas very fully, providing the good padding that is important for a rugmaking stitch. It tends to pull the canvas badly out of shape, however, especially when worked horizontally, and should not be used to work extensive areas of the canvas. But it is an excellent stitch for filling in small areas or outlining designs.

When worked horizontally, the continental stitch is made from right to left. If more than one row is to be done, start at the top of the area to be stitched and work downward; then rotate the canvas 180 degrees (turn it upside down so the bottom becomes the top)

to work the next row; turn the canvas again to work a third row, and so forth (Figure 17).

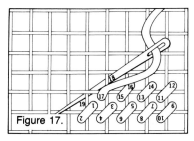

Figure 17.

Working vertically is generally done only in single rows for purposes of outlining, and the rows are stitched from the top downward (Figure 18).

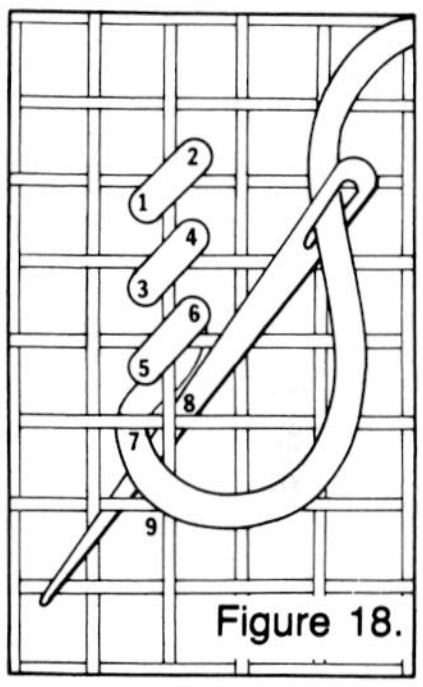

Figure 18.

BASKET WEAVE (DIAGONAL TENT) STITCH

This tent stitch variation, called basket weave because of the interwoven look of the back side of the work, is one of the most durable and frequently used of all needlepoint stitches. It is worked diagonally in ascending and descending rows and, because the stitches are made in two directions, will not pull the canvas out of shape. Basket weave covers the front of the canvas closely and completely, and provides a thick and sturdy padding on the wrong side as well. For all these reasons, it is a preferred stitch for working large solid-color areas of either the design or the background. Although somewhat complex to learn, once you have mastered it, you will find that the basket weave stitch has an easy and regular rhythm and works up quickly.

Start stitching in the upper right corner of the area to be worked and alternate ascending and descending rows, following the numbers in the stitch diagram (Figure 19). Fol-

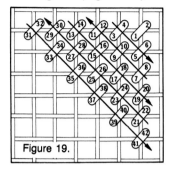

Figure 19.

low arrows to see ascending and descending rows. If you are starting in a squared corner, your first row will actually be only one stitch but counts as an ascending row; and the second row counts as a descending row although it will only be two stitches long. Thereafter, the rows get much longer and are easier to see as well as to work.

On ascending rows, the needle is inserted into the canvas horizontally from right to left and passes under two vertical mesh of the canvas before it is brought out. When working descending rows, the needle is inserted into the canvas vertically and passes under two horizontal canvas mesh before being brought out.

HALF CROSS STITCH

The easiest of the three tent stitches to learn, the half cross stitch is less useful for rug making than the other two. It doesn't cover the front of the canvas as well as do the continental and basket weave stitches, provides very little padding on the reverse side, and, in addition, tends to pull the canvas badly out of shape.

The half cross stitch is very economical on yarn, however, and is appropriate for working small areas and outlining designs. If certain precautions are taken, it can also be worked over larger areas. It should only be worked on penelope or the leno weave rug canvases, not on mono canvas, which is more easily pulled out of shape. Better coverage on the front of the canvas can be achieved by working the half cross stitch over a ground of trame stitching (Figure 13), and the lack of padding on the underside can be alleviated by lining the rug. If you stitch very carefully or, better yet, if you mount your canvas on a frame, you can avoid excessive distortion.

The half cross stitch can be worked either horizontally or vertically. When stitching horizontal rows, work from left to right, following the numbers in the stitch diagram. If more than one row is to be done, begin at the top of the area to be stitched and turn the canvas 180 degrees (so that the bottom becomes the top) to work the second row (Figure 20). Turn the canvas again to

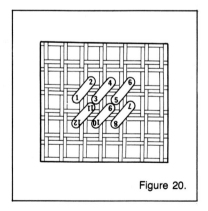

Figure 20.

work a third row, and so on. Vertical rows are usually worked from bottom to top, and the canvas is rotated 180 degrees to begin a new row.

CROSS STITCHES: CROSS STITCH

Used in many types of embroidery, the traditional cross stitch is as appropriate for a needlepoint rug as for a sampler. Although it takes somewhat longer to work than some other stitches, it covers the canvas very well, with good padding on the underside, and will not pull the canvas out of shape when worked. It can be used on a canvas of any mesh size, and is particularly popular for quick point. It can be used in any portion of a rug—the design, the background, or the borders—or the entire rug may be worked in cross stitch.

Cross stitch can be worked in two different ways. The first method is appropriate for all types of canvases; but the second method, while faster, is suitable only for penelope and leno weave rug canvases, not for mono canvas.

Method 1. In this method, each individual cross stitch is completed before the next one is begun (Figure 21). The

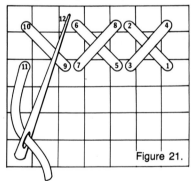

Figure 21.

stitches are worked across the canvas in horizontal rows, and multiple rows are worked from right to left or from left to right, whichever direction you find more comfortable—but be sure to cross all stitches in the same direction. When working more than one row, turn the canvas 180 degrees (from top to bottom) to start each new

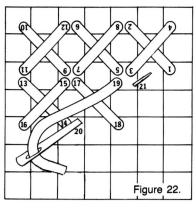

Figure 22.

row (Figure 22).

Method 2. This method is also worked in horizontal rows from the top of the area to be covered downward. But, instead of completing individual stitches, the lower diagonal of each cross is worked across the entire row (Figure 23), and

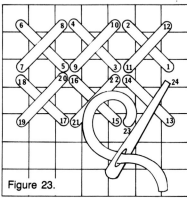

Figure 23.

then all the crosses are completed by working back over the row in the other direction. Since you will work each row in both directions, it doesn't matter at which end you start. If you work the first set of half crosses from right to left, however, the second (or top) set will slant in the same direction as the tent stitch, which is a good idea if you are using both these stitches in your rug.

UPRIGHT CROSS STITCH

Also known as the Greek cross and the St. Andrew cross, this two-part stitch is a variation of the regular diagonal cross stitch and may be used for the same purposes (Figure 24). Each stitch is made individually, working the vertical arm first and then the

horizontal arm; and the stitches are usually made from left to right in horizontal rows, starting at the top of the area to be covered, and working downward. The canvas should be turned 180 degrees (upside down) to start each new row. To work the upright cross stitch, follow the numbers in the stitch diagram (Figure 24).

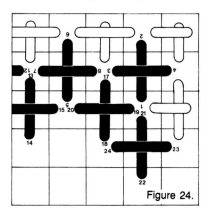

Figure 24.

SMYRNA CROSS STITCH

The Smyrna cross stitch is a large combination stitch with a bumpy texture, and is made by working an upright cross stitch on top of an ordinary diagonal cross stitch (Figure 25).

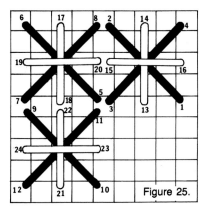

Figure 25.

The entire stitch can be worked in one color, or a contrasting color may be used for the top cross of the stitch. Either version can be worked over four mesh of the canvas,

as shown here, or over two mesh, which is worked in the identical way.

LONG-ARMED CROSS

This attractive braidlike stitch, which is sometimes also called the long-legged cross, is used extensively in Portuguese needlepoint rugs. The full, plaited texture makes it an excellent rug stitch. Use it for design accents, or for backgrounds and borders. Though it looks complex, it is actually quite simple to work once you break it down into separate steps.

The long-armed cross stitch is generally worked in horizontal rows, starting from the top. Two different rows are alternated, the first one worked from left to right and the second one from right to left. The first and last stitch of each row (shown as the shaded-in stitches in the diagram) are always made half the length of the other stitches to which they are parallel in order to maintain straight edges along the sides of the pattern. To work the long-armed cross stitch, follow the numbered stitch pattern (Figure 26).

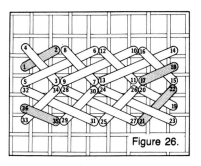

Figure 26.

THE GOBELIN STITCHES:

Named after the French Gobelin tapestries, these stitches resemble tapestry work and are excellent for rug making. They are all long flat stitches made over two to six mesh of the canvas, and work up very quickly without pulling the canvas out of shape. They are appropriate for working areas of the design or for backgrounds; but for rugs, it is best to work them over two or three mesh because the longer versions tend to snag.

UPRIGHT GOBELIN STITCH

Upright Gobelin Stitch is also called straight Gobelin and Gobelin Droit. It is easy to do and is worked over two to six mesh—though for rugs it should usually be limited to about three mesh. It can be made either vertically or horizontally. Long rows may be worked, or small blocks of vertical and horizontal stitches may be alternated for interesting checkered effects. Since it is an upright stitch, extra yarn may be required in order to cover the front of the canvas completely, or a trame ground may be stitched underneath to give the Gobelin stitch a padded look (Figure 13).

Vertical Gobelin stitches are worked in horizontal rows, starting at the top of the canvas. Alternating rows are stitched from right to left and from left to right, as shown in the numbered stitch diagram (Figure 27), without turning the

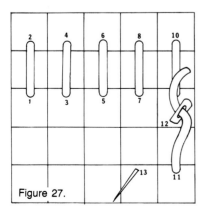
Figure 27.

canvas. But if you find it more comfortable, you can turn the canvas 180 degrees (upside down) to begin each new row.

The upright Gobelin stitch can also be made horizontally, working from the right edge of the canvas toward the left, in alternating ascending and descending vertical rows.

SLANTING GOBELIN STITCH

The slanting Gobelin stitch looks like a tilted upright Gobelin or a large tent stitch (Figure 28). For rugs, it is best

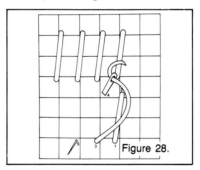
Figure 28.

when worked over two or three mesh of the canvas, though for other purposes it is often done over as many as six mesh. It is a good stitch for backgrounds and borders, design accents and geometric patterns.

Work in horizontal rows, starting at the top of the area of the canvas to be covered. Alternating rows are worked from right to left and from left to right without turning the canvas. If you find it more comfortable, however, you can rotate the canvas 180 degrees (upside down) to begin each new row and work them all from right to left.

VARIATIONS. The slope as well as the height of the slanting Gobelin stitch may be varied, if desired. The stitch can be worked over two horizontal and one vertical mesh of the canvas, for example, or over

two horizontal and two vertical threads. Similarly, it can cross over three horizontal threads and either one, two, or three vertical threads of the canvas. Depending on the size and slant of the stitches, you may need to fill in empty spaces in the canvas at the beginning and end of each row with shorter compensating stitches, as shown by the shaded stitches in Figure 29.

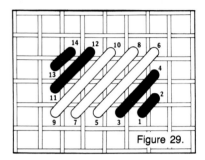
Figure 29.

ENCROACHING GOBELIN STITCH

This stitch is a variation of the slanting Gobelin stitch in which the stitches of adjacent rows are intermeshed. It can be made over as many as six horizontal mesh, but for rugs, a height of two or three mesh is best (Figure 30).

Work in horizontal rows, starting at the top of the area to be covered. Alternating rows are worked from right to left and left to right without turning the canvas, though you may turn the canvas upside down to begin each new row.

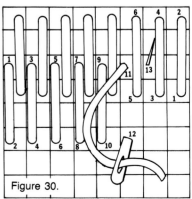
Figure 30.

BRICK STITCH

A variation of the upright Gobelin stitch, brick stitch is made in staggered interlocking rows, which simulate the look of brickwork (Figure 31). It will

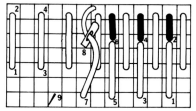

Figure 31.

cover mono and rug canvas very well, but is not as successful on penelope canvas. It has good padding on the underside, works up fast and will not distort the canvas. An excellent background and border stitch, brick stitch can also be effective as a design accent.

Brick stitch can be made vertically, working in horizontal rows starting at the top of the canvas. Alternating rows are worked from right to left and left to right without turning the canvas, though you may do so if you find this way more comfortable. Short vertical compensating stitches must be made along the top and bottom rows to fill in empty spaces in the canvas. These, shown as shaded stitches in the stitch diagram, may be worked as you go along or filled in last.

Horizontal brick stitches are worked in alternating ascending and descending vertical rows, starting at the right edge of the canvas. Compensating stitches will be needed along the right and left edges of the area stitched to fill in empty spaces in the canvas.

KNOTTED STITCH

The knotted stitch is an encroaching Gobelin stitch tied down with small crossed stitches. Thick, firm, and well

padded, with an interesting nubby texture, it is a perfect stitch for filling in areas of the design as well as for backgrounds.

Work the knotted stitch in horizontal rows, starting at the upper right corner of the area of the canvas to be covered. Stitch each row from right to left, rotating the canvas 180 degrees to begin each new row (Figure 32).

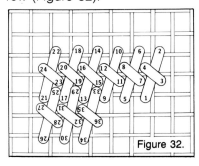

Figure 32.

KALEM (OR KNITTING) STITCH

This stitch, which looks like knitting, is ideal for rugs. It covers the canvas well on both the front and underside, has an attractive texture and won't distort the canvas. It is made of short slanting Gobelin stitches that slope in opposite directions, giving the effect of knitted work. It can be stitched in vertical or horizontal rows, and although the rows look paired, each is made separately.

To work the Kalem stitch in vertical rows, begin in the upper right corner of the canvas. Alternate descending and ascending rows, following the numbers in the stitch diagram (Figure 33).

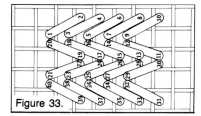

Figure 33.

If you wish to work the stitch horizontally, begin in the upper left corner of the canvas. Work alternating rows from left to right and right to left, following the numbers in the stitch diagram.

DECORATIVE STITCH PATTERNS:

When the various tent and Gobelin stitches are combined in different ways, an endless variety of decorative pattern stitches can be created. A sampling of the most popular ones, all suitable for rug making, are shown here.

MOSAIC STITCH

A stitch pattern composed of little square units of tent and slanting Gobelin stitches, the mosaic stitch can be used very effectively for backgrounds and borders, and makes an interesting design accent. The individual three-stitch units may be worked in horizontal or vertical rows, as well as diagonally. Working diagonally causes the least distortion of the canvas. Colors may be alternated in a variety of ways to produce interesting checkered effects.

To make horizontal rows, work from right to left, rotating the canvas 180 degrees to begin each new row. You can start at the top of the canvas and work down, or begin at the bottom and work up, whichever you prefer (Figure 34).

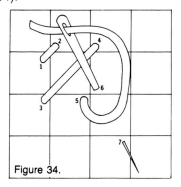

Figure 34.

Vertical rows are worked from the top of the canvas to the bottom, starting at the top right corner, and the canvas is rotated 180 degrees to begin each new row.

CONTINUOUS (OR DIAGONAL) MOSAIC STITCH

A variation of the mosaic stitch, the continuous mosaic stitch is always worked diagonally, in alternating ascending and descending rows. It works up quickly and is a good stitch for covering large background area (Figure 35).

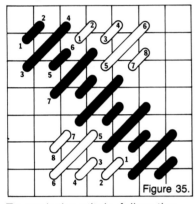
Figure 35.

To work the stitch, follow the numbers in the stitch diagram. The shaded stitches in the diagram are worked as part of the pattern but actually are compensating stitches made to maintain straight lines along the edges of the stitching.

CASHMERE STITCH

The cashmere stitch is quite similar to the mosaic stitch, except that it forms small rectangles instead of squares. It is useful for geometric designs and makes an excellent background or border. The pattern stitch can be made in one color, or may be worked in different colors to create any number of effects.

This stitch pattern is usually worked in horizontal or vertical rows. Horizontal rows are stitched from right to left, and the canvas must be rotated 180 degrees to begin each new row. You can work from the top down or from the bottom up, whichever you prefer. To make vertical rows, begin at the upper right corner of the canvas and stitch downward, rotating the canvas 180 degrees to begin each new row (Figure 36).

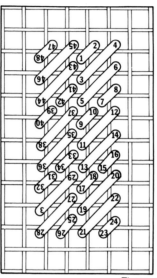
Figure 36.

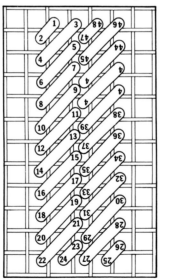
Figure 37.

RIDGED CASHMERE STITCH

This variation of the cash-mere stitch produces a vertical ridged look and is particularly suited for backgrounds and borders. An even more distinct ridging can be made by working the stitches over padding of tramé.

Work vertical rows of the ridged cashmere stitch from bottom to top, starting in the lower right corner of the canvas. Rotate the canvas 180 degrees to begin each new row (Figure 37).

SCOTCH STITCH

Also called the flat stitch and the diagonal satin stitch, this is another interesting square stitch that is particularly useful for geometric patterns. It makes an excellent border or background, and may be varied in numerous ways by alternating colors, slanting the individual squares in different directions, and outlining them in tent stitch. The individual squares that make up the Scotch stitch may be worked over either three or four vertical and horizontal mesh of the canvas. The smaller three-mesh squares are better for rug making because the shorter stitches will be less likely to snag.

Follow the numbers in the stitch diagram to work an individual Scotch stitch square. Horizontal rows are worked from left to right, starting in the upper left corner of the canvas, and the canvas must be rotated 180 degrees to begin each new row (Figure 38). Ver-

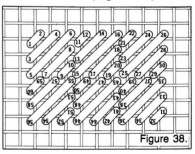
Figure 38.

tical rows are stitched from top to bottom, starting in the upper left corner, and the canvas must be rotated 180 degrees to begin a new row.

VARIATION 1: CHECKERBOARD SCOTCH STITCH. By stitching groups of four Scotch stitches in alternating directions, you can create the illusion of a single large square. Make a number of these large squares for an overall checkerboard effect. To work the Scotch stitches for this variation, follow the numbers in the stitch diagram (Figure 39).

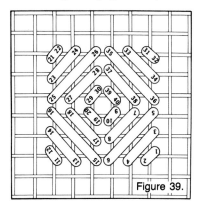

Figure 39.

Start the first stitch unit at the upper left edge of the area to be worked, then give the canvas a quarter turn to begin each of the remaining three units.

VARIATION 2: OUTLINED SCOTCH STITCH. For an interesting contrast in texture, surround individual Scotch stitch units (Figure 38) with an outline of continental stitching, worked in the same or in a contrasting color (Figure 40).

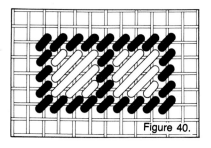

Figure 40.

BYZANTINE STITCH

One of many stitch patterns that zigzag diagonally across the canvas, the Byzantine stitch looks much more complicated than it really is. It consists of equal numbers of slanting Gobelin stitches worked horizontally and vertically in steps. The steps usually consist of four to six stitches, though you can make any number you wish, and each stitch is worked over from two to four horizontal and vertical mesh of the canvas. (See slanting Gobelin stitch, Figure 29.) For rug making, the two-mesh stitch shown in the accompanying diagram (Figure 41) is the best size.

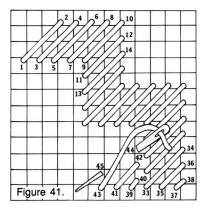

Figure 41.

The pattern may be worked in one or more colors. To make the Byzantine stitch, follow the numbers shown on the center row of stitches in the diagram. Surrounding rows are stitched in the same way, following the zigzag steps established by the first row. The small stitches at the beginning and end of the rows are worked as part of the pattern but actually are compensating stitches, used to fill in empty spaces along the edges of the pattern area.

JACQUARD STITCH

The Jacquard stitch is similar to the Byzantine, but in-

stead of working the diagonally zigzagging rows of slanting Gobelin stitches right next to each other, they are separated by rows of tent stitches, usually worked in a second color. Work the first zigzag row in Byzantine stitch, following the numbers in the stitch diagram (Figure 42). Then com-

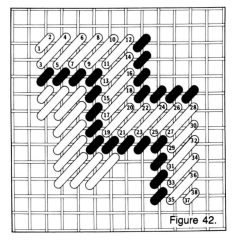

Figure 42.

plete a row of tent stitches (use either the continental or the half cross stitch) on each side of the first row. To continue, alternate rows of Byzantine and tent stitches.

STAR STITCH

Also called the Algerian eye stitch, this unusual stitch can be used for dramatic accent in a design, and is excellent worked alone or in combination with other stitches for borders. It is made over a square of four or six vertical and horizontal mesh of the canvas, and is always worked by bringing the needle out in a hole along the perimeter of the square and inserting back into the canvas in the center hole. Bring the needle up from underneath first at the midpoint of the one edge, then work the stitch on the opposite side, and so on around the square, following numbers in stitching

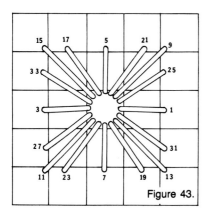

Figure 43.

diagram (Figure 43).

VARIATION. The Star stitch can also be made in a diamond shape, and is worked in the same way, except that the first stitch is at the base of the diamond (Figure 44).

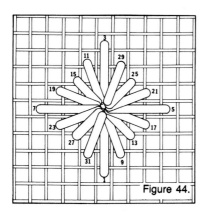

Figure 44.

PILE STITCHES: TURKEY KNOT STITCH

This is the needlepoint version of the familiar Ghiordes or rya knot (Figures 45-49). It can be used to fringe the edges of a rug, worked over the entire canvas, or combined with other needlepoint stitches for interesting contrasts in height and texture. The loops can be made in uniform or in varying heights, and may be cut or left as they are.

Turkey knots are stitched around the vertical mesh of the canvas, between rows of horizontal threads. They work best on the double mesh of penelope canvas and the twisted vertical threads of the leno-weave rug canvases. To make them on mono canvas, two vertical canvas threads must be worked as one, or the knots will slip down to the next mesh.

Stitching is always done from the bottom of the canvas to the top and in horizontal rows from left to right. On 10-mesh canvas, work across every other horizontal row; the larger mesh canvases can be worked across every row. If

you wish to fringe all four edges of a rug, work each row completely around the perimeter, giving the canvas a quarter turn to begin each edge. (On the side edges, you will have to stitch the knots over pairs of horizontal threads.)

To make the first knot, follow the numbers in the stitch diagram shown inserting the needle from right to left under the vertical mesh of the canvas. Start the second knot, holding your thumb down on the yarn to create a loop of the desired size. If you prefer, however, the yarn loops can be formed around a pile gauge. (See Rya Knotting.) Complete the second knot by inserting the needle from right to left under the next vertical mesh, and then drawing the yarn through. Make each succeeding knot in the same way.

SURREY STITCH

The Surrey stitch is a looped stitch similar to the Turkey knot, but it is made over the intersection of vertical and horizontal canvas threads rather than over vertical mesh alone. It makes a very firm knot and works equally well on all types of canvas. Like Turkey knots, the stitches are worked from the bottom of the canvas toward the top, and in horizontal rows from left to right. A knot may be made over every intersection of the mesh (rows need not be skipped), and the thick looped pile may be left as is or sheared.

Begin to work the stitch by inserting the needle from the front of the canvas under one horizontal thread (or a pair, if working on penelope or rug canvas). Draw the yarn through, leaving a tail of the desired length of the pile, and flip the yarn end downward.

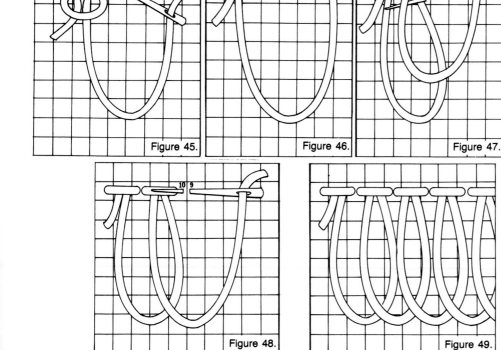

Figure 45.

Figure 46.

Figure 47.

Figure 48.

Figure 49.

Then insert the needle from right to left under the next vertical mesh to the right. Draw needle and yarn through to complete the knot (Figure 50).

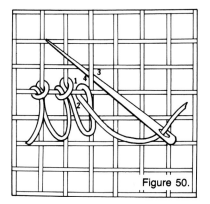

Figure 50.

Start the second knot, holding your thumb down on the yarn to create a loop of the desired size; and complete the knot. Make succeeding looped knots in the same way.

OTHER USEFUL STITCHES: BACKSTITCH

The backstitch is a standard sewing stitch, and should be added to your needlepoint repertoire as well. Backstitching is useful for outlining and separating areas of the design or of different stitches and—importantly—for concealing canvas threads that show through between lines of stitching. It also makes a very strong seam and is often used for joining sections of canvas. Backstitches can be worked in any direction and, though usually made over one or two mesh of the canvas, the stitches may be longer when-

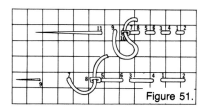

Figure 51.

ever necessary. Follow the numbers in the stitch diagram (Figure 51) to work the backstitch.

BINDING STITCH

The Binding, or Edging, stitch, is an attractive and super-sturdy finishing stitch with a braided look, and is used to bind edges and join the pieces of a rug made in sections. It is worked over one or two mesh just beyond the design area and is always made on a folded edge (Figures 52-55).

Make the stitch from left to right. If a single edge is being bound, work with the wrong side of the canvas facing you; when joining sections of canvas, place them together right sides out. Anchor the yarn by weaving it through the wrong side of the neighboring stitches for at least one inch, and bring the needle out one hole below the fold (or two holes below for a deeper edge finish) on the side of the canvas facing you. Begin the stitch by inserting the needle toward you from back to front in the same hole, and pull the yarn through. Repeat the process in each of the next two holes to the right of the first one, always inserting the needle toward you from back to front. The next two stitches will establish the actual pattern for the remainder of the edge: first insert the needle from back to front two holes to the left, and pull the yarn through; then insert the needle from back to front three holes to the right of the stitch just made, and pull the yarn through. Continue stitching in this pattern along the edge, working two holes to the left and then three holes to the right, and always inserting the needle toward you from back to front.

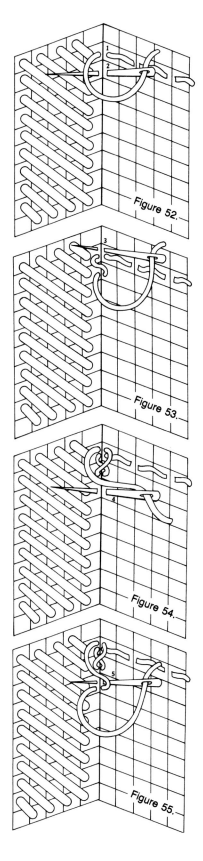

Figure 52.

Figure 53.

Figure 54.

Figure 55.

LATCH HOOKING AND RYA

Latch hooking and rya are two equally enjoyable but very different methods for making luxuriously deep pile rugs that resemble each other quite closely. Both crafts stem from the same ancient tradition of rug making (of which the classic Persian and Turkish carpets are probably the most celebrated examples) and both involve knotting loops of yarn into a backing to create a thick pile of various heights. In each case, the type of knot used is a variation of the Ghiordes or Turkish knot used for Persian rugs, and both latch hooking and rya are easy crafts to learn. But there the similarity ends.

Rya is a venerable craft, practiced in Scandinavia for many centuries. The original rya rugs were woven on looms, and the pile was knotted in as the weaving progressed. This technique is still used, but today rya—a word that actually means "rug"—is more popularly associated with another technique, in which a length of yarn and a tapestry needle are used to stitch knotted loops into a prewoven cloth backing. When the pile is quite short—½ to 1 inch high—and the knots are made very densely so the pile will stand straight up, the effect is actually known as flossa, not rya, but the knotting technique is identical. Rya pile generally ranges in height from 1½ to 4 inches, and several heights are often used in different portions of the same rug. The loops may be made very uniformly, using a pile gauge, or they may be uneven; sometimes they are left uncut, but often they are sheared. The characteristic depth and intensity of color often associated with rya rugs is achieved by blending closely related shades of yarn instead of using only a single color.

Latch hooking, on the other hand, is a twentieth century innovation (first developed in England about fifty years ago) and uses individual precut pieces of yarn, which are knotted into a canvas mesh backing with a special type of tool known as a latch (sometimes latchet) hook. The thick and springy pile created is uniform and velvety, and is usually about 1 inch deep—though you can actually make it any depth you wish by cutting the yarn yourself.

Both crafts, but particularly latch hooking, have become so popular in recent years that prepackaged rug kits are available in literally thousands of different sizes, designs, and color schemes. Most kits include all the materials you will need, though not always the tools—latch hooks, for example, are not always included. Many stores also carry prepainted latch-hooked rug canvases separately, which allows you to choose your own yarns.

Kits and pre-marked backings are convenient, of course, but they tend to be very expensive, and they limit you to someone else's choice of designs, colors, and even pile depths. Creating and marking your own designs for latch hooking and rya can be far more satisfying, and is certainly less expensive. All kinds of suitable ideas—as well as actual patterns that can be used just as they are or adapted to suit your own tastes—can be found in many books and magazine, in museums, and in the world of nature that you can see all around you. Abstract and free-form designs, and patterns based on natural shapes are very effective, and you can even make simple pictorial representations. But avoid intricate details, slender lines, and minute shapes, because the high pile of both latch-hooked and rya knots tend to blur tiny details so they become unrecognizable and sometimes even disappear entirely.

Equipment

EQUIPMENT FOR LATCH HOOKING

LATCH HOOKS. The only essential tool for latch hooking is the hook itself. Latch hooks are very cheap and can be found in most art needlework departments and in many five-and-ten-cent stores. They vary slightly in size and shape, depending on the manufacturer, but all are basically the same. They consist of a handle, made of wood or plastic, and a straight or curved shaft (or shank) with a hook and a hinged latch at the tip. Some people prefer a hook with a curved shank because it allows the hand to rest above the canvas and the finished work, while others like the balance of a straight hook better. Before purchasing any hook, you should hold it in your own hand, and select the type you find most comfortable.

YARN CUTTERS. If you prefer to cut your own yarn for hooking instead of using packaged precut yarns, you may want to purchase an automatic yarn cutting device. These inexpensive gadgets will cut a continuous strand of yarn into uniform-size pieces—usually about 2½ inches long—simply by cranking a handle.

Uniform pieces of yarn can also be cut by hand, using a homemade cardboard pile gauge. To make one, simply cut a piece of heavy cardboard about 8 to 12 inches long and as wide as the desired length of your yarn strands (see discussion of Materials for Latch Hooking). Lightly score the cardboard lengthwise down the center and fold it in half (Figure 1). The yarn will be wrapped crosswise around the gauge and the long open edge will act as a groove to guide your cutting blade.

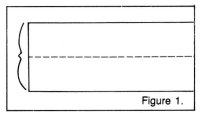

Figure 1.

EQUIPMENT FOR RYA KNOTTING

NEEDLES. Tapestry or rug needles, which are long, blunt-tipped needles with large, oval eyes, are the only special tools you will need to buy for making a rya rug. The blunt tip is important in order to avoid splitting the yarn or the threads of the backing. Tapestry needles come in many numbered sizes, ranging from size 13 for the largest to size 24 for the finest. The highest quality needles are made of nickel-plated steel and come in all sizes. The larger sizes are also made in plastic. For rya knotting, you will generally need to use the largest needle size (size 13) or one just slightly smaller. Since needles are so inexpensive, to avoid constant rethreading it is a good idea to purchase several, at least one for each yarn color or color combination you plan to use.

PILE GAUGE. For an even pile, the loops may be formed around a pile gauge (Figure 1).

Materials

Both latch hooking and rya require a backing or foundation fabric and yarn—and little else. But since the type of yarn and backing required and the methods of their preparation are different for each craft, they are discussed separately below. In addition to these primary materials, to finish a rug of either type you will need only ordinary sewing basket items and, if you wish, rug binding. For latch hooked rugs, sturdy fabric for lining or a liquid rubber backing may also be used. (These are not usually necessary for rya rugs).

MATERIALS FOR LATCH HOOKING

BACKING. Open mesh rug canvas is the preferred backing for latch hooking. This is a very sturdy and stable needlepoint canvas, made of cotton and highly stiffened with size. It looks and is worked as though it were made of single vertical (warp) threads crossing single horizontal (weft) threads, but actually is a type of leno weave, consisting of double warp threads that are twisted around double weft threads. Rug canvas is made in widths of up to 72 inches and in several sizes. Size is determined by the number of mesh (threads) per inch and, for latch hooking, the 3½, 4, 5 mesh per-inch canvases are the most suitable ones.

Penelope canvas, which is another type of needlepoint canvas, may also be used as a backing for latch hooking. Penelope is also a double-

thread cotton canvas, with two warp threads crossing two weft threads but, unlike rug canvas, the warp threads can be separated because they are not twisted to lock them in place. This makes penelope a little less stable than rug canvas but also more versatile, particularly if you wish to make a rug that combines latch hooking and needlepoint. Though the latch-hooked portion will always be worked over pairs of horizontal threads and between pairs of vertical ones, the threads may be separated if you wish to work finer detail in the needlepoint portions of the rug. Penelope canvas is made in widths of up to 54 inches and in many different sizes. Like other needlepoint canvases, size is determined by the number of mesh or threads per running inch; but for penelope canvas it is usually indicated by two numbers rather than one—12/24 or 5/10, for instance. The first number indicates the number of stitches per inch that can be worked over pairs of canvas threads, while the second number refers to the number of stitches per inch that can be made if the threads are separated and worked individually. For latch hooking, 3½/5, 4/8, and 5/10 mesh penelope canvas are the most suitable sizes.

PREPARING THE BACKING. Cut your canvas 6 inches longer and wider than the desired finished dimensions of your rug to allow for hemming. Always measure length in the same direction as the vertical (warp) threads of the canvas—that is, parallel to the selvages; and measure width in the direction of the horizontal (weft) threads—across the canvas from selvage to selvage.

Sections of canvas can be joined if you find that the rug you wish to make is wider than the standard available canvas widths, or if you prefer to work a large rug in smaller, more manageable and portable sections. Joining may be done before you begin to work, or after most of the work has been done, whichever approach best suits your own particular needs. The method is the same in either case: trim away any selvages along the edges to be joined and overlap the pieces about 2 inches, carefully matching the vertical and horizontal threads. Whip the layers together with sewing thread along the top and bottom ends. If the pieces are very long, you may also want to whip the overlapped horizontal threads at several additional points along the length so that the sections won't flap around as you work (Figure 2).

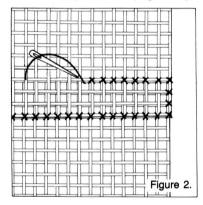

Figure 2.

Bind all cut edges (selvages need not be bound) with masking tape on both the back and front sides of the canvas to keep them from raveling. To make and enlarge an original design, and to mark it directly on the canvas, follow the directions given in the Appendix. If, instead of marking the canvas itself, you intend to follow a graphed design to make your rug, it is a good idea to mark center lines lengthwise and widthwise on the canvas, using a soft pencil or fine-tipped indelible felt marker; outline the edges of the design area as well, counting the exact number of mesh required to complete the design very carefully.

YARNS. Most wool and synthetic rug yarns are appropriate for latch hooking, but beware of mixing yarns of different fiber content because they will often wear unevenly. Avoid ordinary knitting yarns as well, they are too softly spun and are not made to withstand the hard wear that most rugs will receive. The bulkier rug yarns work well on 3½ mesh canvas, and for a very thick, plush pile most of them can also be used with the smaller spaced 4 mesh and 5 mesh canvases. The thinner rug yarns are usually worked on 4 or 5 mesh.

PRECUT YARNS. The ready availability of packaged precut rug yarns prepared especially for latch hooking is a great convenience. Marketed by many different companies, precut yarn is usually about 2½ inches long or slightly longer, and can be found in wool and in various synthetics, in different weights, thicknesses, and number of ply. They usually come in packages of from 240 to 350 pieces and in a sizable number of colors. Some companies market the same yarns in both precut and bulk versions, and you may often be able to fill in colors not available in precut lengths by buying the missing hues in uncut skeins. Precut yarn requires no preparation whatever.

UNCUT YARNS. Some people prefer to buy rug yarn in bulk form and cut it themselves. Uncut rug yarn is appreciably cheaper than the packaged precut pieces and, if you consider the additional choices that buying yarn in skeins will open up, you may decide that the extra time spent in cutting yarn is quite worthwhile.

In addition to a far greater choice of colors, you will also have a larger choice of yarn types. There are quite a few yarns—rug yarns and others—suitable for latch hooking that are not marketed in precut form. Rya yarns, for example, can also be used for latch hooking—in single or multiple strands depending on their weight—and so can multiple strands of tapestry and Persian yarns. If you want to make a really unusual latch-hooked rug, you can even work with ⅛- to 3/16-inch-wide strips of heavy, closely-woven woolen fabric or of felt. Then, too, when using precut yarn, you are limited to a finished pile depth of about one inch, whereas if you cut your own yarn with a pile gauge, you can make the strands any length at all, and create as high or as shaggy a pile as you wish, or you can vary the lengths for different effects.

To determine the length of the strands you will need, double the desired height of the pile and add ½ to ⅝ inch for the knot. Experiment with strands of various lengths until you are satisfied. Then make a simple pile gauge for each strand length you plan to use. Wrap the yarn around the gauge, making a single layer if you want very uniform pieces, or multiple layers if you prefer an uneven, shaggy look. Then place a rubber band, or tie a cord, lengthwise around the yarn to hold it in place, and slice the yarn along the long, slit edge of the gauge, using a scissors or a single-edge razor blade (Figure 3).

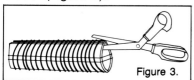
Figure 3.

DETERMINING YARN RE-QUIREMENTS. Making a rough estimate of your yarn requirements will involve doing some arithmetic. The first thing you will need to do is to determine the number of yarn pieces you will need per square inch by multiplying the mesh size of your canvas by itself (3½ mesh, for example, will use 12¼ pieces per square inch, 4 mesh canvas will use 16 pieces, and 5 mesh canvas will require 25 pieces per square inch). Next, figure out the total number of square inches in your project, and roughly divide up this figure proportionately among the various color areas in your rug. To get the total number of pieces you will need in each color, multiply the number of square inches of each color by the number of pieces required per square inch.

When buying precut yarns, you will usually find the number of pieces marked on the package. To determine how many packages of a given color you must buy, divide the number of pieces per package into the total number of pieces you will need for that particular color.

Bulk yarns will require a little additional arithmetic. A yardage figure is often marked on rug yarn skeins, but if it is not, you may have to buy a skein and measure it. (Try asking a salesperson first, however.) To figure out how many

pieces you will be able to cut per skein, convert the total skein yardage into inches, multiply by 36 and divide your answer by the strand length you plan to use. Then, to determine how many skeins of a given color you must buy, divide the number of pieces per skein into the total number of pieces you will need in that particular color.

MATERIALS FOR RYA

If you can't find rya backing, other sturdy rug-backing fabrics may be substituted—but you must choose a durable one or your rug will not wear well. Heavy rug warp cloth and Dura-Back are both suitable, and come in widths up to 200 inches. If the weave is too close to stitch through easily with heavy rug yarns, you can pick out a horizontal thread every half inch to expose the warp and allow you to make the rya knots more comfortable. Since only three or four rya knots are made per running inch, you will have to take care to space them evenly on fabrics that are woven with more than six or eight vertical threads per inch. Another backing suitable for rya rugs is called "Knot-On" and is marketed by Paternayan Brothers. This is a very heavy, eight-thread-per-inch, cotton fabric that looks something like woven string. It comes in 40-inch widths. Rya knots can be worked over pairs of individual vertical threads, spaced between each set of four horizontal rows.

To determine the amount of backing fabric you will need, add 5 inches for a hem allowance to the desired finished length and width of your rug. In the case of imported Scandinavian rya cloth, however, if

you can find a width that is the same as the desired finished width of your rug, the closely woven selvages can serve instead of side hems and you need not add any extra allowance for hemming to your widthwise measurement.

If you are using rya cloth or Knot-On and want to make a rug wider than the standard available widths, you can join two pieces of backing. To do this, simply butt two selvages, carefully aligning the horizontal threads and openweave rows, and whip the edges together with carpet thread. Since rug-warp cloth and Dura-Back are available in such great widths, you will not have to piece these backings for even the largest rug.

Hems can be turned under and finished either before or after the rug has been worked. (Directions for doing this are given in the section on Finishing and Trimming.) If you prefer to complete the hem after you knot the rug, run a line of machine zigzag stitching around all raw edges of the backing fabric, or bind them with masking tape, to keep them from raveling. To make and enlarge an original design, and mark it on the backing fabric, follow the directions given in the Appendix.

YARN. In Scandinavia, rya rugs are worked with special tightly-spun two-ply wool yarns, with a pronounced twist that gives them a ropelike look. Two different weights, in a large selection of jewel-like colors, are made. The heavier weight is most suitable for rugs and the lighter weight is best for pillows, wall hangings and similar articles. Multiple strands are usually used, the exact number depending on the weight of the yarn, the type of backing, and the number of knots made per inch. With Scandinavian rya backing, for instance, three or four strands of the heavier rya yarn will work up into a lush, thick pile. For special effects, the lighter weight rya yarns can be intermixed in small amounts with the heavier ones. These sturdy, imported Scandinavian yarns are carried by many needlework stores and can also be ordered by mail from several sources. They are usually sold by weight in skeins or hanks.

Some of the yarns commonly used for other types of handcrafted rugs can also be used for rya knotting. Of these, the most tightly spun and twisted, long-fibered wool rug yarns are the best suited. The number of strands that should be used for rya knotting may be as few as one or as many as four, and will depend on the thickness of the particular yarn—so you will have to experiment until you get the effect you want. Small amounts of Persian and tapestry yarns, used in multiple strands, may be intermixed with the rug and even the rya yarns, but should not be used in large quantities because the ply are not twisted tightly enough and the cut ends will open up with wear. Rug, Persian and tapestry yarns are made in hundreds of colors. They all come in skeins or hanks and are usually sold by weight, although sometimes by yardage.

DETERMINING YARN REQUIREMENTS: Making general estimates is risky, because the quantity of yarn needed for a rya rug will depend not only on the size of the rug, but on a combination of several variable factors: the thickness of

the yarn, the height of the pile, the type of backing used, and the number of knots made per inch. To make an approximate estimate for your own particular project, first experiment with a small swatch and decide how high you wish to make the pile loops, how many strands you will use, and how many knots you will make per running inch. Then determine the strand length you will need for one knot by doubling the desired pile height and adding ½ inch for the actual knotting. Next, figure out how much yarn you will need for one row of knots by counting the number of knots you will make across one row, multiplying this number by the strand length per knot, and then multiplying the total by the number of strands you plan to use. Count the total number of rows and multiply by the amount of yarn per row. The result will be the approximate total yardage you will need for your project. (The figure will be in inches, so divide by 36 to get the number of yards.) Make a rough estimate by eye of the proportional amount of each color you will use, and divide up the total yardage accordingly. To be sure of matching dye lots, buy a little more yarn of each color than you think you will need.

Preparing the Yarn. Untwist the skeins, and cut through each skein once at the point where the two ends are tied. This will give you strands approximately 55 to 60 inches long. Beginners sometimes find such long strands unwieldy and you can, if you wish, cut them in half. But if you do this, you will find yourself re-threading your needle every few stitches, so try to get used to working with the

longer strands.

Latch Hooking Technique

Knotting the cut pieces of yarn into the canvas mesh backing is a simple procedure, and once you have practiced it for a short time you will find that you will be able to establish a regular rhythm and build up great speed. To work, place the canvas on a table or hold it in your lap—whichever you find more comfortable. Keep the selvage edges at the sides and, especially if your canvas is very large, roll up the end you are not working on (the top end) and secure it with a few safety pins. Keep small amounts of cut yarn, in each color you'll be using, near at hand—right on the canvas if you like—so you can get to it easily for each knot.

METHOD

1. Fold a piece of yarn around the shank of the latch hook, keeping the ends even. If you are right-handed, hold the yarn between the thumb and index finger of your left hand, and the hook in your right hand; reverse hands if you are left-handed (Figure 4).

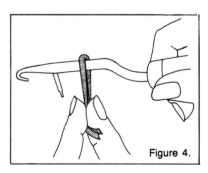

Figure 4.

2. Flip open the latch, insert the hook down into the canvas in the space below a pair of horizontal threads, and bring it up in the space directly

above, pushing the hook through beyond the end of the open latch (Figure 5).

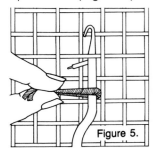

Figure 5.

3. Slowly draw the hook toward you, stopping as soon as the latch is above the horizontal threads and begins to close. Then, still holding the ends, place the yarn over the latch and under the tip of the hook (Figure 6).

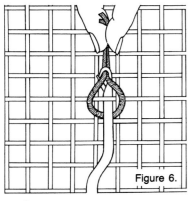

Figure 6.

4. Continue pulling the hook toward you. Once the latch closes over the yarn, let go of the ends and pull both hook and yarn ends through the yarn loop and under the canvas mesh, forming a knot. Tug on the yarn ends to tighten the knot (Figures 7 and 8).

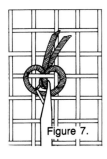

Figure 7.   Figure 8.

Repeat the process to make each succeeding knot.

ORDER OF WORK

Hook a piece of yarn into each horizontal mesh of the canvas, working row by row from the bottom of the design toward the top. You can start in either lower corner of the design area and work horizontally across the row to the right or to the left, whichever direction you find more comfortable. But always continue in the same direction and complete the entire row before starting on the next one above it—and always work row by row from bottom to top. If you work in this fashion, the pile will stand up straighter and look more even than if you jump around, and you will also be less likely to skip meshes by accident.

Change colors as necessary as you work across each row, following your design graph or the painted canvas.

After you complete a number of rows, you can roll up the finished portion if you wish, and let it hang down from the edge of the table or hold it in your lap. This will allow you to get closer to the remaining unworked areas. But never turn the rug to work from the sides or the opposite ends: if you do this, the pile will run in different directions and you'll find it parting unbecomingly every-which-way.

If you are making your rug in sections, work in the same way as just described, except on each section leave two inches unworked along the edge to be joined. If the overlapping part of the design has been painted on both the sections to be joined, trim each section along the design edge. But if the design has been

painted so that one part starts where the other ends, trim one section along the design edge and the other one two inches beyond the design. Then overlap the edges and whip the ends together (Figure 2). Continue hooking the unworked portion row by row from bottom to top, working through both layers of mesh.

Rya Knotting Technique

Stitching rya knots with long strands of yarn and a tapestry needle is very easy to do and, because you make only three or four knots per row and two rows per inch, it is surprisingly fast as well. All kinds of effects are possible by varying pile height and combining yarns of different textures, colors, or tones of the same color; but only one simple knotting technique—the classic Ghiordes knot—is ever used.

Three or four strands of rya yarn are usually threaded on the needle at one time, but with other types of yarns the number of strands will depend on the weight and thickness of the particular yarn. Many people like to form the pile loops around a cardboard gauge, but for a more shaggy, uneven look, you can use your fingers as a gauge instead.

To work, place the backing fabric on a table or other flat surface, with the selvages as the side edges. If your rug is a very large one, you can roll up the end you are not working on (the top end) and secure it with safety pins. Keep a supply of yarn strands of each color you'll be using within easy reach. If you are using Scandinavian rya backing, the knots will be made around two sets of vertical (warp) threads in the horizontal openweave rows that are spaced every half inch. On other types of backings, you may have to knot between two horizontal rows, or in spaces where you have pulled horizontal threads; and the knots themselves may be stitched over two individual warp threads or over two sets of them, depending on the thread count of the fabric. Knotting is always done from left to right across a row—unless you are left-handed, in which case, reverse all directions.

METHOD

1. Thread a large tapestry needle with yarn.
2. To begin making the first knot, insert the needle from right to left under the first set of exposed vertical threads at the left edge of the row (Fig-

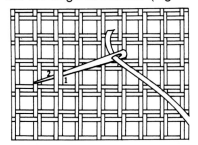

ure 9). Draw the yarn through, leaving an end the length of the pile loops you plan to make.

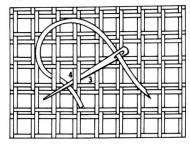

3. Hold the yarn end below the row with one hand to keep it from pulling out. Then, with the strand above the row, insert the needle from right to left under the next group of

vertical threads immediately to the right of the first group (Fig-

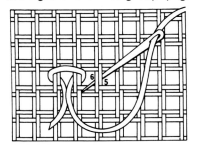

ure 10). Draw the yarn through and pull it tight to complete the first knot (Figure 11).

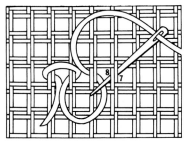

4. To start the next stitch, lay your pile gauge on the backing, aligning the top edge with the bottom of the open weave row. Slide the yarn under and then over the gauge (or under and then over several fingers of your left hand if you aren't using a gauge), and insert the needle from right to left under the next set of vertical threads. Draw the yarn through without pulling it too tightly around the gauge.
5. Keeping the yarn above the open weave row, complete the knot by inserting the needle from right to left under the next set of vertical threads, drawing the yarn through, and pulling the knot tight (Figure 12).
6. Repeat steps 4 and 5 to make each succeeding knot along the row, always working in the set of vertical threads immediately to the right of the previous knot. Slide the pile gauge along as you progress, pulling it out once you have completed the final knot in the row. Then cut the yarn, leaving

an end the same length as the loops. Always complete a knot and cut the yarn, before adding new yarn or changing colors along a row. Start new strands, then continue in the usual way. The looped pile may be left as it is or cut with a scissors, as you prefer.

ORDER OF WORK

Rya knotting is always worked from the bottom to the top of the backing, and from side to side across each horizontal open-weave row (or at ½-inch intervals between horizontal threads for backings without open-weave rows). If you are right-handed, start at the lower left corner of the bottom open-weave row and knot to the right across the entire row. If you are left-handed, begin in the lower right corner and proceed to the left. Always complete a row before starting the next one, and work succeeding rows one above the next, without skipping around. Change colors along each row as required by your design, following the markings on your backing fabric or on a design graph. If you wish to cut the knotted pile loops, do so as you complete each row.

Finishing

Clip any uneven yarn ends on the surface of latch-hooked rugs. Rya rugs never need blocking, and latch-hooked ones do only rarely. But if a latch-hooked rug has pulled badly out of shape, it should be blocked. Trim hem allowances to two inches, turn under and hem. Add rug binding if you wish, or, for latch-hooked rugs, add a lining or latex coating. Rya rugs do not require lining or latexing. Directions for blocking, hemming and other finishing touches are given in the section on Finishing.

KNITTING

Although literally thousands of variations are possible, the basic techniques on which all knitting is based are easy and few in number. However it would be advisable (if you are not already adept at the craft) to learn the basic techniques from one of the many books on the subject and experiment on one or two smaller projects before attempting a rug. This book assumes that you are somewhat familiar with knitting and are ready to apply it to rug making.

The main difference between knitting a garment and making a rug is not difficulty, but simply size. Rugs are more cumbersome to knit and require more yarn than scarves or sweaters—but don't let this deter you. Except for needles and perhaps a few inexpensive accessories, the cost of the yarn will be your entire expense. And the awkwardness of working with a lot of heavy yarn in your lap and a great number of stitches on your needles can be alleviated by using circular needles instead of the usual straight ones, and by making your rug in sections—much like knitting a series of scarves—and joining the pieces once all the knitting has been completed.

Equipment

KNITTING NEEDLES

There are four different kinds of knitting needles—single pointed, double-pointed, circular, and jumper—and all of them may be used for one or another purpose in rug making. Made of aluminum, nickel-plated steel, plastic, nylon, and wood, they come in a variety of lengths and in more than twenty different numbered sizes (or diameters),

ranging from the wire-slender No. 0000 to the giant 1-inch diameter No. 50. Most are available in several colors. You will find it much easier to see your stitches as you work if you choose different colors for your needles and your yarn.

For rug making you can safely eliminate all the finer-sized needles from consideration. Most rugs will be made on No. 10 needles or even larger-sized ones, and rarely will anything more slender than a No. 7 or a No. 8 be called for. You may need pairs of needles in more than one size for some rugs, but usually no more than two sizes will be required.

Knitting instructions always indicate the kind of needle to be used and recommend a combination of needle size (or sizes) and yarn weight or type. But since yarns and occasionally even needles are not always consistent, and since every "hand" is different, your own knitting may not work up to the exact gauge (number of stitches and rows per inch) specified by the pattern. In such cases, you will have to experiment with needles of different sizes, or try a different weight yarn, in order to achieve the required gauge. Gauge is important and is discussed at greater length later in the section. If you find it more comfortable, you can usually substitute circular or jumper needles for straight ones.

SINGLE-POINTED NEEDLES. Sold in pairs, these needles have a tapered point at one end and a knob or cap at the other end to keep the stitches from slipping off. Used for knitting across and back in rows, they are available most commonly in 10-inch and 14-inch lengths. For rug making,

the longer ones are usually more appropriate. Needle sizes from the slender No. 0 to the giant No. 50 are available in both aluminum and plastic, the larger numbered sizes generally only in 14-inch lengths. For those who prefer the feel of wood, these are also available in 14-inch lengths and nearly all sizes from No. 7 to No. 50.

CIRCULAR NEEDLES are large, flexible hooplike cables, nowadays usually made of nylon, with a nylon, plastic or aluminum tip at each end. They are most commonly used for knitting large tubular items, but are useful for knitting back and forth in rows when the number of stitches required is too great to be worked on straight needles. Circular needles are made in all sizes from No. 0 to No. 15 and in several lengths. All sizes up to No. 10½ come in 11-inch, 16-inch, and 24-inch lengths, while the larger-sized needles most often used for rug making— No. 10½ to No. 15—are also available in 29-inch and 36-inch lengths.

JUMPER NEEDLES are a kind of cross between straight and circular needles and are excellent for knitting a project such as a rug where bulky yarns and large numbers of stitches are involved. Jumper needles are used in pairs in the same way as straight needles. But instead of having the rigid shafts of ordinary straight needles, the shafts of jumper needles are made of extremely flexible nylon or plastic, with a firm tip at one end and a knob or cap at the other end to keep the stitches from falling off. This allows you to keep the bulk of the work resting comfortably in you lap so that you don't have to support a great deal of weight in your hands as you knit.

CROCHET HOOKS are almost a necessity. Use a crochet hook, of a size equivalent to that of your knitting needles, for picking up dropped stitches, making seams, and finishing edges. The numbered size designations on aluminum and plastic crochet hooks are the same as knitting needle sizes.

TAPESTRY NEEDLES are used for weaving yarn ends, making seams and embroidering decorative motifs. Choose a needle with a large enough eye to allow the yarn to slip through easily.

STITCH HOLDERS are large safety-pin-like devices used for holding groups of stitches that are removed from the needles for any of various reasons. Large safety pins make satisfactory substitutes.

CABLE STITCH HOLDERS are used to remove stitches from the needles when knitting cable stitch patterns. A double-pointed needle, a long toothpick, or even a bobby pin can be used as a substitute.

YARN BOBBINS are used for holding small amounts of yarn for knitting multicolor patterns, and come in several sizes. You can make your own from squares of cardboard.

ROW COUNTERS are small dials that slip onto your needles and are convenient for keeping track of the number of rows you have knit.

ROW AND STITCH MARKERS are rings that can be slipped onto stitches or needles to mark the beginning and end of rounds or of pattern stitches, points where increases or decreases are to be made, and the like. Safety pins or loops of yarn can be used with equal facility.

GAUGE AND NEEDLE MEASURES are devices that com-bine a 6-inch ruler, a 2-inch square gauge for determining the number of stitches and rows per inch, and a series of graded holes for determining the size of knitting needles and crochet hooks.

NEEDLE GUARDS slip over the points of your needles to keep the stitches from falling off when the needles are not in use. Small rubber bands wrapped at the tip can be substituted.

Materials

To complete a knitted rug from start to finish, the only material you will need is yarn—or a substitute for yarn. Unlike many other kinds of handmade rugs, no backing fabrics are used, nor are bindings or other finishings required.

CHOOSING MATERIALS

When choosing yarn for a knitted rug, as for any hand-crafted rug, the most important practical consideration should be wearability. The stronger the yarn, the better your rug will wear—and it is foolish to put a great deal of time and effort into a project as large as a rug only to have your handi-work wear out after it has been walked on for a short time. The weight of the yarn is another practical consideration: the heavier and bulkier yarns not only make thicker, more substantial fabrics than do the thin yarns, they also work up much faster.

For a floor rug, the best type of yarn to knit with is rug yarn. This is a broad category covering a number of yarns of different weights, thicknesses, fiber contents, number of ply, and type of twist. What they all have in common is strength. They are all spun of longer fibers or filaments, have a harder finish, and are often more tightly spun than other types of yarns—all characteristics that enhance their durability. Rug yarns come in a great number of colors, and are made in light, medium and heavy weights. There are wool, synthetic, and cotton rug yarns, as well as various blends. They come in two- to six-ply; some have a pronounced twist, others are smooth. In general, the light weight yarns are thinner, the heavy-weight yarns are thicker; but some of the bulkiest yarns are surprisingly light in weight and, in any case there is no real uniformity among the yarns of different manufacturers.

Besides rug yarns, the long-fibered, hard-finished Persian and tapestry yarns used for needlepoint are also appropriate for knitting rugs. Three strands of Persian or one of tapestry yarn will be about as thick as most lightweight rug yarns or knitting worsteds, but the number of strands can easily be doubled or trebled to duplicate the bulk of the heavier rug yarns. Heavy crochet cottons, as well as raffia and other straws—in single or multiple strands, depending on the bulkiness desired—can also be used for knitting rugs.

Knitted rugs can be made with materials other than these more or less traditional yarns. Again, keep strength and weight in mind when selecting them. Many of the different kinds of cord used for macrame—cotton, jute, hemp, and sisal twine, for instance—work up into very interesting and extremely durable knitted rugs. Cotton cable cord, rattail, and commercial, fabric-covered upholstery cording can also be used; and if you want a material that will knit up very fast, try using cotton, nylon, or polyester seine cord, clothesline or venetian blind cord, worked on jumbo-sized needles (No. 17 or larger). The color selection in these materials is far more limited than for yarns, but many are dyeable to any hue you wish.

If you are working from a pre-tested commercial pattern, the instructions will indicate exactly how much yarn is required and of what type; you can buy this amount or add an extra skein just to be safe. When making changes in a pattern, or designing one yourself, you will have to determine your own yarn requirements. An easy way to do this is to buy a small amount of the yarn you intend to use and knit a 3- or 4-inch square in the pattern stitch you plan to make, measuring and weighing the yarn beforehand. Then figure out the number of equal-size squares you will have to make to complete your rug, and multiply this number by the amount of yarn used for your sample square. The result will be the approximate amount of yarn you will need to buy.

Most macrame twines are also sold by weight, though occasionally by yardage, and are usually packaged in balls or spools. Rattail, cable cord, upholstery cording, ribbon, braid, and lacing are sold by the yard. Determine the amount of material you will need in the same way as for yarn. Purchasing all you will need at the same time is a good idea, though for natural color materials, you will probably not be able to match tones exactly.

Yarn requires little if any preparation. Wind hanks or ordinary skeins into balls to make them easier to work with, but leave pull skeins as they are. Unless you plan to dye them, twines and similar materials require the same preparation.

The precut flat materials—ribbon, braid, lacing—also require little preparation, though you may want to preshrink washable ribbon and braid.

Advanced Stitches and Variations

PATTERN STITCHES

Texture can be one of the main design elements in a knitted rug. You can make a rug with inserting textural contrast, using only the simple garter and stockinette stitches. But hundreds of other variously textured stitch patterns can be created merely by combining the basic knit and purl stitches in different ways. Several appropriate stitch patterns are described below, and many others can be found in pattern leaflets and in general books on knitting. In fact, simply because there are so many stitch patterns, it is important to learn the characteristics that make some patterns better suited for rug making than others.

When selecting stitch patterns for a rug, keep in mind that—unless you are making a lap rug or a bed throw—your rug will be trod on, scuffed, soiled, and flattened down. Any pattern stitch you choose, therefore, must work up into a closely knit, firm, stable (and preferably thick) fabric that will be able to withstand such treatment. Lacy openwork patterns, for example, are not appropriate for floor rugs: they won't wear well and, in addition, are easily caught in the heels of shoes, which can be a safety hazard to both rug and walker.

For rugs, it is best to pick stitches that work up into stable fabrics that have as little give as possible, because when walked on for a while, pattern stitches with too much give will flatten out, stretching the rug badly out of shape. Ribbed patterns, for instance, must be chosen very carefully—some of them work very well, but others are much too elastic for rugs.

Another factor to consider is the type of surface texture produced by the pattern stitch. Low or moderately raised textural effects are fine for rugs, but avoid pattern stitches that produce extremely raised surfaces. Cable stitch patterns, for example, can be used in rug making, as long as they are not too deeply sculptured. The same is true for the various other stitch patterns used in Aran (or fisherman) patterns: use the low or moderately raised stitches and avoid the very high ones.

Once you have selected a stitch pattern, double check its suitability by making a swatch—and check your gauge at the same time.

SEED STITCH. Also called rice, or moss stitch, this simple pattern stitch works up into a firm, thick fabric. It produces a low pebbly surface texture that looks the same on both sides of the work (Figure 1). The

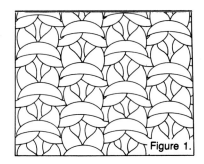

Figure 1.

seed stitch is worked on an uneven number of stitches. All rows are made by alternating one knit and one purl stitch across the row, always beginning and ending each row with a knit stitch.

TEXTURED RIBBING. This stitch has the look without the unusual elasticity of ribbing. It holds its shape very well, even without being blocked. To work the pattern, cast on a multiple of two stitches plus one. On Row 1, knit all stitches; on Row 2, purl all stitches. Row 3 is worked by alternating one knit and one purl stitch across the row, starting and ending with a knit stitch. Row 4 is worked by alternating one purl and one knit stitch across the row, beginning and ending with one purl stitch. To continue the pattern, repeat Rows 1 through 4 as many times as desired.

BASKET WEAVE STITCH. Small blocks of stockinette and reverse stockinette stitch are alternated to create a reversible fabric wiith the look of woven basketry. This simple version is one of a large number of basket weave variations

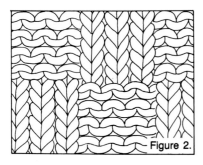

Figure 2.

(Figure 2). It is made on a multiple of six stitches. Rows 1, 2, and 3 are each worked by alternating three knit and then three purl stitches across the row, starting with knit and ending with purl. Rows 4, 5 and 6 are each worked by al-

ternating three purl and then three knit stitches across the row, starting with purl and ending with knit. To continue the pattern, repeat Rows 1 through 6 as many times as desired.

CABLE STITCH. Cables are made by crossing two or more groups of stitches at various intervals to give the look of flat, twisted or braided ropes. Simple cables are formed by dividing an even number of stitches into two equal groups, and then crossing the groups of stitches; in some of the more intricate variations, three or even four groups may be crossed. Knitting instruction books give complete row by row directions for literally dozens of cable stitch patterns of varying complexity. To make a simple two-group cable, for example, when you have worked up to the group of stitches that will be crossed to form the cable, slip the number of stitches indicated in your pattern instructions (usually half the total number in the group) off the left needle without working them, and place them on a cable stitch

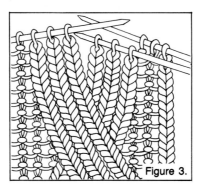

Figure 3.

holder (Figure 3). Position the stitches on the holder either in front or in back of the work, as specified in your instructions, and work the other half of the group of stitches off the left needle and onto the right one

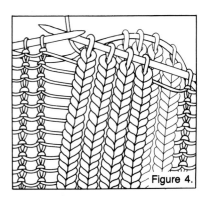

Figure 4.

(Figure 4). Then slip the stitches on the cable holder back onto the left needle and work them off onto the right needle—or work them directly from the cable holder onto the right needle, if you prefer (Figure 5).

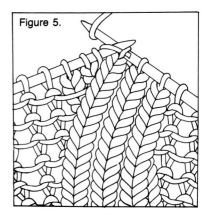

Figure 5.

KNITTING WITH MORE THAN ONE COLOR

Color can be used as a design element in knitting in many ways. Joining individual blocks of different colors to form checkerboard or diamond patterns, and alternating stripes of different colors are just two of the simplest ways. Here, one color is knitted at a time. The individual blocks are simply seamed together or, if the rug is made all in one piece, a new color is joined when the first color area has been completed.

Completely different effects can be created by knitting with more than one color yarn simultaneously. For a tweedy look, work an entire piece with two strands of yarn, each in a different color, using them as though they were a single strand. The yarns may be of equal weight and thickness, or use one light weight and one heavier strand. Almost any pattern stitch can be knitted with two strands in this manner, but you should work up a small swatch before starting your rug to see the exact effect you will be getting, and to check your gauge as well. If you are designing your own rug, you will need to know the gauge in order to figure out how many stitches and rows you will need to work. If you are planning to follow a pretested knitting pattern, you will probably need to make some adjustments to achieve the gauge or overall measurements specified in the instructions.

Geometric and even simple floral and pictorial designs can be worked in stockinette stitch by alternating two or more colors at different points across the rows of knitting. The popular Argyle and Fair Isle (or Scandinavian) designs are of this type. Instructions for which stitches must be knit in which colors are usually given in graph form.

When knitting Argyle, Fair Isle, and other similar designs, each new color is usually tied into the work at the point where it first appears. This is done without breaking off the original color. Any color needed in small amounts can be wound onto a bobbin, which is less unwieldy than carrying along the entire skein. When colors are needed in larger amounts, however, the skeins should be left intact, or can be wound into balls if you find this easier to manage. The various colors are held at the back (wrong side) of the work until needed.

If colors alternate in large blocks, a separate bobbin or skein should be used for each block, and switching colors is done by simply twisting the two strands so there will be no hole in the work at the point where the color change was made. To do this, place the strand you have just finished using over the new strand, bring the new strand up from underneath, drop the old strand, and continue working with the new strand (Figure 6).

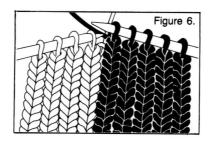

Figure 6.

Repeat the same procedure on each succeeding row at the point where the color change occurs.

When two colors alternate every few stitches across each row of the design, as is often the case with Fair Isle patterns, the strand not in use is carried loosely along on the wrong side of the work until it is needed, and the colors are then changed. If the strand not in use is to be carried across more than three or four stitches, however, you must twist it around the strand that you are using every few stitches to avoid producing long loops across the back of the work.

DUPLICATE STITCH

Duplicate stitch, known also as Swiss darning, is a method of embroidering designs over fabric knitted in plain stockinette stitch. It is done with tapestry needle and contrasting color yarn of the same or a slightly heavier weight than that used for the knitted work. The embroidered stitches are worked directly over and imitate the knitted ones, in effect duplicating them. An excellent technique for decorating plain knitting, duplicate stitch can also be used as an alternative to knitting in small areas of color. (The lines in Argyle patterns are often worked this way.) Any design given in graph form can be used as a pattern for duplicate stitching, each square on the graph representing one stitch.

To work the duplicate stitch, thread a tapestry needle with a long strand of yarn of the desired color. Insert the needle from the wrong side of the knitting and bring it out through the center bottom of a knitted stitch, leaving several inches of loose yarn at the back of the work. Slide the needle horizontally from right to left under both strands of the stitch above and draw the yarn through. Then reinsert the needle into the base of the stitch and draw the yarn through to the back. Work additional stitches in the same manner, consulting your design chart for placement. Always make the stitches loose enough to lie flat on the surface of the knitting. If you find the yarn you are using does not fully cover the knitted stitches underneath, switch to a heavier weight. To finish, weave the yarn ends through the back of the work for about an inch and trim.

Finishing

One of the many nice things about making a knitted rug is that once you have finished stitching it, there is very little work left to be done. Unlike most other types of hand-crafted rugs, knitted ones have no backings to be hemmed or bound, nor do they need to be lined. All you need to do to finish a knitted rug is conceal loose yarn ends and stitch the sections together if the rug has been made in pieces. Then add a knitted border, crocheted trim, or a fringe, if you wish, and block the rug. Blocking is a must if you want a smoothly finished professional looking rug and, if the rug is soiled, it should be washed as well. If you've knitted your rug in sections, the pieces can be washed and blocked individually or after you have assembled them. Instructions for washing and blocking, and for making fringes are given in the section on Finishing and Trimming.

WEAVING YARN ENDS

Pull all loose ends through to the wrong side of the work. Open any loose knots or bows securing joined strands of yarn. Correct stitch tension so that stitches around a join are the same size as the rest, and retie the ends in a single knot. Then thread each end on a tapestry needle and weave it through the back of the stitches for about an inch. Trim close to the work (Figure 7).

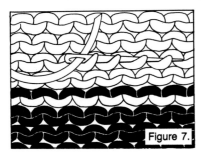
Figure 7.

JOINING KNITTED PIECES

Any of several types of seams may be used to assemble a rug that has been made in sections.

METHOD 1. Backstitched seam. This is a good general purpose method, producing a strong yet elastic seam. Place the pieces to be joined together, wrong sides out. Align the edges to be seamed, matching rows and stitches as closely as possible, and pin. Thread a tapestry needle with matching yarn and backstitch fairly loosely one stitch away from the edges of the knitted pieces. Anchor the yarn at the beginning and end of the seam by making several small running stitches, one over the other. Check the tension of your seam every few stitches to make sure the seam will have the same amount of give as the knitting (Figure 8).

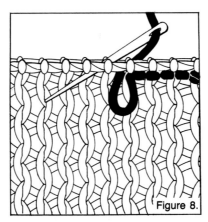
Figure 8.

METHOD 2. Crocheted seam. Crocheting is an excellent alternative to sewing, and makes a seam that is even stronger and more elastic than backstitching. Use a crochet hook of the same size as your knitting needles (the size numbers will be the same), and the yarn used for knitting. Place the pieces to be joined together, wrong sides out. Align the edges, matching rows and stitches. Pin if de-sired, or just hold the pieces together with your fingers. Place the yarn behind the back layer of knitting, insert the crochet hook from front to back through the top stitch of both pieces and draw a loop of yarn through to the front. Insert the hook into the next stitch on both pieces, and draw a loop of yarn through the knitted work and the loop on the hook (Figure 9). Con-

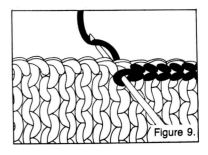
Figure 9.

tinue in this manner to draw a loop of yarn through the knitted work and the loop on the hook until you have worked a slip stitch in each matching pair of knitted stitches along the edges of the work.

METHOD 3. Woven seam. Weaving with yarn and a tapestry needle produces flat, unobtrusive seams and is a very good method to use when joining the vertical side edges of knitted pieces. The edges to be joined must be straight, however, and of exactly the same size and number of rows. Place the pieces next to each other on a flat surface—they can be right side up or down, whichever you prefer. Align the edges to be joined so that the rows and stitches match. Thread a tapestry needle with a length of the knitting yarn, insert it through the small "pip" of the first stitch on each edge, and pull the yarn through, leaving an end several inches long. Secure the first stitch by weaving the needle through the same two pips once more. Then, working row by row and alternating sides, weave the needle through the pip at the end of a row on one edge and then through the pip at the end of the matching row on the other edge (Figure 10).

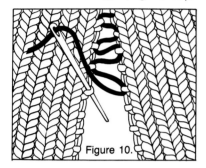
Figure 10.

When you reach the end, check the tension of the weaving to be sure that the seam will give with the work, then secure the last stitch in the same way as the first. Draw the yarn ends through to the wrong side of the work, weave them through the back of the stitches for about an inch, and trim.

PICKING UP STITCHES ALONG AN EDGE

Stitches are often "picked up" along an edge when a band or border is to be added. This can be done along vertical side edges as well as across horizontal cast-on or bound-off edges. Despite the name of the technique, the stitches are not actually picked up but are, in fact, knitted into the edge.

With the right side of the piece (usually the knit side) facing you, attach a new skein of yarn at the point along the edge where you wish to begin picking up the stitches. Insert the needle from front to back (right side to wrong side) through the first stitch along the edge, wrap the yarn from the skein around the tip of the needle as if to knit, and draw the needle and loop through to the front of the piece. Keeping

this loop—and each succeeding one picked up—on the needle, repeat the process until you have picked up the number of stitches required.

Patterns will usually indicate how many stitches are to be picked up along an edge. To be sure the stitches are evenly spaced, divide the edge into short segments of equal length, and pick up the same number of stitches in each segment. The needle is usually inserted through both strands of the stitch along the edge, but for a flatter finish on vertical side edges, or for a ridged effect on cast-on and bound-off edges, the needle may be inserted through just the outer strand of the stitch. If the knitted border is to go around two or more sides of a square, use a double-pointed needle for each side of small pieces and one (or even two) circular needles for large pieces.

CROCHETED EDGES

A row of single crochet stitches worked around a knitted rug makes a neat and attractive edge, and several rows make an interesting border. Use a crochet hook of the same size as your knitting needles (an equivalent-size hook will have the same number as your needles), and a new skein of yarn. To begin a crocheted edge, make a slip-knot a few inches from the end of the yarn and place it on the crochet hook. Then work the single crochet stitch inserting the crochet hook through a stitch along the edge of the knitted piece in the same way you would insert it through a stitch of a crocheted foundation chain. Work one single crochet stitch in each knitted stitch along a straight edge, and three single crochet stitches in each knitted stitch to turn a corner.

CROCHET

While crocheting is a good needlecraft for the beginner because of the minimal investment in tools and the simplicity of stitches and techniques, it would be advisable to learn the basic techniques from one of the many books on the subject and experiment on one or two smaller projects before attempting a rug.

Equipment

The only tools you'll need to purchase to make a crocheted rug are a crochet hook, or perhaps several, in different sizes, and a tapestry needle.

Materials

To crochet a rug, the only material required is yarn or something similar to yarn. This is only one of several characteristics that crocheting shares with knitting. In fact, the yarns and yarn substitutes most appropriate for making a crocheted rug are exactly the same as the ones best suited for making a knitted rug. Methods for determining amounts and for preparing materials are the same as well—except, of course, that when swatches are called for they are crocheted, not knitted.

Advanced Stitches and Techniques

A variation of crocheting, afghan stitch is worked in a different way, with a different kind of hook. Afghan stitch works up into a very firm, strong, and thick fabric that is excellent for floor rugs as well as for afghans. See Appendix for complete instructions.

WEAVING

A handwoven rug is not only a sturdy, practical floor covering, it is a creative personal expression of which any craftsperson can be proud. If you are a beginner and are hesitating to take up a "new" craft, remember that weaving has been practiced for 20,000 years, and for all but a short time it has been done by hand on the simplest, most primitive of looms.

Glossary Of Weaving Terms

To the novice, weaving instructions may at first appear to be written in a foreign language, and in a sense they are, for weaving has a technical vocabulary all its own. But don't let this discourage you: if you take a little time to study the glossary of weaving terms until you have the terminology well in hand, you'll discover that most weaving instructions are quite easy to understand.

Bobbin. Spool made of wood, paper, or other materials around which the weft thread is wound before insertion into the shuttle. Also called a quill.

Bubbling. A method of easing in the weft before beating it, to ensure that the cloth will not buckle.

Butterfly. Weft yarn wound in figure-eight fashion around the fingers and used instead of a regular bobbin.

Chaining. Forming the warp threads into a crochet-like chain to keep them from becoming tangled.

Comb. A fork-like comb, usually made of wood or metal, for beating weft threads in place; used particularly in tapestry weaving. See also *sword.*

Draft. A graphed diagram for a weaving pattern.

End. An individual warp thread.

Filling. See *weft.*

Harness. The frame or bar on which are hung the heddles used for raising or lowering selected warp threads.

Heading. A tightly woven plain weave band, often of string, rags, or heavy yarn, worked at the beginning and sometimes also at the end of the fabric.

Heddle. Vertical wire, string, or metal strip with a loop or eye at the center through which the warp threads are passed. The heddles are attached to the harness and can be raised to form a shed for weaving.

Pattern weave. A design formed by the regular repetition of a given arrangement of warp and weft threads.

Pick. A single passage of the weft thread or threads through the shed. Also called a *shot.*

Pile. Weft yarns used to make a surface that is raised above the basic weaving.

Plain weave. The basic weave formed by the simple alternation of the weft over and under every other warp thread.

Quill. See *bobbin.*

Ratchet. A wheel with notches or teeth, fastened to ends of warp and cloth beams to hold proper tension and to prevent unrolling.

Selvage. The finished lengthwise edges of woven fabric.

Sett. The number of warp ends threaded per inch.

Shed. The opening made by raising or lowering selected warp ends in order to make a passageway for the shuttle carrying the weft thread.

Shot. See *pick.*

Shuttle. The device used for passing the weft thread through the shed.

Sword. A thin, flat stick, often pointed at one end, used to make the shed openings and for beating down the weft on simple looms. Also called a pick-up stick.

Take-up. The tightening of the warp caused by its curving under and over the weft threads.

Tapestry technique. A particular method of weaving used for creating pictorial designs with different-colored yarns.

Twill weave. A basic weave in which the weft and warp threads cross over each other in such a way as to form a pattern of diagonal lines.

Warp. The lengthwise threads of the fabric, which are stretched taut on the loom as the foundation through which the weft (filling) threads are interlaced to form the fabric. When the warp threads are spaced closely enough to predominate over the weft threads, the resulting fabric is known as a warp-face fabric.

Weft. The crosswise threads of the fabric, also called the filling. A weft-face fabric is one in which the weft threads cover and conceal the warp threads completely.

Equipment

Choosing a loom should be given a great deal of thought. A large floor or upright loom has many advantages and may be a good choice if you are an experienced weaver, but it is also expensive, takes a great deal of space, and is usually rather complicated to set up and prepare for weaving. A much simpler loom can do just as well for a beginner: it is far less expensive and will give you a chance to see how well you like weaving and what kind of weaving you like best before you make a major investment in a large piece of professionally-built machinery. Moderately-priced table looms are another option; though smaller, they share many of the features of larger floor looms, and can be used for rug making by piecing together several woven strips.

SIMPLE LOOMS

The most basic equipment can be used quite successfully to weave a rug—in fact the beautiful tapestries of the Indians of Guatemala and Peru, Navajo rugs, and even the celebrated carpets of Persia were traditionally woven on the most primitive of back-strap and frame looms. These and other types of simple looms can be made easily and inexpensively at home or purchased at very moderate prices.

SQUARE LOOM: A simple, inexpensive practice loom can be made with a piece of cardboard. Draw vertical lines to mark each warp position and notch the cardboard at the top and the bottom (Figure 1).

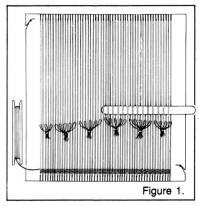
Figure 1.

A loom can be constructed very easily from a few strips of wood and some nails, and if you make it yourself, it can be oblong as well as square and any dimensions—from potholder to room-size—that you wish. A flat wooden picture frame or two pairs of artists' canvas-stretchers assembled with wedges will be strong enough for a small loom; four lengths of 2 x 2 lumber, squared-off at the corners and fastened together with 3-inch

nails or wood screws, should be used for larger rugs (Figure 2). Reinforce all but the small-

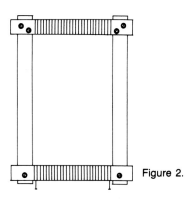
Figure 2.

est frames at the corners with angle braces. Mark guidelines for placement of the nails around which you will weave by drawing a line down the center of each side of the frame. Then mark off points at regular intervals along each side, making sure the points on each pair of opposite sides line up, and hammer in a finishing nail at each point (Figure 3). The points can be from

Figure 3.

¼ inch to 1 inch apart, and the finishing nails from ¾ inch to 3 inches long, depending on the size of the frame and the bulkiness of the weaving materials you plan to use.

FRAME LOOM: Frame looms are not only an excellent way to acquaint the novice with the art of weaving;

they allow the experienced rug maker the utmost freedom and direct control over the entire weaving process. You can buy a basic frame loom very inexpensively, or make one of practically any size from a picture frame, canvas stretchers, or some lumber. Make a guide for the placement of the warp by drawing sett marks at ¼-inch intervals across the top and bottom sides of your frame, or by grooving the edges with a saw or file. Add a removable tension stick—a long flat piece of smooth wood such as a yardstick, or a strip of ⅜-inch lathing or heavy cardboard—the width of your frame, and you can use the frame as your loom just as it is. Tape the tension stick to the lower front edge of your loom. To warp the loom, simply tie the end of your warp thread to the nail at the left with a slipknot and then, unreeling the yarn directly from the spool, wrap it around and around the frame, using the sett marks to space the ends evenly, until you have completed the number of ends you need. Then tie off the warp around the nail at the right. To weave, you can open a shed for the weft by manipulating the warp with your fingers, or you can "automate" the process to a degree by using a shed stick (Figure 4).

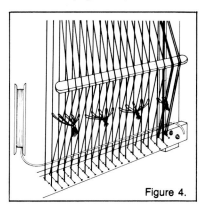
Figure 4.

A somewhat more sophisticated frame loom variation involves the use of a heavy dowel rod (or, for a very large loom, a broomstick may be used) for attaching the warp. This method allows you to rotate the warp around the frame as you weave, and thus to make a rug nearly twice the length of your frame. Cut the dowel the same width as the loom, lay it across the back of the loom (near the bottom), and tape it down temporarily. Then tie the end of your warp thread securely to the left end of the rod with a slipknot. Bring the warp down and around the front of the loom, over the top, down again and around the rod. Then bring the warp up over the top of the loom, down the front, around to the back, and wrap it around the rod again (Figure 5). Continue in this manner, al-

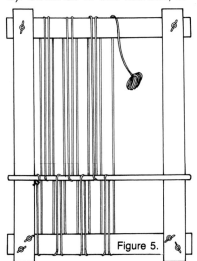

Figure 5.

ternating directions and using the sett marks drawn on the frame to space the warp ends evenly, until you have completed the number of ends you will need for the width rug you wish to make. Tie the last warp end securely to the dowel, cut it off, and remove the tape holding the rod down. If you wish to make strong sel-

vages, you can wind two warp ends close together at each side edge.

To weave on any loom, you must be able to open a shed through which the weft can pass. On a frame loom, this can be done by simply manipulating the warp threads with your hands, pulling each warp end up or pushing it down with your fingers as you approach it with the shuttle, butterfly, needle or bodkin carrying your weft yarn. If you wish, however, you can speed up the process somewhat by using a shed stick, which is inserted across the loom in and out of alternate warp ends and, when turned on edge, will create the shed opening (Figure 20). You can buy shed sticks or make them with 1½ x ¼-inch lathing strips or even a couple of yardsticks, cut a few inches longer than the width of your loom and sanded smooth.

Plain weaving can be done with a shed stick alone, but you can save even more time by buying a frame loom with string heddles, or adding one or more sets of them to your own homemade loom. You can use one heddle plus a shed stick, or two heddles if you prefer, to create two permanent sheds for plain weaving; adding up to four heddles to your loom will allow you to create the multiple sheds required for a variety of pattern weaves (Figure 6). Making your own

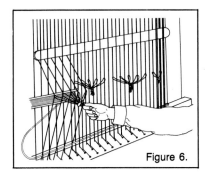

Figure 6.

string heddles is very easy and requires few additional materials. All you will need is a sturdy dowel for each heddle (the diameter should be at least ½ inch, but will depend on the size of your loom), two small pieces of 1-inch board (grooved along the top edge to hold the dowel rods), a few nails and a ball of string. To attach the warp ends to your heddle rod(s), tie one end of the string securely to the end of the dowel, make several half hitches with the string around the rod until you are even with the first warp end you want to tie up, then loop the string under the warp end. Make another series of half hitches on the dowel until you reach the next warp end to be tied up, loop the string under this warp end, make another series of half hitches on the rod, loop the string under the next warp end to be attached, and so forth (Figure 7). For a

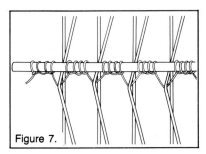

Figure 7.

plain-weave rug, attach every other warp end to one heddle rod, and use a shed stick or a second heddle rod to make the alternate shed. If you have multiple heddle rods and plan to make a pattern weave of some sort, use your pattern draft as a guide for attaching the string loops of each heddle rod to the appropriate warp ends. When a given series of string heddles is not in use, just rest the heddle rod in the grooves of the wooden side pieces. The slackened

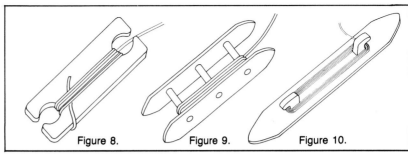

Figure 8.　　Figure 9.　　Figure 10.

string loops will not interfere with the warp and you can make an alternate shed. To use the heddles, simply lift the rod high enough for the string loops to pull the warp ends up into a shed. You can hold the bar up with one hand while you pass the weft across with the other or, to free both hands for weaving, insert a shed stick on edge into the shed and release the heddle rod.

MISCELLANEOUS EQUIPMENT

In addition to the loom, to make a rug you will need a number of incidental tools and accessories, including shuttles, bobbins, yarn winders, and other items. The type and number of accessories required will vary with the kind of loom you plan to use.

SHUTTLES. These are the devices that carry the weft yarn or other filling materials across the width of the loom through the shed opening. They come (or can be made) in a variety of sizes and shapes. The choice of a shuttle depends on a number of factors: the weight and type of filling material, the width of the loom, the size and depth of the shed opening, and the type of weaving that will be done.

The stick shuttle is the simplest type and is usually used for heavy yarns and filling materials, and particularly with looms that have narrow shed openings. It can be purchased but is easy to make, being nothing more than a long strip of smooth flat wood (or even of heavy cardboard) deeply notched at both ends to keep the yarn from slipping off. The long edges are sometimes beveled so that the shuttle can be used to beat down the

woven weft—a good idea if you are using a frame loom without a built-in beater (Figure 8). Stick shuttles can range in length from about 6 inches to a yard or more. Some weavers like to use a length slightly greater than the width of the warped area of the loom so that the shuttle can be passed across the entire shed opening in one operation. Others find this unwieldy and prefer a shorter shuttle.

Rug and ski shuttles are enlarged variations on the stick shuttle, and can be thrown through the shed opening. Both are made of smoothly sanded wood and come in different sizes, the rug shuttle consisting of two flat slats positioned on edge and held together by pegs (Figure 9), while the ski shuttle has a single flat slat into which two shaped wooden hooks have been inserted for holding the yarn (Figure 10). They are generally used for heavy yarns, while the rug shuttle—a particularly popular type for rug making—is also excellent for rag fillers.

The wooden boat shuttle is the only type that unwinds by itself as it is thrown through the shed opening. It is used to carry fine-to medium-weight yarns and comes in a variety of sizes and types (Figure 11).

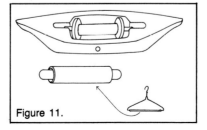

Figure 11.

The base is a boat-shaped wooden block with a hollowed out or open center holding a long steel pin. The yarn is wound around a bobbin or quill, which is then slipped onto the pin and rests in the hollow of the boat. Some boat shuttles hold two bobbins, others are equipped with rollers. Bobbins are made in wood, plastic, and cardboard. You can make extra ones yourself by rolling a tube of heavy wrapping paper 1 inch shorter than the opening in the shuttle (Figure 11). Bobbins can be wound by hand or, to save time and ensure more even winding, a hand-turned or electric bobbin winder can be used (Figure 12).

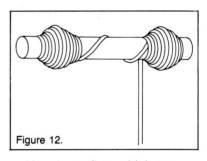

Figure 12.

Yarn butterflys, which are formed by hand and require no extra tools or equipment to make or use, are commonly used instead of shuttles for weaving small areas and for tapestry and other hand-manipulated techniques. Tapestry bobbins, blunt-tipped rug-lacer and tapestry needles, bodkins and long homemade wooden needles are also useful for these purposes, as are small knitting bobbins.

BEATERS. If you are weaving on a frame or simple upright tapestry loom without a reed, you'll need some sort of implement for beating down the weft yarn—and this is also the case for tapestry techniques, whatever type of loom is being used. Tapestry combs, which are made in various materials, weights, shapes, and sizes, are excellent for beating down small areas at a time and can be purchased from weaving suppliers; but an ordinary sturdy hair comb with large teeth, or even a table fork will often do just as well. Use a heavy, weighted comb when forceful beating of thick filling materials is necessary, and lighter, finer combs for thinner yarns (Figure 13). A long weaver's

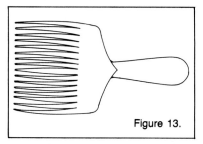

Figure 13.

sword (or pick-up stick), bevel-edged stick shuttle or shed stick can also be used as a beater, especially if the weft is to be packed down across the entire width of the loom.

STRETCHERS. These gadgets, also known as temples, are used to keep the woven piece at its intended width as it is being made by preventing the warp from drawing in. They consist of two interlocking bars that can be adjusted to the desired width. With the bars in a partially folded position, teeth that are located at both ends are pushed through the selvages. The bars are then straightened and locked in position, keeping the edges of the fabric even as the weaving progresses. A stretcher can be used on any loom but for frame looms,

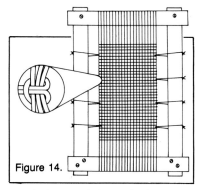

Figure 14.

cords knotted through the selvages and tied around the sides of the frame at regularly spaced intervals make an easy and inexpensive substitute (Figure 14).

Materials

Yarn is what weaving is all about, and to enjoy the craft to its fullest, the weaver should develop a basic understanding of the major factors that should be taken into account when choosing warp and filling yarns: fiber content, ply, twist, size and thickness. In addition, yarn for rug making must be chosen with special attention to its strength and wearability.

FIBER FACTS:

FIBER TYPES. Yarn fibers come from three basic sources: natural animal and vegetable fibers, and man-made fibers with vegetable and chemical bases. Sheep's wool and silk have always been the most common types of animal fibers used for yarns, though horse, goat, camel, rabbit, llama, and other animal hairs are also used. Of these, wool—strong, resilient, flexible, warm, easy to spin, dye, and weave with—remains the staple filling yarn for rug making, while novelty yarns spun from horse and other animal hairs can also be used for some purposes. Silk though lustrous and beautiful, is both difficult to work with and generally too fragile for rugs.

Cotton and linen have been the most common vegetable-fiber yarns used for weaving cloth throughout history. Both are excellent for rug making, particularly for the warp. Ramie (a rough but very strong grass fiber), jute, sisal, and hemp are also commonly used yarn fibers and are appropriate for rug fillings and sometimes for the warp, as well. Various other grasses and reeds, such as raffia and bamboo, can also be used for woven rugs (though these, generally, are not actually spun into yarn).

Man-made fibers are available in great variety. Though each type of fiber has its own particular characteristics, most of them are spun in forms appropriate for rug making.

PLY AND TWIST. Most natural fibers are too short to be used directly but, instead, must be spun. If the fibers are twisted to the left as they are spun, the result is called an S-twist; if the twist is to the right, a Z-twist results (Figure 15). A

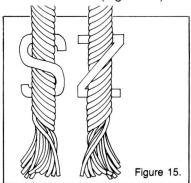

Figure 15.

single strand produced by such spinning is called a one-ply, or a singles, yarn. Many yarns, however—including most of those appropriate for weaving—are multiple-ply yarns, made by twisting together two or more single-ply strands. Twisting together the ply is done in many different ways, resulting in a variety of yarn textures, including all sorts of novelty effects that can add surface interest to a woven rug.

YARN COUNT. Yarn requirements for weaving are usually estimated in terms of yardage, but when you go to purchase your materials, you may look in vain for an indication of the number of yards contained in each of the yarn packages you have chosen. Instead, you will often find the weight of the package noted, along with references to the yarn count and number of ply. If you understand the significance of these terms, you will be able, with a little arithmetic, to figure out the yardages yourself.

The size, or thickness, of yarn is measured by a system of numbering called the count, which for spun natural yarns (such as cotton, linen, and wool) is based on how much singles (one-ply) yardage of a given yarn can be spun from one pound of the raw fiber. Although the method of arriving at the base number in the system varies with the type of fiber, in all cases, No. 1 count yarns are the heaviest ones and contain the least number of yards per pound; and as the count number gets higher, the yarn gets finer and the yardage greater. The yardage for one pound of No. 1 count yarns of different fiber content is as follows:

cotton	840 yards
linen, ramie, jute, hemp	300 yards
wool	1600 yards
worsted wool	560 yards

For a No. 2 count yarn of each of these types, the yardage will be twice that indicated for the No. 1 count; a No. 3 count yarn will have three times the yardage of a No. 1 count, and so forth. Remember, however, that these count numbers and yardages refer to a single

strand. Plied yarns (those containing more than a single ply) are usually indicated by two numbers separated by a slash mark, such as 4/3, the first number referring to the count of the yarn and the second one indicating the number of ply. To determine the yardage for a plied yarn, multiply the yardage for a No. 1 count yarn of the particular fiber type by the actual count number of the yarn in question, then divide the total by the number of ply in that yarn. For a 4/3 cotton yarn (No. 4 count, three ply) for example, the equation would be:

$$\frac{4 \times 840}{3} = 1120 \text{ yards per pound}$$

Choosing the Warp

The warp are the lengthwise threads that are stretched tautly on the loom to provide a structure through which the weft (filling) can be interlaced. Stronger yarn is always required for the warp than for the filling. Also the warp used in rug weaving must be particularly strong because of the heaviness of the yarns usually used for the weft and the extreme force used to beat it down, as well as because of the considerable wear to which rugs are generally subjected.

To be appropriate for use as a rug warp, a yarn should be multiple-plied and tightly spun, as well as fairly smooth and relatively inelastic. (Yarns with too much give will stretch as you weave, resulting in uneven tension that will distort the work.) Cotton or linen rug warp, which are manufactured specifically for this purpose, are excellent. Linen rug warp is made in natural tones, while cotton warp yarns come in many different colors. Both types are available in various counts and ply, so that you

should have no trouble finding a weight appropriate for the particular type of rug you plan to make. Linen yarns, other than warp yarn, should *not* be used because they tend to fray too easily, but various types of cotton yarn other than cotton rug warp—seine and wrapping twine, and cable cord, for instance—are suitable if they are spun with a tight enough twist and don't have too much give. Similarly yarns and cords made from jute, hemp, ramie, and various synthetics can also be used as warp if they share all the general characteristics required of a warp yarn. Wool rug yarns are good for making warp-faced rugs. Before you use any yarn as the warp (and better yet, before you even buy it), test it for strength and frayability: if you can break it relatively easily with your hands or if it begins to abrade if you rub it roughly over the edge of a table a few times, it isn't strong or durable enough to use as the warp for your rug.

ESTIMATING WARP YARDAGE. To figure out how much yarn you will need for the warp, you'll first have to decide on the finished dimensions of your rug, as well as on how many warp ends per inch will be used. (This is called the sett.) Then determine the total number of warp ends required by multiplying the number of ends per inch (sett) by the overall width of the rug, and add four to this figure for the extra ends you will need for the selvages. Next, to figure out how long each warp end must be, add together the following figures: the desired finished length of the rug; approximately 36 inches for tying, take-up and other waste; plus a hem allowance of several inches or a fringe allowance of up to 20 inches, depending on which method you will use to finish your rug. To arrive at the total warp yardage you will need, multiply the length required for one warp end by the total number of warp ends and, if you have been working in inches, convert this figure into yards by dividing by 36. If, for example, you planned to make a fringed 36 by 48 inch rug, with a sett of 8 ends per inch, your calculations would be:

rug width	36 inches
ends per inch	8
selvage ends	4
Total number of ends:	292

rug length	48 inches
tying, waste	36 inches
fringe	12 inches
fringe	12 inches
Total length per end:	96 inches

TOTAL YARDAGE:
$$\frac{292 \times 96}{36} = 778\frac{2}{3} \text{ yards}$$

CHOOSING THE WEFT

The weft, or filling, is the crosswise thread that is woven in and out of the warp threads to create the fabric. The filling for a rug need not be quite as strong as the warp, but it should be sufficiently sturdy to survive being beaten down during weaving and being walked upon thereafter. Since a great variety of yarns and other materials meet these qualifications, however, the range of choice open to the weaver is far greater than for warp yarns. Wool rug yarns (including Persian, tapestry, and rya yarns) are generally considered the finest filling for woven rugs. While usually

more expensive than other types of rug fillings, wool is also warmer, more resilient, and more durable—and works up into rugs of lasting beauty. You should test these yarns before using them in large quantity, however, because each type has its own particular quirks.

Fillings less flexible than wool, cotton, or synthetic yarns are often used to weave warp-faced rugs (rugs in which the warp largely covers the weft).

ESTIMATING WEFT YARDAGE. Weft yardage will be about the same as warp yardage if both yarns are of similar weight. Purchase a little extra yardage to be safe.

PREPARING FILLING MATERIALS

Preparing weft yarns is a simple process of unreeling them from the cones, spools, skeins, or balls in which they are packaged and winding the required amount onto shuttles and bobbins, threading them onto needles and bodkins, or making them into butterflies.

To fill stick, rug, and ski shuttles, make a slipknot near the end of the yarn and loop it around the notched end, peg, or hook; then wind the desired amount lengthwise around the shuttle. Don't fill your shuttles too full, however, or you will have difficulty passing them through the shed.

Yarn butterflies are often used instead of shuttles for weaving on a frame loom, and they are also handy whenever tapestry and other hand-manipulated techniques are being used. A butterfly is made by holding the end of the yarn against the palm of your hand with the ring and little fingers and winding the strand a number of times around the thumb and index fingers in a figure

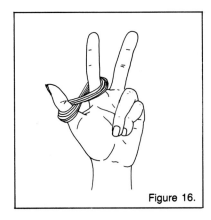

Figure 16.

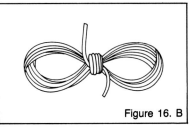

Figure 16. B

eight (Figure 16). When you are finished—and don't wind too many times or the butterfly will be too bulky to weave with comfortably—cut the yarn and make two half-hitches with the second end to tie off the bundle (Figure 16 B). Undo small amounts of yarn as you need it by tugging on the first end that you wound.

Weaving The Rug

THE BASIC WEAVES

The weave is the way in which the warp and weft threads cross over and under each other to form the fabric and, although an almost unlimited number of combinations are possible, most patterns are based on two basic weave constructions: plain weave and twill weave.

PLAIN WEAVE. Also known as tabby, plain weave is the simplest and most basic of all the weaves. It is made by interlacing the weft over and under every warp thread in al-

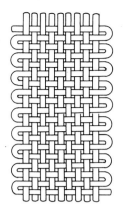

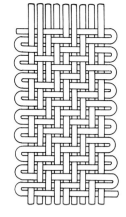

Figure 17.

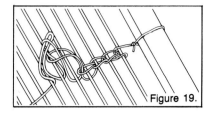

Figure 18.

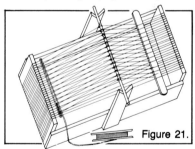

Figure 19.

ternating rows (Figure 17). A complete repeat of the pattern requires only two vertical (warp) and two horizontal (weft) threads; that is, on one row the weft will go over the first warp thread and under the next one, and so forth, and on the second row it will go under the first warp thread and over the next one, etc. The two thread, two row sequence is repeated across the entire width and along the entire length of the fabric. Because it is based on a sequence of only two alternating shed openings, tabby is the perfect weave for a simple frame or other two-harness loom. It can, of course, be woven on any loom equipped with more than two harnesses, and can be easily worked by manipulating the warp threads completely by hand as well. As strong as it is simple, tabby is the most popular weave for rug making, forming the basis for tapestry and knotted pile as well as other techniques. Many variations of plain weave are possible. It can, for example, be weft- or warp-faced; in the former the warp threads are spaced fairly widely and are completely covered by the beaten down weft. In the latter, heavy, closely-spaced warp threads are used and largely or completely cover the weft.

TWILL. A popular and sturdy construction, twill weave is characterized by diagonal lines that are created by staggering the interlacing of the warp and weft threads (Figure 18). These lines can go from left to right or from right to left and a great many variations are possible. Twill patterns are usually based on at least four, and frequently more, vertical and horizontal threads, and are generally woven on looms having four or more harnesses.

WEAVING ON A FRAME LOOM

CHAINING. Most frame looms don't have reeds or other built-in devices for spacing the warp ends evenly, so before actual weaving is begun, a row of chaining is worked across the warp ends to serve this function. Once the rug has been completed, the chain is removed before the edges are finished. Chaining is done with heavy cord (linen is good). You will need a length about five or six times the width of your loom. Work the chain in a straight line near the bottom of the frame, but be sure to leave enough of the warp ends free to tie-off and hem or to make a fringe. To start the chain, tie one end of the cord to the right side of the frame. Then pull loops of cord around each warp end in crochet-like fashion, using your fingers or a crochet hook. Tighten each loop as you finish it so that there will be no slack between loops, and be sure to space the loops evenly. When you finish the last loop, pull the cord end through to lock the chain, and tie off the cord around the left side of the frame (Figure 19).

WEAVING THE RUG. Weaving on a frame loom is extremely simple and involves the repetition of four basic motions: opening the shed, passing the weft (or filling) through the opening, closing the shed, and beating down the filling (Figure 20). Although pattern

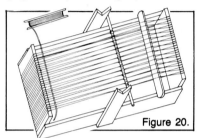

Figure 20.

weaves can be made, frame looms are most commonly used for making plain weave rugs, which require only two shed openings (Figure 21).

Figure 21.

Continue weaving in this manner, alternately raising the first and then the second shed, passing the weft back and forth through the opening, and beating it down. If you have attached the warp so that you can rotate it around the frame to weave a longer rug, you can move the warp to a new position by removing the tension sticks and pushing the warp bar higher up on the back of the frame. Replace the tension sticks once you have repositioned the warp to your satisfaction. As the take-up causes the warp to tighten, however, you can remove the tension sticks permanently. On the other hand, should you find that your warp tension is uneven due to stretching or faulty warping, tighten the loose threads by pulling them up at the top of the frame and inserting a pencil or narrow strip of cardboard. When you have completed the weaving, cut the work off the frame, making sure you leave long enough warp threads to finish the edges of the rug. Knot pairs or groups of the warp threads to keep the filling from unraveling (remove the chain spacer first), and hem or fringe the rug as desired. Instructions for all these techniques are given in the section on Finishing.

STARTING AND ENDING YARNS

Whenever you start a new weft yarn—whether at the beginning of the weaving or as you progress and your shuttle is empty or you want to change colors—try to do it at the selvages. Your rug will be stronger and you will avoid holes or bumps in more visible spots if you do this—even if it means discarding a little yarn that may be left on your shuttle. To start new yarn, leave a 1- to 3-inch end (the length depending on the size of your rug) extending beyond the side (selvage) edge as you make the first pick with the new yarn. After this pick has been beaten down and the next shed opened, tuck the yarn end into the opening, make the next pick, and then beat down the tail along with the new pick (Figure 22). Fol-

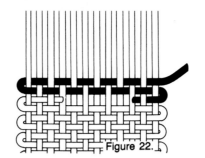

Figure 22.

low the same procedure to end a strand of the weft, leaving a yarn tail extending beyond the selvage as you finish the last pick made with the yarn, and then tucking it in and beating it down with the next pick.

When ending a strand of the weft and beginning a new one of the same yarn or other filling material, you can, if necessary, make the join away from the selvages, but be sure to lap the beginning of the new yarn 1 to 2 inches over the end of the old one, (Figure 23), or you will have a weak

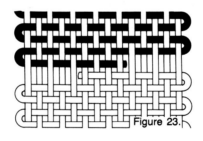

Figure 23.

spot and perhaps even a hole in the middle of your rug.

EASING THE WEFT

As the weft is passed through the shed to make a pick, enough ease (or slack) must be allowed to counteract the effects of the take-up—the length lost as the filling material curves over and under the warp threads. If this isn't done, the weaving will tend to draw in at the edges and become uneven. The process of easing the weft is called bubbling and can be done in several ways. One method (which is very good for weft-faced weaves because it ensures good coverage of the warp) is

to pass the shuttle or other yarn carrier through the shed in little half circles (Figure 24).

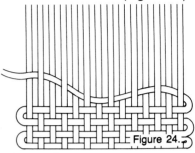

Figure 24.

Another technique is to slant the weft at an angle as the pick is made by pulling the shuttle away from the finished part of the cloth (upward on frame and tapestry looms) as it passes through the shed (Figure 25); or you can arch

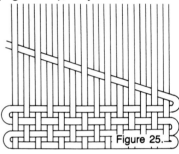

Figure 25.

the pick at the center by pushing the yarn upward or toward the back with your fingers.

There is no neat formula for determining how much ease you will need to allow as you make each pick. It will depend on the weaving materials you are using and the type of weave you are making. Learning how to judge the amount is just a matter of a little practice.

Another way to keep the weaving even and avoid having the selvages draw inward is to use stretchers. This is done in addition to, not as a substitute for, bubbling. On frame looms with a stationary warp, cords can be knotted into the selvages and tied around the sides of the frame at 2 or 3 inch intervals; and if you are weaving on a floor or table loom, stretcher bars can be used instead.

SELVAGES

The selvages of a rug—the finished side edges formed as the weft is turned back and forth on itself to make each new pick—deserve extra attention. They should be straight and firm or your rug will not only look unprofessional, it will not wear well (Figure 26). Ensure even selvages by placing the weft carefully around the first few warp threads as you make each turn. Pull tight enough so that the weft will be firm and even against the outside thread of the warp, with no loop extending beyond the warp, but not so tight that you pull in the edge and make it uneven (Figure 27).

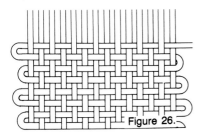
Figure 26.

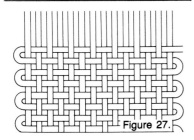
Figure 27.

The edges of a rug receive the hardest wear. Using pairs of threads rather than single strands for the last two or three warp ends on each side (a general practice for all types of fabric) helps strengthen the side edges, but an additional technique can be used if you want to make even firmer and stronger selvages.

To do this, make two turns with the weft instead of a single one to start a new pick, by winding the weft once around the outside warp end, then turning again and making the pick in the normal way (Figure 28).

Figure 28.

CARRYING YARN OVER

When two colors are to be alternated in narrow bands, the filling material need not be cut off every time you want to change colors. You can, instead, carry the yarn along in a selvage until you need to use it again. When you finish weaving with one color, rest the shuttle on the finished fabric or let it hang down from the edge. Then take the shuttle with the new color and bring it up and around the old one from underneath before making the first pick with it; and each time you return to this edge, bring the yarn you are using up and around the old yarn from underneath as you turn to make a new pick (Figure 29). This will incorporate the yarn you aren't using into the selvage, where you can pick it up again whenever required.

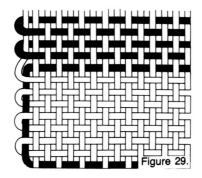
Figure 29.

"FALSE" RUGS: STENCILED FLOORS & FLOORCLOTHS

Have you long imagined the jeweled tones of a large antique Oriental rug covering the great bare expanse of your living room floor, only to have the dream vaporized by thoughts of the expense? With a few stencils and some paint (and perhaps a canvas), you can have your dream "rug"— and at an affordable cost. And you don't have to remove your old linoleum to have that interesting new pattern—just stencil it right onto the old surface.

You need not be a talented artist or craftsperson to stencil a "false" rug or floor. Precut stencils can be purchased in a great variety of beautiful designs, which can be combined in different ways to create any number of overall design schemes; and an even larger array of patterns and design sources are available if you would like to cut your own stencils. Nor is stenciling a floor or floor cloth a long-term project like making most types of hand-crafted rugs. A project of modest size can be ready for use in a week or less, and much of that time you will be waiting for the paint to dry. Since the design is determined by the stencil plate, several people can work on the same project without having the results appear uneven.

Equipment

Stenciling a floor or a floor cloth does require a fairly large array of supplies and equipment, but don't let this deter you. You'll find that most of the items are inexpensive and commonly available. Of all the things you'll need, the most essential are the material from which the actual stencil will be cut, a special cutting surface, a few simple cutting tools, and some brushes or other devices for applying a painted base coat and for stenciling the design.

Some of the items mentioned in the discussion that follows are alternatives (you'll need only one type of stencil material, for example, not all of them) and others are necessary only in specific circumstances. So before you rush out to buy one of everything on the list that you don't already own, read through the directions in their entirety.

CUTTING BOARD

You will need a surface on which to cut your stencils. If you will only be cutting a few stencils, heavy cardboard is cheap and easy to use. A smooth-surfaced medium-weight illustration board is best, and is available at art supply stores. (Avoid corrugated cardboard: the ridged construction makes smooth cutting extremely difficult.) A 24" x 24" square of ¼ inch thick plate glass makes an excellent permanent cutting board. Tape edges to prevent accidents. The slick surface requires greater control of the stencil knife, so practice some sample cuts before beginning work on the actual stencil.

STENCIL MATERIALS

Stencils can be cut from a number of different materials, all usually carried by art supply stores, and sometimes by large paint stores as well. Although these materials vary in price, durability, and ease of cutting, satisfactory stencils

can be cut from any of them. See Appendix for a chart of Stencil Materials.

CUTTING TOOLS

KNIVES. Except for tracing linen, where intricate details can be successfully cut out with a small scissors, stencils are almost always cut with a blade. The versatile craft knife —consisting of a handle, usually of lightweight aluminum, and a removable blade— is the single best tool for cutting stencils (Figure 1). For

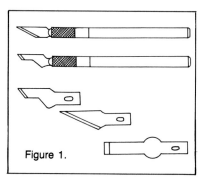
Figure 1.

most stencil cutting all you will need is a No. 1 handle (which is about the length and diameter of a fountain pen), and a supply of No. 11 blades. Be sure to buy plenty of extra blades or sharpen dull blades on a carborundum block. To cut a stencil properly, the blade must be razor sharp. Fortunately, both handle and blades are inexpensive, and can be readily found at art supply and hobby shops. An alternative knife for cutting stencils would be a simple mat knife (Figure 2).

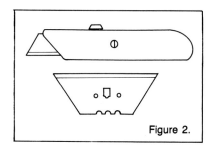
Figure 2.

PUNCHES. Paper punches are useful for cutting small circles. You can find them at any stationery or dime store. Also available are the variously-shaped razor-edged punches used in leathercraft; these can be purchased at craft and hobby shops and from many mail order suppliers.

SCISSORS. Small, sharp, thin-bladed embroidery scissors are useful if you are cutting stencils from architect's tracing linen. And, for cutting canvas or other floor cloth fabrics, you'll also need a good pair of large dressmaker's shears.

BRUSHES AND OTHER COLOR APPLICATORS

STENCIL BRUSHES. Stencil brushes are the classic tools for applying color through a stencil. They are round, blunt-tipped brushes, usually with hog's hair bristles, and come in a variety of sizes, ranging from No. 1 (the smallest) to No. 12 (the largest) (Figure 3).

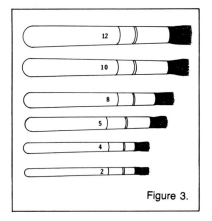

Figure 3.

Since your brush must always be dry and clean before you start to use it, it is wise to have several—at least one for each color you plan to use—on hand. Stencil brushes are not expensive, and can usually be purchased at art supply and paint stores.

AIRBRUSH. This professional tool is actually not a brush at all, but an apparatus that sprays paint onto a surface in much the same way as does a can of spray paint. Consisting of an air compresser, (or aerosol cans of compressed air) hose, tip, and refillable paint container, it can be used with many types of paint, and even with wood stains, to apply a thin coat of paint which dries very quickly. Several coats may be required to get even coverage of the background. The equipment, however, is quite expensive, and this is its major drawback.

PAINT ROLLERS, PAD APPLICATORS, AND BRUSHES. Paint rollers, housepainting brushes, or pad applicators may be used to prime or seal floors to apply a background coat of paint before stenciling, or to apply a finish coat of varnish or polyurethane. A small 2 inch brush or pad applicator may be useful for "cutting in" next to baseboards, while larger brushes, pad applicators, or a low-nap, "tight space" roller may be selected for applying paint or finishes to large areas. Small, low-nap paint rollers and small pad applicators can also be used as a substitute for large stencil brushes when applying paint through simple, large-scale stencils. Use a wide, stiff-bristled housepainting brush if you want to create a spattered effect over a large surface. Choose only good quality tools compatable with the type of finish you will use, and clean and care for them well.

TOOTHBRUSHES. Old toothbrushes are excellent for spatter painting through small stencil openings.

SPONGES. Interesting dappled effects and subtle shading can be achieved by stenciling with sponges. Use household or cosmetic sponges, either natural or synthetic, and cut them into small strips or squares.

CHEESECLOTH. Used when applying wood stains as the stenciling medium, cheesecloth is also an effective strainer for paints that have become lumpy or have formed a skin on the surface.

Materials

To stencil a "false rug" you will need the surface itself and a few items for preparing the surface; the background paint, if desired, the color medium of stenciling, and polyurethane or a similar varnish to form a protective coating over the stenciled design.

STENCILING SURFACES

FLOORS. Any wood floor can be stenciled, as can linoleum or vinyl (both sheet and tile) covered floors. If you like the idea of stenciling, but are unwilling to commit a good hardwood floor to a finish that can be effectively removed only by sanding down to the bare wood, consider stenciling your "false" rug on a "false" floor laid atop the real floor. "False" floors can be created from inexpensive self-stick vinyl or linoleum tiles or from squares of ¼-inch-thick masonite, hardboard, or plywood. Affixing the false floor is simple and will do very little damage (easily repaired at that) to the original floor; vinyl and linoleum tiles are, of course, self-adhesive, and a few nails will hold squares of masonite, hardboard, or plywood in place.

Preparation of each of these surfaces for stenciling is discussed in the section on "Preparing Floors for Stenciling."

Depending on the type and condition of the surface, the following materials may be required: *Paste Wood Filler.* For repairing large cracks or holes in wood floors. *Shellac.* Used to seal unfinished and newly sanded wood floors, as well as plywood for false floors. Use a 4- or 5-pound cut of natural shellac thinned with denatured alcohol.

FLOORCLOTHS. Heavy cotton canvas, of the type used to make sails, is the traditional fabric used for floor cloths. Cotton or linen artists' canvas, however, is an excellent and more readily available alternative. Sold by the yard, it can be found at art supply stores or ordered from a number of mail order houses, comes in several weights that are heavy enough for floor cloths—No. 8, No. 10, or the even heavier No. 12 canvas are all appropriate—and is made in widths up to 165 inches. You can buy artists' canvas unprimed or primed with gesso. If you are going to paint the entire cloth as a background for your stenciled design, you can use unprimed canvas and prime it yourself, or eliminate this task by purchasing the preprimed type of canvas. Buy only unprimed canvas, however, if you want to retain the look of the natural canvas as a background for the stenciled design. Seaming the canvas should be avoided if at all possible, so try to find a width great enough for the project you are planning. To estimate the yardage you will need, decide on the finished dimensions of your cloth and then add a total of 8 inches for hemming (4 inches along each side) to both the length and the width. If you prefer to fringe rather than hem the edges of your cloth, add at least 8 inches, or more if you

want to make any type of knotted fringe or a plain fringe longer than 4 inches.

Heavy cotton duck and denim, which can be found at most yardgoods stores, can also be used, especially for small floor cloths. Estimate yardage in the same way as for canvas, and be sure the goods are 100 percent cotton. Fiber rugs and mats of various sorts—tatami, straw, sisal, cocoa fiber, and the like—can also be effectively stenciled and make interesting rugs; you can find these at specialty import stores, carpet stores, and the rug sections of department stores.

If you are going to use unprimed canvas or other yard goods for your floor cloth, you will also need to buy gesso or acrylic polymer medium for clear sealer or primer (available at art stores) to prime any areas of the fabric that will be painted, as well as some ordinary white household glue—or fusible web porous materials—for finishing the hems. Hemming will not be necessary if you will be using any of the fiber rugs or mats, since these come with prefinished edges.

COLOR MEDIUMS

A variety of different paints can be used for stenciling, and several of them are appropriate for painting a base coat or background as well. Wood floors can also be stenciled with stains. Paint used as an all over base coat, or background, should be of a consistency that will coat well yet flow easily when brushed or rolled onto the floor. For most stenciling, however, the color medium should be quite thick or it will tend to seep under the stencil, making the edges of the design fuzzy. (The color medium must be strained—and thinned—for use in the air-

brush.) Most paints can be used for stenciling directly as they come from the container, without being thinned. A few are normally very thin and must be stenciled onto the surface very sparingly and several coats applied, if necessary, to achieve the desired finished effect.

For floor stenciling projects, the best all-around combination of paints is oil base deck enamel for the base coat and easy-to-apply acrylic artist's paints for stenciling. Most of the following paints and stains, are appropriate for use either as a base coat or a stenciling medium, on floors—and all can be found in paint or art supply stores. Some latex paints may not bond well to vinyl or linoleum floors, and neither the latex paints nor wood stains described below are appropriate, for stenciling a floor cloth. For this type of project, acrylic artists' paints or any of the oil-based paints discussed can be used for painting the background as well as for stenciling, and spray enamels are especially good for stenciling rough-surfaced fiber mats. See Appendix for a quick-reference chart of floor finishes.

OIL-BASE ENAMEL PAINTS. These can be used on all types of floor and floor cloth surfaces, for both base coat and stenciling. Although tough, these paints may become brittle with age, and will be more likely to crease and crack on a floorcloth than the plastic- or acrylic-based finishes. The slow drying time is a disadvantage when they are used for stenciling, as each stencil must be left in place longer to allow drying before repositioning. These paints provide a tough, durable finish, however.

FLOOR AND DECK PAINTS. Also known as porch and patio paints, this family of paints is extremely weather and abrasion resistant. They can be used both indoors and out, and will bond well to many surfaces.

SPRAY ENAMELS. Aerosol spray paints will adhere to all types of floor and floorcloth surfaces as well as the painted base coats described in this section. They are excellent for all stenciling because they dry quickly and require no separate applicator, and are particularly recommended for stenciling on floorcloths made from fiber rugs and mats.

ACRYLIC PAINTS. These artists' paints are the easiest to use and most popular medium for stenciling. They are available in a full range of colors, opaque as well as translucent, and can be mixed to obtain any hue desired. Acrylics dry to a matte finish but can be mixed with a special polymer emulsion if a glossy finish is desired. The thick consistency of the paint is perfect for stenciling just as it comes from tube or jar. For floorcloths, acrylics are appropriate for both stenciling and painting the background.

JAPAN PAINTS. These are flat oil-based paints that adhere well to slick, glossy surfaces. When used for floors or floor cloths, they are more appropriate for stenciling than for painting an all-over background. The consistency of japan paints is quite thin and, to avoid seepage under the stencil, they should be applied with a well-pounced-out brush, using several coats if necessary.

ARTISTS' OIL PAINTS. These can be used for painting the background on canvas floor cloths as well as for stenciling floors or floor cloths. They dry very slowly, however, unless japan drier is added to

the paint to speed drying. As they come from the tube, artists' oils are extremely thick, and will often need to be thinned somewhat with turpentine. Colors can be mixed to obtain any tone desired.

WOOD STAINS. To create the effect of inlaid parquet, bare or partially sealed wood surfaces can be stenciled with stains. Use a high-quality penetrating oil stain, and apply it very sparingly with an almost dry pad of cheesecloth or air brush.

PROTECTIVE FINISHES

Whatever stenciling medium and/or base paint is used, all stenciled floors should—and when latex paints are used they *must*—be varnished to protect the surface and give it a finished look.

Planning A Stenciled Design

SOURCES OF STENCIL DESIGNS

If you prefer to cut your own stencils but aren't quite ready to design them yourself from scratch, you'll find a wealth of stencil patterns in craft anthologies and books on stenciling, as well as in many of the popular craft, homemaking, and decorating magazines. To use these designs, all you have to do is trace them and, if they are small scale drawings rather than full-sized patterns, enlarge them to whatever size is appropriate for your own particular project. If you can't find an overall design scheme that you like well enough to use exactly as is, you can mix and match components that you like from different projects, rearranging them any way you wish until you arrive at an overall look that pleases you and suits the proportions and

decor of your room.

Designing your own stencils is a more ambitious undertaking than using already prepared patterns or precut stencils, but it isn't really difficult and you needn't have a special talent for drawing to attempt it. There are any number of sources for designs characterized by the kind of firm, sharp outlines, and clearly defined internal shapes necessary for cutting a good stencil—tracings of real leaves or ferns, quilt designs, wallpaper and textile patterns, Persian carpets and American Indian rugs, Pennsylvania Dutch decorative motifs, and the floral and geometric traceries found in so many forms of Islamic art, to name only a few.

TYPES OF STENCIL DESIGNS

There are only three basic categories of designs for stenciling: spots, diapers, and borders; and, however simple or complex the individual units of any particular stenciled pattern or the overall effect of their repetitive arrangement may be, all stenciled patterns are made up of one of or a combination of these three types of designs.

SPOT DESIGNS. This term is a very inclusive one, and refers to any individual design—of any shape or size—that is a complete entity in itself (Figure 4). Designs of this

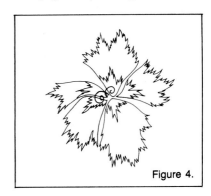

Figure 4.

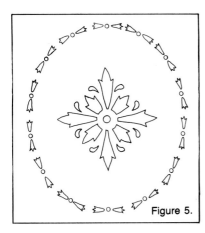

Figure 5.

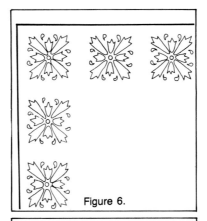

Figure 6.

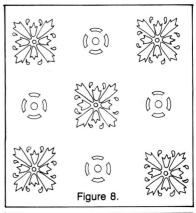

Figure 8.

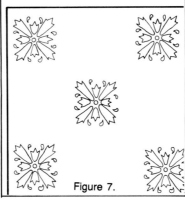

Figure 7.

Figure 9.

type may be used in a multiplicity of ways. A single spot can be used once—as a large central motif, for instance (Figure 5)—or reproduced as many times as desired to create a repetitive pattern for a border (Figure 6) or for an overall ground (Figure 7). It may be used alone or in combination with other spots (Figure 8), or with diaper designs (Figure 9).

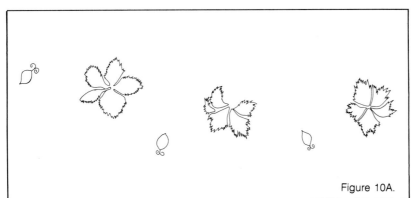

Figure 10A.

Figure 10B.

DIAPER DESIGNS. A diaper is a particular type of repetitive pattern in which the individual units of the repeat are interconnected on all sides by means of common edges or outlines, so that the overall design appears to be continuous in all directions. The complete design may consist of a single unit that is repeated in all directions (Figure 10A), or it may be composed of one or more individual spot designs— framed by an overall interlocking figure, often some sort of scrollwork or series of lines that form geometric patterns (Figure 10B). Extremely effective for stenciling over an entire floor or as the main element on a large floor cloth, diaper designs can be used alone or in combination with bands and borders. They are generally the most complicated of all stenciled designs, however, and must be planned and laid out with great precision.

BORDERS. Border designs usually consist of a continuously repeated motif—either a single component or a composite of several elements—arranged to form a band or strip. The border motif for a floor or floor cloth may be simple or complex, and the band itself may be as narrow as an inch or as wide as 18 inches or more.

Several methods can be used to end a border and to turn corners. If your border design is a continuous repeat unbroken by secondary motifs, the easiest way to end it is simply to stop stenciling the motif just before you wish the border to terminate, masking the stencil if necessary, and then to stencil a vertical bar immediately beyond the motif. To stencil the bar, you can apply masking tape directly to the floor or cloth, or cut a separate stencil, if you prefer (Figure 11). If your border design

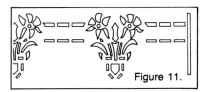

Figure 11.

consists of a main band interrupted by a secondary motif, you may want to end with the secondary motif; measure carefully and, if necessary, extend the band motif so that the spot will fall at the desired point of termination (Figure 12). To turn a corner, the design of the band can be mitered at a 45 degree angle and the sections on each side

Figure 12.

of the corners butted (Figure 13); or a spot design—either

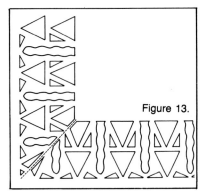

Figure 13.

an independent motif or an enlarged and/or modified version of an element taken from the border itself—can be used, and the stencil for the border masked so the excess portion of the repeat is cut off just before the corner is turned (Figure 14).

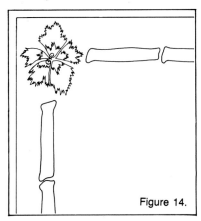

Figure 14.

TYPES AND CHARACTERISTICS OF STENCILS

A stencil, essentially, is a mask from which selected portions have been cut out. To reproduce the design, color of some sort is applied to a surface through the openings in the mask, while the portions of the mask that remain intact protect all surrounding areas from receiving any of the color. If the cutout parts of the stencil represent the design itself, as is the case with the majority of stencil designs, the

image will be positive and may be reproduced in one or more colors depending, of course, on the particular motif you are stenciling and the look you wish to achieve (Figure 15).

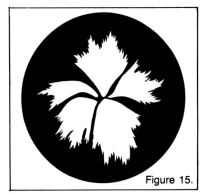

Figure 15.

With some designs, however, the cutouts in the stencil represent the background and, when the color is applied, the image itself appears in the areas that have been masked, that is, in the color of the underlying surface (Figure 16).

Figure 16.

When translating a design into a pattern for a stencil, it is important to remember that the plate must remain physically intact or it will not be able to be effectively used as a mask. This means that the cutout areas must be sufficiently far apart so that a network of stencil material remains to hold the plate in one piece, but this must be done in such a way that the design will still be recognizable. The most common method for accomplishing this compromise between the physical integrity of the stencil plate and the visual integrity of the design is to fracture the design motif into individual segments, either by actually spreading them apart slightly or by shaving down all common edges (or a combination of both techniques), so that each element is separated from all adjacent elements by a space. These spaces, called ties or bridges, not only remain to hold the stencil together when the design has been cut out, they also give the design a characteristically stenciled rather than hand drawn look (Figure 17).

Figure 17.

Some design motifs will require only a single stencil, but it is not advisable—or even possible—in all cases to reproduce a design motif from a single stencil (Figure 18-A). Some designs, for example, look more attractive if the elements overlap or butt, and the only practical way to do this and keep the stencil structurally sound at the same time is to separate the elements

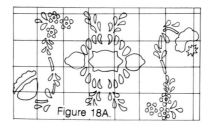

Figure 18A.

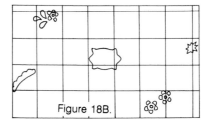

Figure 18B.

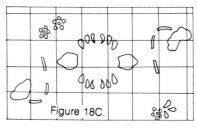

Figure 18C.

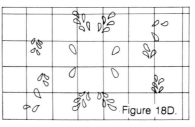

Figure 18D.

that make up the motif into a series of two or more plates, dividing them up so that adjacent elements appear on different plates (Figures 18B, C, D). Then, too, although a single plate can often be stenciled in more than one color, it is frequently more practical to make a series of plates, one for each color to be applied. Some motifs, on the other hand, need not be broken into more than one stencil, but can be, if you prefer to have the option of being able to rearrange individual design elements in a variety of different ways.

ALL-IN-ONE STENCILS. This type of stencil has the complete design motif cut into it and is often used for spot designs. Such a stencil can be used for a design that will be stenciled only once in the overall design scheme or for repeats, so long as the entire design motif will be repeated. All-in-one stencils are particularly appropriate for motifs to be stenciled in a single color; but, in many cases, if the color areas do not actually butt and their arrangement is not overly complicated, the cutout parts of the stencil can be selectively masked so that you can use a single plate for multicolor stenciling, thus avoiding the necessity of cutting a series of stencils (Figure 19).

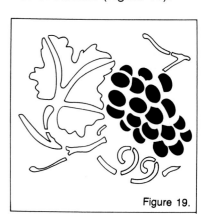

Figure 19.

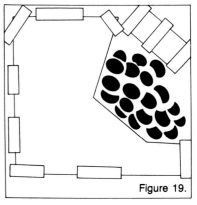

Figure 19.

MODULAR STENCILS. A modular stencil is one that

contains an individual design component—either a segment of a large repetitive pattern such as a diaper or border; or a single shape or element that, alone or in combination with other components, can be rearranged in many ways to create a variety of designs. Modular stencils will allow you to make the fullest—and often most imaginative—use of the reproductive possibilities of stenciling, which is, of course, the most essential characteristic of the medium itself.

Diaper designs, for instance, though usually extensive in scope as well as intricate in overall effect, generally require only a single or at most two modular stencils, or—if several colors are to be used—one or two sets of color separation plates. One complete repeat of the elements of the design is all that the stencil need contain, and the overall pattern is created by reproducing the partial motif contained in the stencil over and over again in all directions (Figures 10A and 10B).

Most border designs also consist of a single motif—some with as few as one or two individual elements—that is repeated many times, and will usually require but a single stencil. In this case, however, at least several repeats are usually included in the stencil, thus reducing the number of times you will have to reposition the plate in order to finish the pattern.

Stencils containing individual shapes—a diamond, a teardrop, a leaf, a blossom, even a single petal—or very simple combinations of several elements offer the stenciler great latitude for experimentation and the play of imagina-

tion. Easy to work with and even easier to cut, such stencils can be arranged in endless combinations and the very same components can be used to create totally different designs. A few examples of the possibilities of this approach to stenciling, using only a handful of design elements, are shown. Try arranging these—or modules of your own creation—in different ways, using a graph paper grid and small-scale cutouts of the elements made from stiff paper, and you'll see how easily you can invent your own overall design schemes.

STENCILS FOR STRIPES. One or more stripes, of the same or of different widths are often used to separate an overall design from a border, and to act as a buffer between the overall or border design and the baseboard moldings around the walls. Simple, straight-edged stripes do not require the cutting of actual stencils. All you need to do is to mark the exact length and width of the stripe(s) you wish to stencil in the desired location on your floor or floor cloth, and then apply masking tape along the markings. To ensure a good bond between tape and floor (or cloth) so that your paints or stains will not bleed under the edges of your masking tape "stencil," be sure to use a continuous length of tape along each edge rather than overlapping short strips. Corners are the only exception to this rule, and here you *must* overlap the two tape ends completely and securely. Then, once you have applied the tape, run a smooth hard object over it, taking care to press out all ripples or air bubbles.

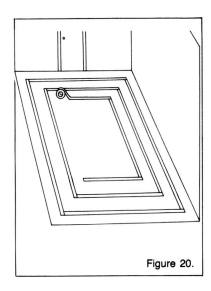

Figure 20.

GRAPHING THE DESIGN

Roughing out the design for your stenciled floor or floorcloth on graph paper in a scale drawing is good preparation for the work of making patterns, cutting stencil plates, and actually stenciling. It is not only an excellent way to experiment with different motifs, their arrangement and their relative sizes and proportions, it will allow you to visualize what the finished design will look like on the floor of your room, and to resolve any difficulties with the design—before you have progressed far along in your project.

If you are going to stencil a floor or a false floor to be laid on top of your present surface, carefully measure the dimensions of the room, and draw the shape—including all doorways, windows, fireplaces, alcoves, etc.—on graph paper, using whatever scale is most practical (Figure 21). For a floorcloth, simply decide on the size and shape you wish to make and mark this to scale on your graph paper. Then tape a sheet of tracing paper over the grid so you can experiment with design motifs without having to redraw the room plan each time you change your mind about the design.

To plot your design on the grid, begin by delineating each of the major areas—large central motifs, diapers or other overall patterns composed of repeated spot designs, borders, and the like, including any spaces you intend to leave or stripes you may want to use to separate any of the primary areas from each other (Figure 21). Then, working

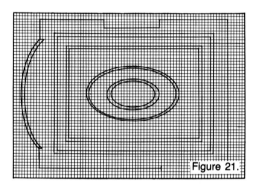

Figure 21.

from the center of the room (or floor cloth) plan outward, block out the repeats for overall diaper or spot designs with a network of crisscrossed lines representing the edges of each repeat, and mark individual elements as well (Figure 22).

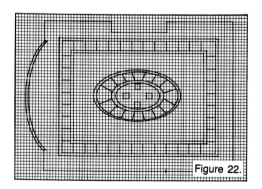

Figure 22.

You must do this carefully, measuring your design elements exactly, because you will use the scale drawing for

marking your finished design on the floor. Mark the repeats for any border design you plan to use in the same way, working from the center of each side of the floor or cloth plan outward toward the corners.

As you mark the major sections of your design as well as the blocks for individual motifs and repeats, try to accommodate the size of each of these areas to any existing demarcation lines on your floor that you can make use of as a natural grid—the edges of floorboards or tiles, for instance. If you can do this, you will save a good deal of time later when you have to block out the design on the floor in preparation for stenciling.

Using the framework you have blocked out, draw in all the important elements of your design. This should be done to scale but need only be a rough sketch of the major shapes and outlines (Figure 22). This is the best way to tell not only whether all the various elements will fit, but whether they are well balanced and will work well together. This is the stage at which you will be able to identify your design problems, and the necessary adjustments can be made. Try tracing several full-size repeats of border, diaper, spot, on tracing paper and moving them around on tile floor to check scale relationships.

Preparing The Stencil Pattern

ENLARGING THE DESIGN

If the design or design component you have chosen is the exact size you need to make the pattern for your stencil, all you have to do is trace it onto a large sheet of tracing

paper. Often, however, you'll need to re-scale the design, enlarging or reducing it to fit the proportions of your specific project. The process is the same in either case. Begin by tracing the design onto a sheet of tracing paper, then scale it to the size you want on graph paper, as shown in the Enlarging section of the Appendix.

KEYING THE DESIGN

When several stencils will be required to produce a design or design component, keying the design will make it easier to determine how many stencils you will need and which portions of the design will be cut into each stencil. When a separate stencil is used for each color of a design, for example, only the colors need be keyed on your tracing paper or graph paper pattern. You can do this by actually sketching in each area of the design with different colored pencils, by writing the names of the colors in the appropriate design areas, or by using a code of letters or other symbols.

GUIDELINES AND REGISTRATION MARKS

GUIDELINES. These are helpful for placing stencils in the proper position on the floor (or whatever surface you will be stenciling). Mark them first on the pattern and then transfer the markings to the stencil with pencil, china marker or carbon paper tracing. Whatever the actual shape of the design, draw a square or rectangle around it just beyond the farthest edges, carefully centering the design within it. Next, mark a border by drawing another square or rectangle 1 to 3 inches outside the inner one. Then mark the guidelines by drawing lengthwise and crosswise lines that bisect the squares (or rectangles). Each of these lines should form a right angle with every line it crosses. (Figure 23). If you find it difficult to differentiate the guidelines from lines in the design, mark the guidelines in a different color.

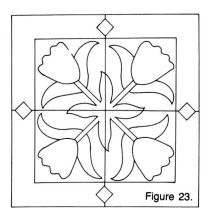

Figure 23.

REGISTRATION MARKS. An aid to matching designs, registration marks are essential for designs composed of a single continuously repeated module or segment, as well as for those that are to be divided into a series of color or design separation stencils. These marks should be drawn first onto the pattern and then cut into the stencils. Depending on the purpose, registration marks can be made in two different ways, or both methods can be used simultaneously.

Registering Color and Design Separations. Mark four small diamonds just outside the squared-off design area, centering one on each side of the square (or rectangle). Place each diamond along a guideline, at the same distance from the edge of the square. If an individual design for which separation stencils are to be cut will also be used repetitively—and the repeats will be placed close together—you can use the registration marks for lining up the repeats as well as for matching the separations. To do this, decide how far apart the repeats are to be placed, halve the figure, and draw each of the diamond-shaped registration marks this distance from the edges of the square enclosing the design. Although this type of registration mark is cut into the stencil, it is used only for chalk-marking the stencil alignment of the floor and is not stenciled in as part of the design (Figure 23).

TRANSFERING THE DESIGN

Once you have scaled the design into a full-size pattern, keyed it, and marked the guidelines and registration marks, it is ready to be used for preparing the stencil. There are a number of ways this can be done, depending on the type of stencil material you are using.

USING THE PATTERN AS A CUTTING GUIDE. Retrace the pattern and work from the tracing, leaving the original for reference and for future use. Trace with a fine-tipped black felt marking pen so the lines of the design will be clearly visible. Include the guidelines, registration marks, and the square or rectangular marking surrounding the design area. Transfer any details which will not be cut, such as guidelines, directly to the stencil material, using a china marker for acetate, or dressmaker's carbon for stencil paper or stencil board. Then glue the tracing to the stencil material with spray adhesive or rubber cement and smooth out the paper to eliminate any air bubbles.

Cutting a Stencil

Experiment first on a small sample of your stencil material before attempting to cut your actual stencil. Use a duplicate of a small part of your stencil pattern, and practice cutting along the traced lines.

PREPARATIONS

Trim the stencil material into a square or oblong 1 to 3 inches larger on each side than the dimensions of the inner markings surrounding the design area of your pattern. The extra inches will act as a border, and will increase the stability of the stencil. *Note:* Whatever the actual shape of the design, the stencil should always be square or oblong.

Begin cutting with a new blade, and change blades or sharpen them frequently. The blade must be sharp at all times to produce cleanly cut edges, which will make crisp, clean stencils.

CUTTING TECHNIQUE

Hold the knife near the base of the handle much as you you would hold a pencil, positioning it so the shaft is perpendicular to the cutting board (Figure 24). Exert just enough

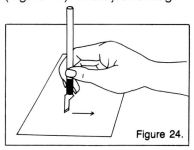

Figure 24.

downward pressure so the tip of the blade penetrates the stencil material and you can lightly feel the resistance of the cutting board beneath. Always cut towards you, using only the tip of the blade. Make each cut with a single, clean stroke. Turn the stencil whenever necessary to position the line you are about to cut in the position most comfortable for you. To cut curves or circles, use one hand to turn the stencil smoothly and continuously, while holding the knife blade almost stationary with the other hand.

ORDER OF CUTTING

Cut your registration marks first, so you won't forget them. Since the stencil will become increasingly weakened as more and more segments are cut from it, it is best to cut all the small shapes before starting on the large ones.

REPAIRING STENCILS

If you accidentally tear the stencil or cut through a tie, tape over the damaged area on both sides with transparent tape and recut carefully along the correct lines.

Preparing The Surface For Stenciling

The steps you'll have to complete to ready your surface for stenciling will depend to a great extent on the type and condition of the surface—whether it is a cloth or a floor, and the particular kind of cloth or floor—as well as on whether the stenciling is to be done on the natural surface or on a painted ground. If you read through the entire section before beginning any preparations, you'll be better able to decide exactly what treatment your own particular surface will require. Often you may start these preparations even before you finish cutting your stencils—you'll have ample time to work on the stencils as sealers, primers, or painted base coats are drying. Remember that primers, sealers, paints, and even some of the powerful cleaning agents give off fumes that may be irritating or even toxic; so, as a basic safety precaution, *always* work in well-ventilated conditions, and always wear a face mask when sanding or spraying.

WOOD FLOORS

Stenciling looks terrific on either an unfinished or a stained wood floor, a fabric, or a painted background. If your floor is not in great shape, painting is an easy and attractive way to avoid the laborious and expensive process of sanding the floor down to bare wood and refinishing it.

Whether you plan to stencil directly on a finished natural wood floor or apply background paint, every trace of dirt and wax must be removed first, so that the surface is completely clean. Scrub the floor with any good heavy-duty commericial cleanser. Then wipe it down well with denatured alcohol, using a clean cloth. Let the floor dry *thoroughly*—from 24 to 48 hours, depending on the temperature and humidity conditions. If you are going to paint the floor, fill in any large cracks or holes with a paste wood filler, and allow this to dry for 24 hours before sanding smooth with fine sandpaper mounted on a block. Lightly sand any small rough spots on the floor at the same time. If you are going to stencil directly on the existing floor surface, you can lightly sand any spots that are particularly rough, but don't use wood filler—the filler will be a different color than your floor and will show up more obtrusively than if you leave the cracks as they are. Vacuum the floor thoroughly and wipe with a tack cloth to be sure all traces of dust have been removed. The floor is now ready for stenciling or for the background paint, if you have chosen this method.

Deck enamel is the best type of paint to use for backgrounds on most floors. If you can't find the exact color you want, buy white deck paint and tint it as desired with small amounts of flat japan paints or other tinting medium recommended by your paint dealer. Before starting to paint, protect all baseboard moldings with masking tape. Apply the paint with a 2½ to 3 inch wide housepainter's brush, following the manufacturer's directions. Make sure the brush is clean and pull out loose bristles before dipping the brush into the paint. Make long strokes and paint in the same direction as the grain of the wood. Clean the brush in the medium suggested by the manufacturer as soon as you are finished with it, and close the paint can tightly so a skin doesn't form on top. Let the first coat of paint dry for 24 hours, then apply a second coat and let it dry for another 24 hours before marking your guidelines and beginning to stencil.

Luxurious parquet and inlaid effects can be created by stenciling with wood stains. For sanding, sealing and stencilling wood floors with wood stains, see Wood Stain Stencil, page 150.

VINYL AND LINOLEUM FLOORS

Vinyl and linoleum floor coverings, both the sheet and the tile forms, can be spruced up with stenciling (See page 153). On these floor coverings, stenciling is usually done over a base coat of enamel deck paint—the background color serving the dual purpose of obliterating the original pattern of the floor covering and concealing surface damages.

Paints won't adhere well to these types of surfaces, however, unless they are spotlessly clean, so scrub the floor well with a potent wax-removing cleanser, making sure to get off every trace of wax and dirt, and rinse thoroughly. (Light sanding may be necessary if the surface is not smooth.) Allow the floor to dry completely, and then paint two coats of deck enamel, as described in section on wood floors. Once the paint is dry, you can mark guidelines on the floor and begin to stencil.

"FALSE" FLOORS

The only major difference in preparing and stenciling a "false" floor—that is, a floor installed on top of your real floor—from preparing a real floor of similar material, is that you have the choice of preparing, stenciling and varnishing the tiles after *or* before you actually lay the floor. The latter alternative allows you to work on small groups of tiles, or even on a single tile at a time. Thus, you don't have to clear the entire room of furniture—you don't even have to work in the same room in which the floor will be installed.

FLOORCLOTHS

To prepare canvas, duck, denim, or other yardgoods for stenciling, first press the fabric to remove all creases and wrinkles. If you must piece lengths of fabric to get the width you'll need for your project, make a plain, machine-stitched seam, leaving 1-inch-wide seam allowances; then make a second line of stitching directly over the original one and press open the seam allowances. Spread a plastic dropcloth over your floor and cover it with a layer of newspapers. Then place the cloth

wrong side up on the floor, stretch the fabric taut in the area around the seam and secure it with pushpins. Then cement the seam allowances to the fabric with white glue, applying the adhesive according to the manufacturer's directions. Weight the glued area down with flat heavy objects, such as books, and allow it to dry thoroughly. Or heat-bond with a strip of fusible web.

The next step—whether you've had to seam the fabric or not—is to turn your cloth right side up (this means seamed side down for pieced goods, gesso side up for primed canvas, and the smoothest side up for all others) and lay it on the floor on top of the protective layer of drop-cloth and newspapers. Without distorting the shape, stretch the fabric taut and tack it down every few inches with rustproof pushpins. Then, using a soft pencil or tailor's chalk, mark the desired finished shape of your floor cloth on the fabric, taking care to center the shape on the fabric and leave 4-inch hem allowances on the sides. When you've done this, apply masking tape in the hem allowances, aligning the edge of the tape along the markings you have just completed (Figure 25). Protect the unmasked

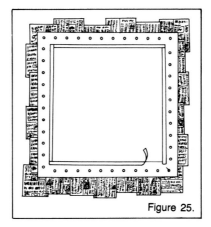

Figure 25.

portion of the hem allowances from spatters by covering them with newspaper.

If you are planning to stencil your design on the natural surface of the fabric rather than on a painted ground, apply two good coats of clear acrylic polymer medium to seal the surface. When this is dry, chalk or pencil in guidelines for your design and proceed to stencil it. Applying a painted ground over the entire surface (except for the hem allowances) is the more traditional method, however, and if you plan to do this but are using ordinary fabric or unprimed canvas, you should prime the cloth first with gesso, which is available at art supply stores. Apply the gesso according to the manufacturer's directions and allow it to dry thoroughly. To paint the background, use deck paints, spray or other oil-based enamels, or even artists' acrylics, and apply the paint thinly but evenly over the entire surface of the cloth (except the hem allowances) with a large brush, or a tight-space roller. You will need to apply at least three coats, allowing each to dry for 24 hours or longer before painting the next one. Once you have finished painting and the cloth is bone dry, you can chalk in guidelines for your design and start to stencil.

Stenciling on fiber mats and rugs is usually done directly on the natural surface rather than on a painted background and, since the edges of these rugs are already finished, little preparation is necessary. All you have to do is to spread your dropcloth and a layer of newspapers on the floor, place the mat or rug finished side up on the newspapers, stretch it taut without distorting the shape, and tack it down.

MARKING GUIDELINES ON THE STENCILING SURFACE

In order to place your stencils in the proper position on your floor or floorcloth, the design must be blocked out on the actual stenciling surface in much the same way that you blocked it out on graph paper. The only circumstance in which this need not be done is if your floor is composed of equal-sized tiles and you have arranged your design to fit neatly within the edges of this ready-made grid.

Depending on the surface, marking may be done with pushpins and tautly-stretched string (a good method for natural wood floors to be stenciled with stains), or with chalk, pencil, or even a china marker. Whatever marking device you select, test it first to be sure you can wipe it off or paint over it without leaving any traces, and if you have any doubts, use the pushpin and string method.

Begin by dividing your overall space into quadrants: measure and mark the midpoints of each side, then connect each pair of opposite points. If your floor or floorcloth is very large, the simplest way to do this is to use pushpins and tautly-stretched string. (On painted floor cloths, however, be sure to anchor the pushpins in the hem allowances, not in the painted ground where they will leave permanent holes.) You can leave the strings in place or use them as a guide for marking with chalk and then remove them. Then, using your design graph as a guide and these crossed lines as your basic points of reference, and working from the center of the area to be stenciled toward the outer edges, block out the spaces that will enclose each component of your design. For an overall design, for example, this means starting at the point where the lines cross at the center of the room or cloth, and for borders it means starting at the midpoint of each side.

If your design consists of one or more continuously or frequently repeated motif, you can save a great deal of time by cutting cardboard templates—one for each different-sized motif. Then, instead of having to measure each repeat with a ruler, you can simply place the template on the surface, trace around it, and pick it up and move it to the next spot to be marked. For continuous repeats, the size of your template should be equal to the design repeat itself; but for motifs that will be separated from one another by a space, make the template the size of the motif plus half the space that will separate it from adjacent repeats. Once you have completed the basic grid, add crossed lines, duplicating those that you marked on your pattern and stencil, in each space that will actually contain a motif. This will ensure that the motifs will be centered properly in their allotted spaces (Figure 26).

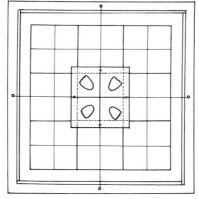

Figure 26.

Stenciling

PREPARATIONS

Before you begin to stencil on your floor or floor cloth, practice the method you plan to use until you feel comfortable with the technique. Try to make your test on the same type of surface as that of your actual project—an extra square of fabric, or a piece of wood or tile similar to that of your floor—but if this isn't feasible, use a sheet of paper or cardboard. Experiment with different methods if you wish, and test the consistency of your paints and stains, the degree to which your brush or other applicator should be loaded, and the pressure and rhythm with which you apply the color to the surface until you are satisfied with the results.

Then, when you're ready to start your "real" stenciling, cover your floor or floor cloth with a plastic dropcloth or some newspapers, except for the area where you are going to stencil first. Assemble all of your materials and supplies—paints or stains, brushes or whatever applicators you plan to use, paper plates or other containers for your mixed paints, spoons for ladling out paints, palette knife and stirrers, solvents and jars for cleaning brushes, paper towels, a thick pad of newspapers for pouncing out your brushes, and the like—and place them all on the dropcloth close to where you are about to work. Whatever type of paints or stains you plan to use, if you are going to custom-mix colors, it is a good idea to make a fairly large batch of each color you'll need (omitting japan drier, if you plan to use it) and store the mixed paints in very tightly sealed containers. When you are ready to begin work, put a small amount of each color that you will need on paper plates (use a separate plate for each color) or some other type of shallow containers, and if you are using slow-drying oil paints, stir in a few drops of japan drier. Replenish your palettes as required, but to ensure freshness only add a little paint at a time.

Select the stencil you wish to use, double-checking with your design graph and keyed master-patterns if you have any doubts about what motif goes where on the floor or which of a set of separation plates should be used first and for what color. Then place the stencil on the surface, using the guidelines marked on both stencil and surface as well as any registration marks already present, to align it properly, and secure the plate with a few small pieces of masking tape. Occasionally, you may want the stencil to adhere more closely to the surface than is possible just by taping the edges down—if, for example, the cutouts are very intricate, the natural consistency of the color medium is very thin, or an airbrush or spray enamels will be used. If this is the case, brush a thin coat of rubber cement onto the back of the stencil or spray lightly with an aerosol adhesive before placing it on the surface; then position the stencil very carefully and press down to bond it to the surface. (Later, once you have carefully removed the stencil and the colors have dried completely, you may need to rub the area lightly with a kneaded eraser to remove any adhesive residues that remain. Then chalk in any registration marks; and if you

are going to stencil with more than one color, mask all the openings in the stencil except those for the first color you plan to use by covering them with masking tape or pieces of paper (Figure 19).

BASIC METHOD OF STENCILING: STIPPLING WITH A STENCIL BRUSH

Stippling—applying the color through the cutouts of the stencil with a special round, blunt-tipped stencil brush—is the most common method of stenciling and can be used for just about any combination of paints or stains and floor or floor cloth surfaces you are likely to encounter. Your brushes must be dry and absolutely clean, so be sure to have a supply of them handy—at least one brush for each color you plan to use.

Hold the brush between your thumb and index finger, supporting it against the middle finger, and position it so it is perpendicular to the surface to be stenciled (Figure 27).

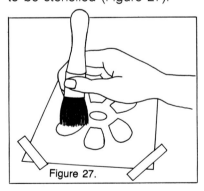
Figure 27.

Dip the tip of the bristles—never the whole brush—into your paint and then pounce out the brush on a pad of newspapers to distribute the paint evenly in the bristles and remove any excess. Pouncing is the basic motion of the stippling procedure and consists of dabbing the tip of the bristles perpendicularly against the

surface with an up and down motion of the entire forearm—practice it until you develop a regular and rapid rhythm. Continue to dip the bristles into the paint and pounce out the brush on the newspaper until you can get an even, speckled coat, but avoid loading the brush with too much color. The brush should be quite dry, particularly when working with thin paints or stains, or you'll run the risk of having the paint seep under the edges of the stencil.

When you are ready to begin stenciling, place your free hand on the stencil to hold it flat aginast the surface in the area where you want to work or, if the cutout you are about to stencil is surrounded by narrow ties, use the tip of a pencil to hold it flat against the surface (Figure 28). Apply the

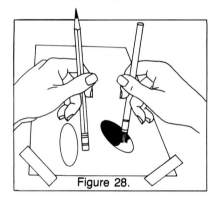
Figure 28.

color with the same up-and-down pouncing motion, working in a circular direction first around the edges and then inward toward the center of the cutout. Keep the movement of the brush continuous, overlapping each succeeding dab that you make. Coat the surface evenly and completely, but do not build up the paint too heavily, especially around the edges of the cutout, or it will form ridges and may also bleed under the stencil. Apply several thin coats if necessary, rather than one thick one, to achieve the intensity and degree of coverage you want and, if your paints are runny, leave the stencil in place and let each coat dry to the touch before applying the next one.

If you have masked portions of your stencil in order to work with more than one color, allow the first color to dry before going on to the next one. Then remove the tape or paper masking the unstenciled cutouts, place a new mask over the completed portions, and proceed to stencil as before, using a clean, dry brush for your second color.

Continue working in this manner until you have applied the desired amount of color through all the openings in the stencil (but *don't* paint the diamond-shaped registration marks cut into color and design separation stencils). Blot gently with clean paper towels, then clean with solvent. If you make a mistake, wipe it up immediately with a clean rag moistened with a solvent appropriate to the particular type of paints or stains you are using. When you are finished, let the paint set for a few minutes, and then carefully take off the masking tape holding the stencil in place and remove the stencil, lifting it straight up to avoid smudging the design. Allow the color to dry thoroughly before positioning additional stencils on the same spot—the remaining plates of a set of color or design separations, for example. The same stricture applies to working in immediately adjacent areas if the edges of the stencil will extend far enough to overlap any still-wet paints or stains. Before repositioning a stencil you have just used, check the back of the stencil to see if it has picked up any

color, and gently wipe it clean with a rag or paper towels dipped in the appropriate solvent. After several repeats have been stenciled, the entire stencil should be cleaned.

ORDER OF WORK. Stencil borders first, then fill in overall designs such as diapers or repetitive spot motifs and, finally, apply masking tape for long stripes that are to separate major sections of your design and fill these in. In all instances, if you are using a series of color or design separation stencils to build up the finished motif, complete the entire section of the design that you are working on (in the manner described below) with one plate, then go over the section with the second plate, then the third one, and so forth, until you have used all the plates in the set.

Borders. Start working on your border at the midpoint of one side, positioning and taping down the stencil in the blocked-out space straddling or directly to the right of the midpoint marking on your floor or cloth. Once you have finished stenciling this first repeat, remove and clean the plate. Then, if you are using very fast-drying paints, position the stencil in the space directly to the right, aligning guidelines and matching registration marks, and stencil as before. Continue working to the right until you are one repeat from the corner; then repeat the entire procedure working to the left of the midpoint until you are one repeat from the corner. Stencil the remaining sides in the same way, ending one repeat from the corner. (Stenciling alternate sides allows you to work faster).

Should you be working with slow-drying colors, however,

you won't be able to immediately reposition the stencil in the adjacent spot to the right without disturbing the still wet paints or stains. Instead, position your stencil at the midpoint of the next side of the floor (or cloth) and stencil in the design; then continue to the midpoint of the third side and so forth until you work your way around all sides. By this time, the repeat you stenciled on the first side should be dry and you can stencil the next repeat to the right of the original one. Continue in this fashion, working your way around each side until you are one repeat from each of the corners. Then duplicate the entire process, working to the left of the midpoint, until you are again one repeat from each corner.

To turn the corners, you can either miter your continuous repeat motif or use a separate spot motif. If you prefer to miter the corners, position the stencil for your continuous repeat motif in remaining empty space at the right end of one side of the floor (or cloth) and tape it down. At the very corner, mask the stencil at a 45 degree angle by applying a strip of masking tape extending from the inner to the outer corner (Figure 13), and add additional strips of tape or a piece of paper to cover all cutouts beyond this 45 degree line. Stencil in the unmasked cutouts and remove the stencil in the usual way, but leave the mask intact. Repeat the procedure in each of the remaining right corners. Then remove the mask from the stencil, position it in one of the empty left corners, again masking the plate at a 45 degree angle from the inner to the outer corner, and stencil in the unmasked cutouts; then repeat this procedure in the remaining left corners.

To turn corners with a spot motif, position the appropriate stencil in the space you have marked for it at one of the corners, tape it down, and stencil the motif; repeat in the remaining corners. You'll then have to fill in the empty spaces between the corner spot motif and the point where you left off with your continuous repeat motif. To do this, position the stencil for your continuous motif in each of the empty spaces, aligning your registration marks with the adjacent repeat. If there isn't enough room for a complete repeat, tape a mask over the excess portion of the plate, and then stencil in the unmasked areas.

Overall Designs. Diaper patterns should be stenciled from the center outward toward the edges. Once you have finished the first repeat of the pattern at the center of your floor or cloth, you can alternate sides or work in one direction at a time, as you prefer. But, if you have partial repeats at the edges, do all the complete repeats first before starting on the partial ones. Mask the floor, not the stencil.

If you are stenciling an overall design consisting of separate but frequently repeated spot motifs, the direction as well as the order in which you should work will depend strictly on the nature of your particular design scheme and the method you find most convenient. If, for example, your design is arranged in blocks in which two separate motifs will be alternated, you will probably find it most practical to complete all the blocks for one motif (and if separation stencils are involved, to work one plate at a time), progressing across the floor or

cloth from one side to the other in rows, before going back to stencil all the intervening blocks with the second motif. But, if you prefer, you can also work from the center outward toward the edges, or finish one entire row at a time, alterately stenciling one and then the other motif.

VARIATIONS

STENCILING WITH SPONGES. Applying the stenciling colors with a sponge is another very popular technique, and one that is especially appropriate if you want to create interesting dappled textures. Try a variety of different types of sponges—you'll get a different texture with each one. Cut your sponges into small squares or long narrow strips, and pour your colors into saucers (in this instance, don't use paper plates), diluting them to a much thinner consistency than you would use with stencil brushes. Dip the flat surface of a sponge square or the tip of a long strip into the color, squeeze it out to distribute the color evenly and eliminate any excess, and pounce on a pad of newspapers to test the effect and make sure the sponge isn't too saturated (Figure 29). To stencil, you can

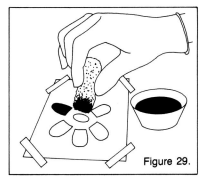

Figure 29.

pounce gently or rub the color in, or a combination of both techniques (Figure 30). Work

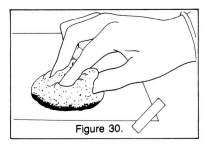

Figure 30.

first around the edges of the cutout area and then inward toward the center, using your free hand to hold the stencil against the surface. When you are finished, be sure to let the paints set before lifting off the stencil. Follow the same order of work outlined in the discussion of the Basic Method of Stenciling.

STENCILING WITH SPRAY PAINTS AND AIRBRUSHES. Stenciling with a spray enamel is probably the simplest method of all. Effective on all types of horizontal surfaces, it is particularly good for rough-textured fiber rugs and mats. The only drawback to using spray paints is that they are rather expensive especially if your project is a large one, and are available in a more limited range of colors than most other types of paints.

When preparing to work with any kind of aerosol, be sure to spread your dropcloth and/or newspapers over everything in sight beyond the edges of your stencil or you'll find the surrounding area covered with a fine and extremely hard to remove paint mist. And unless you are going to stencil on unsealed raw wood or a very rough-textured natural (rather than painted) fiber rug surface, affix your stencil in the desired position with rubber cement or a spray adhesive—this will prevent seepage of the thin paints. Shake the can well to mix the paint and test spray on some newspaper to be sure the paint is flowing properly from the nozzle. To stencil, hold the can about 10 or 12 inches from the surface with the nozzle pointing straight down, and spray lightly, moving the can closely back and forth across the surface until it is thinly but evenly coated (Figure 31). Spray sev-

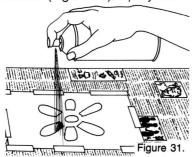
Figure 31.

eral light coats in this manner, letting each coat set before applying the next one, until you achieve the color intensity and degree of coverage you want. Allow the paint to set before you carefully remove the stencil; then let it dry thoroughly before using any additional stencils in the same spot or overlapping stencils for adjacent areas. Follow the same order of work outlined for the Basic Method of Stenciling. Be sure to remove all overspray before varnishing.

In both technique and effect, stenciling with an airbrush is very similar to using a can of spray paint, except that the airbrush can be used with practically any of the paints or wood stains appropriate for floors and floor cloths and it is, of course, refillable. (However latex and metallics may dry too quickly and clog the brush.) Your paints or stains will need to be diluted to a much thinner consistency than is appropriate for strippling with a stencil brush, and it is best to refer to the manufacturer's instructions for the proper proportions of color and solvent, as well as for directions concerning assembling the equipment, filling the paint well, and adjusting the pressure of the air compressor.

SPATTER STENCILING.
Spattering is another easy special effect technique that can be used over an entire background (many early American painted floors and cloths were decorated this way), or to give an interesting look of irregular speckling to the stenciled design itself (Figure 32). Depend-

Figure 32.

ing on the effect you want to create, spattering can be done in a single color or in several and, for stenciling, it can be used as the primary method or to highlight an already stenciled design.

To spatter-stencil small areas, the tool to use is an ordinary toothbrush; and for larger stencil cutouts or for spattering an entire background, buy a stiff-bristled housepainter's brush and shear off the bristles about an inch or so from the base. Be sure to have a separate brush—clean and dry—for each color you plan to use. If you are going to spatter through the cutouts of a stencil rather than cover an entire background, mask the area for several feet around the stencil with a dropcloth or newspapers. Dilute your paint with the appropriate solvent until it is quite thin, and pour it into a saucer. Dip only the tips of the bristles in the color and

pounce out the brush on a pad of newspapers. Then hold the brush in one hand with the bristles positioned perpendicular to the surface you want to spatter; and with your free hand, draw the narrow edge of a paint stirrer or other flat stick (or use your index finger) across the bristles (Figure 32). As the bristles spring back they will propel tiny paint drops onto the surface, creating the spattered effect. Move the brush as you work to get an even coverage of the entire surface, and wipe the stick (or your finger) frequently to avoid a buildup of paint that may drip down onto your stenciling surface. Since you are working with a fairly thinned-out medium, once you have finished stenciling, leave the plate in place until you are sure that the paints have set.

Cleaning Stencil Equipment

To keep your stencils and brushes in good working order, it is important to clean them promptly and properly. If you can't stop to clean a brush as you finish using it, don't just put it down and let the paint dry on it. Instead, before you start to work, fill a coffee can or large jar with the solvent appropriate for the type of paint or stain you will be using and keep it on hand along with the rest of your stenciling supplies; and when you are done with a brush, place it in the container until you can take time to clean it well.

Stencils should be cleaned immediately after use. Place them on a flat surface over a layer of paper towels and wipe gently, first on one side and then on the other, with a clean cloth or sponge saturated with soapy water or turpentine, depending on whether you have been using water-soluble or oil-based paints or stains. Once the plates are clean, wipe again with a plain damp cloth or sponge, and then pat dry with paper towels. Store your stencils flat (never rolled up or standing on edge), placing them between layers of cardboard.

Finishing Stenciled Floors and Floor Cloths

Applying a Protective Coating
When you have completed your stenciling, close off the room and let the paints or stains dry for at least 24 hours, or even longer if you stenciled with slow-drying oil-based paints. Leave floor cloths tacked to the floor during this period and until after you have varnished them. Once the floor or floor cloth has dried thoroughly, wipe off all remaining traces of your stenciling guidelines and vacuum, taking care not to mar the surface. Then, using a large brush, roller, or pad applicator, and working in well-ventilated conditions, varnish the surface with polyurethane, following the maufacturer's directions. If you want a very shiny surface, use high-gloss polyurethane or, for a semi-gloss finish, mix equal parts of high-gloss and satin polyurethane. For floors, apply two coats of the varnish, allowing the surface to dry for 18 to 24 hours between coats (not longer than 24 hours, or the coats won't bond well). Floor cloths should be given three or four coats or polyurethane, again spacing the applications 18 to 24 hours apart.

Finishing the Edges of Floorcloths
When the polyurethane has dried, remove the tape masking the hem allowances and pull out the pushpins. You can finish your cloth either by hemming or by self-fringing the edges. Directions for fringing and making glued hems are given in the section on Finishing Handcrafted Rugs.

FINISHING HANDCRAFTED RUGS

No rug is fully finished when the stitching, hooking, weaving, or painting of it has been completed. If the rug has been pulled out of shape while being worked, blocking will be necessary and, if soiled, you may also have to clean or launder it. Then the edges must be dealt with (finished, if raw, or perhaps decorated with fringe, or both) and sometimes the entire underside must be protected with a lining or latex coating as well. Whatever type of finishing you want or need to do should be carefully planned before you begin to work your rug—in fact before you even cut your backing fabric (if any). Preparations and sometimes the order of work will vary with the finishing method or combination of techniques that you select, and if you plan in advance you will avoid unnecessary work as well as eliminate the possibility of unpleasant surprises.

Blocking

Blocking—reshaping needlework by dampening, stretching and, sometimes, pressing it—is necessary for any handworked rug that has become misshapen during the process of producing it. Needlepoint, knitted, and crocheted work will almost always require at least minimal blocking and, occasionally, handwoven and latch-hooked rugs will also need to undergo the treatment. Blocking is not necessary for hooked, braided, and rya rugs, but light steam pressing with a damp press cloth will help flatten out any ruffling or unevenness in a braided rug; and steaming the surface of a hooked or rya rug, by holding a steam iron just above the pile, will help restore the bloom.

As you make your rug—needlepoint particularly, but other types as well—keep in mind that while blocking will correct a great deal of distortion, it cannot entirely restore a piece that has been worked so tightly or unevenly that the canvas backing (or the stitches themselves, in the case of knitting and crocheting) has been pulled permanently out of shape. If you work with an even, slightly loose tension, you will not have to cope with this problem.

A rug made in sections can be joined before blocking, particularly if the sections aren't badly out of shape. But in most cases, the size alone makes it easier to block the sections individually before joining them; and badly distorted pieces may need to be blocked several times, at least once before they are seamed together and again after the complete rug has been assembled.

NEEDLEPOINT. To block a needlepoint rug, you'll need a board (plywood is excellent) several inches larger all around than the size of your

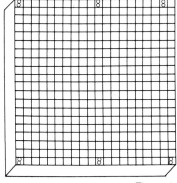

Figure 1.

canvas. If you do a lot of blocking, rule the entire surface of the board into a grid of 1-inch or even ½-inch squares, using an indelible, waterproof black marker such as a laundry pen; this will allow you to block pieces of many different sizes on the same board (Figure 1). Should you prefer not to mark directly on the board, you can tape a large sheet of brown paper to the board and draw a square or rectangle the size of the worked part of your canvas on the paper; center the shape on the paper and use a T-square and ruler to be sure the lines are straight and the corners square; then mark vertical and horizontal center lines across the square or rectangle, extending them to the edges of the paper. Protect your board and paper pattern by spreading a plastic sheet over it and taping or tacking it down.

If your needlepoint piece is badly out of shape—or if it is only mildly distorted but has been worked with a combination of flat and raised or textured stitches—you'll have to dampen it before pinning it to the board. To do this, you can moisten both sides of the canvas with a clean wet cloth or sponge (use cold water), spray it with a water-filled atomizer, or roll it in a wet but wrung-out terrycloth towel until the piece is quite damp. Whichever method you choose, however, don't remove the masking tape binding from the edges of the canvas, don't saturate the canvas with water, and *never* soak the entire canvas. Don't try to wash needlepoint either: if the piece is quite dirty, send it to a reputable professional dry cleaner, and have it cleaned (and blocked at the same time); and if it is just slightly soiled from handling, you can clean it yourself, once it has been dampened, with one of the spray cleaners made especially for the purpose and sold in needlework stores. Place the well-dampened canvas face down on the board (that is, unless you have worked the piece with stitches that are quite raised and textured, in which case it should be blocked face up). Aligning the edges of the worked area of the needlepoint with the markings on your board or brown paper pattern, tack the canvas to the board with *rustproof* (aluminum) pushpins. Insert the pushpins at least 1 inch outside the worked area and preferably along the tape-protected edges, between—not into—the threads of the canvas (you may cut the threads if you tack directly into them). *Never* pin into the worked part of the canvas. Start by tacking at the midpoint of each side, matching the guidelines on board and canvas, and work outward toward the corners, stretching the canvas as you work and placing the pushpins 1 inch apart or even as close as every ½ inch if you are having difficulty squaring up the canvas (Figure 2). If you have

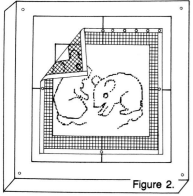

Figure 2.

such difficulties along selvage sides of the canvas, you may

have to clip the selvages and, if the canvas has already begun to dry by the time you finish tacking it in place on the board, sponge or spray it again lightly with water. Then allow it to dry naturally, away from artificial heat, a process that will take at least 24 hours and perhaps even several days. Once your needlepoint is completely dry, remove the pushpins and turn the work right side up, but leave it on the board for a while to make sure the canvas doesn't start to creep back into a distorted shape. If this does happen, repeat the entire blocking procedure, once or even several times if necessary, until the canvas will stay put in the correct shape. When you are satisfied with the blocking, place the work right side up on the board and steam it lightly to restore the bloom to the yarn by holding a steam iron above (but not touching) the surface and moving it back and forth across the worked area.

Blocking needlepoint that is only mildly distorted (needlepoint worked with flat stitches, that is) is a much quicker and simpler process. Just tack the dry canvas right side down to your board, as described for badly distorted work. Then place a damp press cloth over the worked area and press lightly with a steam iron, picking the iron up and placing it down again in the next spot without sliding it around. When you are done, remove the press cloth and leave the canvas in place on the board until it is dry; then turn it right side up and steam lightly without allowing the iron to touch the surface.

OTHER RUGS. Handwoven pieces that are out of shape should be blocked in much

the same way as needlepoint—that is, if the work is badly distorted, it should be dampened and pinned face down to a board over a tracing of the correct shape, and then left to dry; or, if the piece is only slightly distorted, it should merely be pinned down over the tracing, pressed with a steam iron and damp press cloth and left in place until dry. Latch-hooked rugs that are slightly out of shape (this type of work will rarely become seriously distorted) can be dampened on the wrong side, tacked right side up to a board over a tracing of the proper shape, and left to dry naturally.

Knitted and crocheted rugs should also be blocked on a board, but the board should be padded with several layers of toweling, and the outline of the shape for blocking should be marked on a piece of muslin or an ordinary sheet rather than on paper, and then tacked or taped over the toweling. If washing is necessary, use *only* cold water and cold water soap, and rinse thoroughly; then place the piece between layers of toweling and gently pat out as much of the moisture as you can. Thereafter the procedure is the same as for needlepoint: dampen badly distorted pieces (if they aren't already damp from washing) as well as *any* pieces made from synthetic rather than wool yarns, tack right side down on your board, and allow to dry naturally. Steam press slightly distorted wool pieces with a damp cloth and steam iron, picking the iron up and putting it down again very lightly, rather than gliding it along or letting it rest with any weight against the surface of the work.

Hemming

Some rugs—notably braided, knitted, and crocheted ones—have self-finished edges that need no further finishing; but all other types of handcrafted rugs must either be hemmed in some way to conceal and protect the raw edges or unraveled around the edges to camouflage their rawness by turning them into a self-fringe. Fringe can also be attached to any type of rug as a secondary and purely decorative edge finish.

DOUBLE-TURNED HEMS

The classic double-turned hem is an appropriate edge finish for hand-and punch-hooked rugs as well as for woven and rya rugs.

HOOKED RUGS. If you are going to protect the back of your rug by coating it with latex, do this before hemming; if you plan to line the rug, however, complete the hem first. To hem, begin by trimming the hem allowances evenly all around. Large square and oblong rugs may have hems as deep as 3 inches, plus a ½-inch turn-under. Round or oval rugs should be finished with slightly narrower hems: allow 2½ inches, including the turn-under, for large rugs; 1½ inches, including the turn-under, for small rugs. Whatever the shape of your rug, however, if you are going to attach a decorative knotted fringe to any or all edges and plan to do this after completing the hem, be sure to allow room for the fringe before trimming your hem allowances. (In this case, it is a good idea to chalk or pencil in a hem foldline ¼ to ½ inch beyond the worked area of the rug.)

Miter corners of square and oblong rugs by trimming the

corners of the hem allowances diagonally, cutting ½ to ¾ inch beyond the worked area or the marked hem foldline of the rug (Figure 3). Next, with

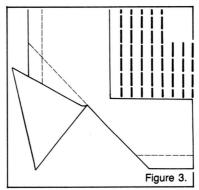

Figure 3.

the rug wrong side up, fold the diagonally-cut corners down just beyond the worked area or along the corner hemline markings, as appropriate; press the folds. Then fold down each of the edges ½ inch and press to hold the fold. Finally, working along one side of the rug at a time, turn down the hem again, folding just beyond the worked portion and pin in place (Figure 4).

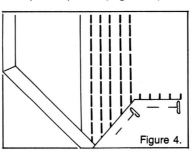

Figure 4.

Slipstitch the folded inner edge of the hem to the back of the rug, using a strong carpet thread and taking care that the stitches are secure but do not show on the finished side of the rug; then slipstitch the mitered corners (Figure 5). Remove all pins, knot in a fringe if desired, and line the rug unless you have already applied a latex coating.

To hem a round or oval rug, turn it wrong side up, turn

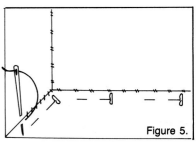

Figure 5.

down the hem edge ½ inch and pin, baste, or press to hold the fold. Then turn the hem down again, folding just beyond the worked portion or along the hem foldline markings of the rug, as appropriate. Space the ripples formed by the excess hem fabric evenly around the circumference, form them into shallow tucks or pleats, and pin them down. Add additional pins along the inner hem edge as necessary. Slipstitch the inner folded edge of the hem to the back of the rug, using a strong carpet thread; then slipstitch the pleated folds to hold them flat (Figure 6). Remove

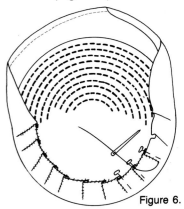

Figure 6.

all pins and bastings, knot in a fringe if desired, and then line.

WOVEN RUGS. Woven rugs have finished selvage edges and require hemming only along the two nonselvage ends. To hem, turn the rug wrong side up and fold down each nonselvage edge ½ to 1 inch, taking care to fold directly along a weft thread of the cloth. Pin the folded hem in place and, using a strong carpet thread or a strand of the weaving warp, slipstitch to the rug fabric. Be sure to catch the back of the rug securely with your stitches, but don't allow them to show through to the finished side of the rug. Remove the pins and press the hem lightly with a steam iron and press cloth.

RYA RUGS. Rya rugs that have been worked from selvage to selvage require hemming only along the two nonselvage edges. This is done in the same way as for woven rugs, except that deeper hems are usually made (2 inches plus a ½-inch turn-under), and the hem is measured and folded from the first openwork row of the fabric backing beyond the worked portion.

If you have had to cut away the selvages of a rya backing or have left wide hem allowances along the lengthwise sides of the cloth, all edges must be hemmed. Hemming the entire circumference is necessary for round and oval rugs as well. For all shapes, mark a hem foldline around the entire rug ⅜ inch to ½ inch beyond the worked portion of the rug. Trim the hem allowances to 2½ inches—including a ½-inch turn-under—beyond these markings. Round and oval rugs can have slightly shallower hems, if desired. Then complete the hems as described for hooked rugs of the same shape.

BOUND HEMS

Any rug worked on a canvas mesh backing, notably needlepoint and latch hooking, should be finished with bound hems. Hemming with rug binding is also an appropriate alternate method for finishing rya rugs, hooked rugs (after latexing or before lining them), as

well as for the nonselvage edges of handwoven pieces. Stitch-on rather than iron-on rug binding should be used. It is made in 1½-inch and occasionally in even wider widths, comes in various neutral colors (which you can dye, if you wish), and is usually found wherever home sewing notions and supplies are sold. If you cannot find actual rug binding tape, any wide, heavy, general-purpose cotton twill tape can be substituted, but it must be at least 1¼ inches wide, or preferably wider.

NEEDLEPOINT AND LATCH HOOKED RUGS. To make bound hems for rugs worked on canvas mesh backings, start by laying the rug right side up on a flat surface and, if you have already knotted fringe around the edges, push the fringe off the hem allowance and back onto the worked area of the rug. Place the rug binding tape along the edges of the worked portion of the rug, extending the outer edges of the tape ¼ inch beyond the worked area (remember, however, to leave room for any fringe you plan to knot into the edge after completing the hem), and pin to hold the tape in place. Fold up the first tape end ½ inch and, when you have worked your way around the rug, lap the second end 1 inch over it (Figure 7). If your rug is rectangular,

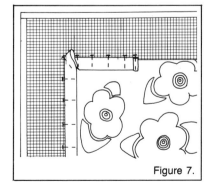
Figure 7.

start and end the binding tape at the midpoint of one side rather than near a corner. Then stitch the tape to the canvas hem allowance just beyond the worked area or the area to be occupied by a fringe (Figure 8). You can sew

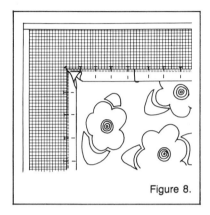
Figure 8.

by machine, or backstitch by hand with carpet thread. For extra strength, make a second seam over or just outside the first one. When you have finished stitching one edge of the tape to the rug, place the rug wrong side up on your work surface, but do not yet turn the binding tape to the wrong side.

Then, for square and oblong rugs, trim the canvas mesh hem allowances so that they will be about ¼ inch narrower than the binding tape (lift up the binding tape temporarily so that you can judge how much you must trim from the canvas), but take great care not to cut into the tape itself. Then trim the corners of the canvas *(not* the tape) diagonally, cutting ½ inch to ¾ inch outside the seam you have just completed. To keep the cut canvas mesh from raveling, apply a little white glue around the edges at the points where the threads intersect, and allow to dry. When the glue has dried, fold the canvas hem allowances against the rug and pin (don't do anything with the binding yet), turning down the diagonally-cut corners first, and then the sides (Figure 9).

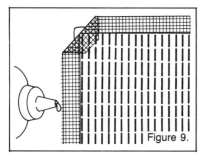

Figure 9.

Whip the inner edges and mitered corners of the raw canvas to the back of the rug and remove the pins (Figure 10).

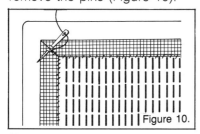

Figure 10.

Then turn the binding to the wrong side of the rug and, folding one side at a time (Figure 11), pin to the back of the

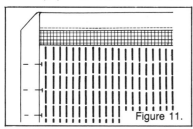

Figure 11.

rug. Hemstitch the unattached edge of the binding to the back of the rug and slipstitch the mitered corners (Figure 12). Remove the pins and

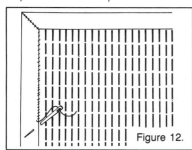

Figure 12.

then, if you wish added protection, line the rug.

To complete the hems of round or oval rugs, trim the canvas hem allowances, glue the edges, and then fold the remaining raw canvas against the back of the rug as for rectangular rugs. Space the ripples formed by the excess canvas mesh evenly around the circumference, forming them into narrow pleats or tucks, and pin them down (Figure 6). Whip the inner edge of the canvas to the back of the rug (Figure 10), and tack down the pleated folds as well. After removing the pins, turn the binding tape to the wrong side of the rug, forming the excess tape into evenly spaced pleats in the same way as before. Hemstitch the inner edge of the binding to the back of the rug and slipstitch the pleated folds. Remove remaining pins and, if desired, line the rug.

WOVEN RUGS. Woven rugs need to be finished only along the two nonselvage edges. To make bound hems along these edges, cut strips of rug binding tape 1 inch longer than the edges. Lay the rug right side up on your work surface and pin a strip of the binding tape along each edge to be hemmed, aligning the outer edge of the tape ¾ inch from the edge of the rug and turning up the tape ends ½ inch so that they are flush with the sides of the rug. Stitch the tape to the rug ¼ inch from the outer tape edge and remove the pins; then make a second line of stitching over or just outside the first seam. You can sew by machine, using a heavy-duty mercerized cotton or cotton-wrapped polyester thread, or backstitch by hand with carpet thread. Then turn the rug wrong side up, fold

down the hems just beyond the stitched edge of the binding tape, and pin in place. Hemstitch the unattached tape edge to the back of the rug and whip the layers together along the short ends (Figure 13). Then remove the pins and

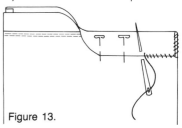

Figure 13.

press lightly with a steam iron and press cloth.

HOOKED AND RYA RUGS. Hooked rugs may be bound in much the same way as those made on canvas mesh backings, except that the trimmed edges of the backing fabric need not be glued and, particularly with rectangular rugs, it is not essential to whip the hem allowances to the back of the rug before turning and stitching down the remaining edge of the binding tape.

The same procedure and exceptions apply to binding the edges of rya rugs that must be hemmed on all sides. In addition, for these rugs, the first side of the rug-binding tape should be stitched on ⅜ inch to ½ inch beyond the worked portion of the rug (rather than immediately beyond that area). To bind only the two nonselvage edges of a rya rug, trim the hem allowances along these edges to about 1½ inches; then apply the binding tape and finish the hems exactly as described for woven rugs.

GLUED HEMS

The edges of stenciled floor-cloths cannot be hemmed in any of the usual ways because stitching into the fabric will mar the painted surface. Instead, the hem allowances may be fringed (see the discussion of self-fringes, next page, or they can be affixed to the underside of the floor cloth with glue. If you have left hem allowances wider than 4 inches, trim them to this width, making sure the edges are even all around. Then, to hem square or oblong cloths, trim the corners diagonally, cutting ½ inch outside the finished area of the cloth (Figure 3). Turn the cloth wrong side up and fold down the diagonally-cut corners ½ inch (up to the finished part of the corner, that is), pressing in a crease with your fingers (Figure 14). Apply

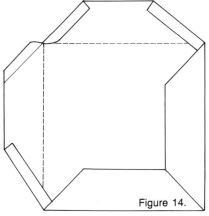

Figure 14.

white glue to the underside of the corners, following the manufacturer's directions, press the layers together firmly, and weigh them down with books or other heavy flat objects. Leave the weights in place until the glue has dried. Then, working on one side at a time, fold down the hem along the edges of the finished area (or slightly further away if you plan to knot in a fringe after hemming), and press in a crease with your fingers. Apply glue to the underside of the hem in the same manner as before and press the layers together firmly—the mitered corners should meet but not overlap.

Weigh down the entire hem with books and allow it to dry.

To hem a round or oval cloth, place it wrong side up and fold the hem along the edge of the finished area (or slightly beyond if you plan to add a fringe), pressing in a crease with your fingers. Form the excess fabric of the hem into perpendicular wedges, spacing them evenly around the circumference, and trim them off. Hold your scissors flat against the surface and cut the fabric away no closer than ⅜ inch from the hemline fold (Figure 15). Then glue the hem to the cloth and weigh it

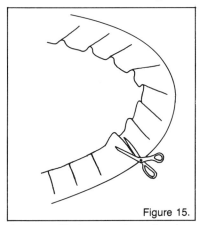

Figure 15.

down until dry, as described for square and oblong rugs.

Fringes

Fringe is often just the little extra touch needed to finish off a rug with flair. It can be knotted into the edges of almost any type of handcrafted rug and, in some cases, can even be fashioned from the threads of the rug fabric itself.

SELF-FRINGE

Fringing, rather than hemming or binding the raw edges, is an attractive way to finish the warp ends of woven rugs, and is appropriate as well for rugs that are made on sturdy but good-looking fabric

backings—hooked and rya pieces, and stenciled floor cloths, for instance. On woven rugs, fringe is made only along the two crosswise edges, since the selvages provide all the finishing required along the lengthwise sides. Square and oblong rugs made on backing fabrics may be fringed on all four sides if the threads of the fabric are appropriate; but here too, fringing only the crosswise edges is more common.

Self-fringes must be planned before the rug is made. For a woven rug, you'll need to leave extra-long warp ends, and fabric-backed rugs will require unusually wide hem allowances. Once you have worked the piece, you can always change your mind and finish your rug with hems, but if you don't provide for fringes at the outset, you won't have the choice. The amount of extra fabric or warp that you will need for self-fringes will depend on how deep a fringe you want to make and also on whether you plan to leave the strands of the fringe loose or knot them into a pattern. A 2- to 3-inch fringe may be wide enough for a small rug, but larger rugs may have fringes as deep as 8 or 10 inches. As you plan, keep design in mind as well as size. Fringe should balance and complement the rug, not detract from it. This may mean making a wider fringe or it may mean making a narrower one, a simple plain fringe or an elaborate knotted pattern, all depending on what will look well with the rug. The safest course is to allow for the widest fringe and trim it down later, if necessary. Remember, too, that knotting requires a greater fringe allowance than does making a plain loose fringe of the same overall length, and with some knotted patterns this amount can be appreciable. You'll be able to judge the amount more accurately if you tie some measured strands of string or yarn around a yardstick and actually knot a sample of the fringe pattern you plan to use.

FRINGING WOVEN RUGS. To fringe the warp ends of a woven rug, the first thing you must do (unless you've already done it as you removed the work from the loom) is to tie the warp threads together in overhand knots. Whatever you plan to do with the fringe thereafter, this initial knotting is essential in order to keep the filling (weft) threads of the rug from unraveling, and may be done in pairs or, particularly if you warp is rather fine, in small groups of threads (but don't include too many threads in each knot). The overhand knot (Figure 16) can be made

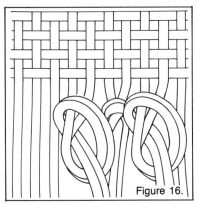

Figure 16.

to the left or to the right, but all knots should be made in the same direction and as close to the filling as possible. If you have difficulty pushing the knot up close without tightening it prematurely, insert a knitting needle into the open loop and use the needle to push the loop into position against the filling; then tighten the loop around the needle (Figure 17), slip the needle

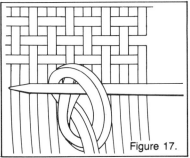

Figure 17.

out, and give the knot a final tug to tighten it. Groups of warp threads can be knotted in the same way. Just count off the threads to be sure each knot will contain the same number of strands (Figure 18); or, to ensure that the

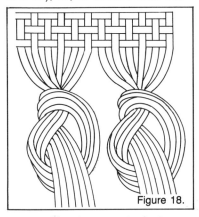

Figure 18.

warp will not separate between each knot and disturb the evenness of your last rows of weaving, cross the two outside threads of each batch and include them in the adjacent knot rather than in their own contiguous group (Figure 19).

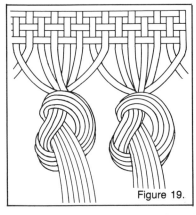

Figure 19.

To complete a fringe of loose strands, comb out the threads with your rug beater or any wide-toothed comb if they have become tangled; then trim the ends to the length desired. A simple way to make sure that you cut the fringe evenly is to lay the rug on a table, extending the excess portion of the fringe over one edge, and place a yardstick or long metal ruler on top of the fringe, lining it up with the table edge. Then, pressing the ruler down firmly with your free hand, cut the fringe with a sharp-bladed dressmaker's shears, holding the blades up against the side of the table (Figure 20).

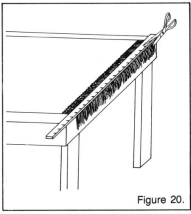

Figure 20.

If you want to make a more elaborate fringe, add one or more additional rows of knotting. A second row of overhand knots, placed far enough from the woven edge of the rug to avoid buckling it, can be made if you wish to group larger numbers of warp threads together to form heavy multiple strands (Figure 21). You can create even more complicated patterns by making several rows of knots and re-dividing your groups of threads in various ways between each row. For patterns with multiple rows of knotting, overhand knots can be combined with square knots, or even more intricate macrame techniques can be used—just be sure your fringe will not overwhelm the rug itself. When you have completed your knotting, trim the strand ends evenly.

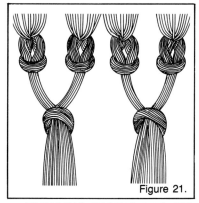
Figure 21.

FRINGING FABRIC-BACKED RUGS. The sturdy, heavy, even-weave cotton, linen, and burlap backing fabrics used for hooked and rya rugs often make handsome fringes, as do the canvas (unprimed *only),* duck or denim underpinnings used for stenciled floorcloths. Fringing these fabrics is a simple process of securing the edges, unraveling all the parallel threads beyond this point, and then, if desired, knotting the ones that remain. It is generally done along the two crosswise edges—that is, the filling (weft) threads are removed to leave the loose warp threads as the fringe. But since the filling threads of these even-weave rug backings are usually as thick and strong as the warp, there is no reason why you can't fringe the lengthwise sides of your rug as well. The only warning that must be given is that the grain of the fabric must be straight in order to fringe successfully. So if you plan to finish the edges of your rug in this way, be sure to check the grain when you buy the goods, and then carefully mark

the outlines of your design area on grain as you prepare to work your rug. You can secure the edge beyond which the fringing will be done at the same time or wait until you've worked the rug, as you prefer. To make these preparations, draw a line parallel to, and about ¼ inch beyond, the edge of the design area by pulling a pencil or waterproof fine-tipped felt marker along a single thread of the fabric. Or if you are marking the line *after* the rug has been worked, simply remove the thread itself from the fabric by picking it out with the point of a needle or pin. Then run a line of machine zigzag stitching (or two rows of very closely spaced straight stitches) along the marking. If necessary you can substitute handworked blanket or buttonhole stitches. If you plan to fringe all four sides of your rug, mark your line or pick out a thread and then stitch around the entire perimeter of the design area (Figure 22). But, if you intend to fringe

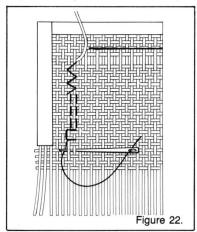
Figure 22.

only the two opposite crosswise edges, mark or pick out the thread and stitch along each side only up to the corner of the design area, not to the edges of the hem allowances. *(NOTE:* This entire procedure should be omitted for

stenciled floorcloths with allover painted backgrounds. And though advisable for a floorcloth with a natural fabric background that extends to the edges of the design area, this must be done before, not after, stenciling.)

Wait until all other work on the rug has been completed—blocking, latexing, varnishing, and the like—before making the fringe. Then, if you are only fringing the two crosswise edges, clip the hem allowances along these two sides at each end of the area to be fringed, cutting up to the corner of the worked area. When you have done this, you can proceed to unravel the threads on the hem allowances to be fringed up to the line of machine or hand stitching, securing the worked part of the rug. You can leave the loose strands of the fringe as they are, simply combing out tangles and trimming the ends evenly (Figure 20); or, if you prefer, you can group them into equal bunches and knot them into a pattern (Figures 18 and 21). To finish the unfringed sides of the rug, trim the extended ends to ½ to ¾ inch, turn them under, and then hem, using any appropriate method. To fringe all four sides of a rug, simply unravel the threads along each side (Figure 22), trimming and leaving them loose or knotting into the desired pattern.

ATTACHED FRINGE

Attaching fringe by knotting strands of yarn into the edges is a decorative touch suitable for all types of handcrafted rugs (except perhaps for braided ones, which are rarely fringed unless by unraveling the braid ends themselves). Round and oval rugs are fringed around the entire curcumference, while those of rectangular shape can have fringe attached along the two crosswise sides or, if you wish, around the entire perimeter. Knitted and crocheted rugs are fringed after the rug has been completed and blocked, while rugs requiring hems can be fringed either before or after the hems are made.

Choose a yarn for your fringe that is equivalent in weight to the yarn with which you worked the rug, and in a color that complements your design—or try mixing different colors of yarn for interesting effects. To determine the strand length you'll need, decide how long you want the finished fringe to be, double this figure and allow at least an inch for knotting—more if you plan to make a pattern involving more than the initial row of knots. If you are uncertain, test-knot a few strands before cutting them all. Since you will need so many individual strands, an easy way to cut them is to cut a piece of heavy cardboard about 8 to 12 inches long and as wide as the desired length of your yarn strands. Lightly score the cardboard lengthwise down the center and fold it in half. Wrap the yarn in a single layer around the cardboard, stretch a rubber band or tie a cord lengthwise around it to hold the yarn in place, and then slice the yarn along the long slit edge of the cardboard, using a scissors or a single-edge razor blade.

FRINGING RUGS MADE ON CANVAS MESH BACKINGS. Fringe for needlepoint and latch hooked rugs should be worked next to the last row of stitches. It is easier to do this before the hems are completed, but it can be accom-

plished after hemming. To attach fringe before hemming, insert a small crochet hook from the back to the front of the canvas through the same hole in which the last stitch of the rug was placed. Fold a strand of yarn in half, catch the loop in the tip of the hook, and pull it through to the back of the canvas. Then insert the crochet hook from front to back into the canvas two holes below, catch the yarn loop and pull it through to the front (Figure 23). Using the hook or

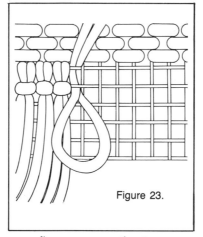

Figure 23.

your fingers, pass the two yarn ends through the loop and pull tight to make a knot on the front of the canvas (Figure 24).

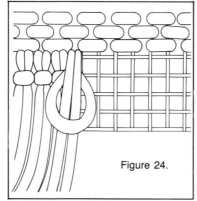

Figure 24.

Continue in this manner along two sides or around the entire perimeter of the rug, until you have knotted a strand of yarn into each hole along the edge. For a thicker fringe, use more

than one strand of yarn in each hole. You can leave the loose strands of the fringe as they are, simply combing out tangles and trimming them evenly, (Figure 20), or group them into equal bunches and knot them into a pattern (Figures 18 and 21). Finish the rug by turning under and binding the hem.

If you want to hem your rug before fringing it, be sure to leave enough room for the fringe by stitching your binding tape four mesh away from the edges of the worked area and then folding the hem two mesh beyond the last row of rug stitching. Then, to attach the fringe, insert a small crochet hook from back to front through the doubled canvas mesh, bringing the hook out through the same hole in which the last stitch of the rug was placed. Double a strand of yarn, catch the looped end with the hook, and pull it through to the back of the rug. Pass the two yarn ends through the loop and pull tight to make a knot along the front edge of the canvas (Figure 25). Continue in this manner

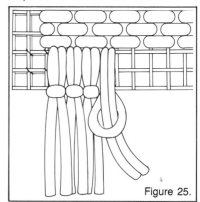

Figure 25.

along two sides or around the entire perimeter of the rug until you have knotted a strand of yarn into each hole along the edge. For a thicker fringe, use more than one strand of yarn in each hole.

FRINGING FABRIC-BACKED AND WOVEN RUGS. Woven and fabric-backed rugs can be fringed before hemming, but attaching the yarn strands is easier to do once the hems have been completed. In both cases, the techniques are quite similar to those used for fringing rugs made on canvas mesh backings. If you plan to hem first, be sure to leave enough room for the fringe before folding back the hem or stitching on binding tape. For double-turned hems, leave ¼ to ½ inch between the last row of rug stitching and the hem fold. Sew binding tape to the hem allowance twice this distance from the last row of rug stitching and fold the hem midway between the end of the worked area and the binding tape. Then attach the fringe. If you have trouble pushing your crochet hook through the hem, use an awl or fine knitting needle to punch a hole through all layers of the fabric just beyond the last worked row of the rug. Knot in your first strand of yarn; then, using the width of this knot as a guide, punch additional holes just beyond the last worked row of the rug, spacing them evenly around all edges to be fringed. Continue attaching the fringe as before until you have knotted a strand of yarn into every hole you have punched. For a thicker fringe, use more than one strand of yarn in each hole. Trim the fringe ends or knot them into a pattern.

To fringe before hemming, use an awl or fine knitting needle to punch a hole into the backing fabric just beyond the last row of rug stitching; then punch a second hole about ¼ inch outside and directly below the first one. (For woven rugs, punch these holes just inside the line along which you wish to fold the hem.) Knot in the first strand of your fringe; then, using the width of this knot as a guide, punch two rows of evenly spaced holes around all edges to be fringed. Continue attaching the fringe as before until you have knotted a strand of yarn into every pair of holes you have punched. For a thicker fringe, use more than one strand of yarn in each hole. Trim the fringe ends or knot them into a pattern, then hem the rug.

FRINGING KNITTED AND CROCHETED RUGS. To fringe the self-finished edges of knitted and crocheted rugs, knot in the yarn strands as described for pre-hemmed needlepoint rugs, inserting your crochet hook between the knit or crocheted stitches. Space the strands evenly, placing them close together but without crowding them. For a thicker fringe, use more than one strand of yarn at a time. Trim the fringe ends or knot them into a pattern (Figure 26).

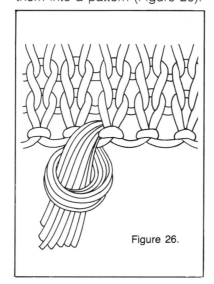

Figure 26.

Latexing

Latexing is a process of sizing the underside of a rug with a liquid rubber-based adhe-sive, and is done before making the hem. It is an essential protective measure for sheared-pile hooked rugs (the clipped yarn or fabric strips tend to come right out of the backing if not held in place by the sizing) and is also strongly recommended for hooked rugs with looped (uncut) pile, since a heel that catches in one loop can easily pull out an entire row. Latexing can also be used on latch-hooked and needlepoint rugs if a non-skid backing is desired, though for these kinds of handcrafted rugs it is a completely optional procedure.

Liquid latex is marketed under a number of trade names. It can be purchased at large needlework and craft stores as well as in the hardware sections of some department stores, or you can order it from several general merchandise and craft mail order suppliers.

Lay a protective plastic dropcloth over your floor (or over a plywood board several inches larger all around than your rug), and tack the rug face down to the surface with rustproof pushpins. Make sure the backing fabric is taut, but do not distort the shape. Insert the pushpins every inch or so into the hem allowance (not into the worked area of the rug). Apply the latex as it comes from the container, spreading it very thinly (as you would butter a slice of bread) with a spatula, brush, putty knife or plasterer's taping knife, or even a piece of sturdy cardboard. Cover only the worked portion of the rug, not the hem allowances, exerting as little force as you can against the backing fabric and coating as thinly as possible to avoid having the latex seep through to the front of the rug

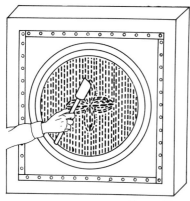

Figure 27.

(Figure 27). Leave the rug tacked to the floor or board until the latex has dried completely—usually overnight. The edges of the rug can be finished in several ways. You can "glue" down the hem allowances, using the latex instead of glue but otherwise following the procedures described in the discussion of glued hems; you can stitch standard double-turned hems; or you can unravel and fringe the edges.

VARIATION: SIZING WITH GLUE. If you can't find liquid latex or simply don't want to bother with it, an easy-to-make and easy-to-apply glue sizing may be substituted. It won't provide a non-skid backing, but will effectively keep the pile of hooked rugs (both cut and uncut) from pulling out of the backing fabric, and is also excellent for preventing blocked needlepoint and latch-hooked rugs from creeping back to a distorted shape. To make the sizing, mix equal parts of ordinary white household glue and water. Tack the rug face down to the floor as described for latexing, and paint on the glue solution sparingly with a wide brush. Allow the glue to dry thoroughly before untacking the rug; then finish the edges as desired.

Linings

Lining a rug is required only for hooked rugs that will not be latexed or sized with glue but, though an optional procedure, it is an excellent way to protect and extend the life of needlepoint and latch-hooked rugs, and can be used for knitted, crocheted, and rya rugs, and for braided rugs made from fragile materials (such as necktie silks) as well. Use a sturdy, closely woven cotton fabric—such as duck, denim, or mattress ticking—or a high quality burlap, and try to find a width that doesn't require seaming. Cut the fabric to the same size as your finished and hemmed rug (not including any fringe), adding a 1½- to 2-inch hem allowance along each side. If you must piece the goods in order to obtain the width you need, trim off selvages and make a plain, machine-stitched seam, leaving ⅝-inch seam allowances; and then press open the seam allowances.

Fold under the hem allowances of the lining and press. If your lining is for a square or oblong rug, open the folded corners and trim them diagonally, cutting ½ inch outside the corner foldlines; then refold, turning down the diagonally-cut corners first and then the sides, press again, and slip-stitch each of the mitered corners together along the fold (Figure 5). When folding and pressing the hem allowances of round or oval linings, shrink in any excess hem fabric with a steam iron, or press in very small pleats, spacing these evenly around the circumference (Figure 15).

Then place your rug wrong side up on a flat surface and lay the lining, right side up, on top of it. Adjust the position of the lining until the edges are even with those of the rug. Starting from the center and working outward toward the edges, insert pins every 6 inches or so to hold the lining flat against the rug, smoothing the lining as you pin. Then pin every few inches around the edges of the lining and slip-stitch it to the rug with carpet thread. To keep rug and lining from shifting unevenly, tack the lining down with cross stitches at regular but widely-spaced intervals, making sure to catch the back of the rug with the stitches without sewing through to the finished side (Figure 28). Then remove all pins and

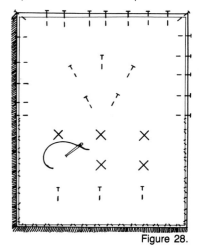

Figure 28.

press lightly around the edges, using a steam iron and press cloth.

SPECIAL
RUG PROJECTS

RYA KNOT RUGS

The latch hook and rya rugs, shown right, are a delightful addition of deep pile texture to room settings that include flat hard surfaces and areas of open space. The bold abstract designs are ideal for this technique because an intricate pattern would be lost in the deep pile. The wall-hung "Sunrise", above right, is 39 inches by 57 inches. "Terra Firma", the smaller companion rug beneath "Sunrise" is 24 inches by 41 inches. The red stripe on beige rug shown at right is 40 inches by 60 inches.

MATERIALS
1 piece scrim rug backing—(the size of rug plus a 2" hem on all sides).
Burlap or woven rug binding
Large blunt tapestry needle
Pile gauge
Yarn—"Terra Firma"—Select rug yarn in shades of rust, coral, deep gold, medium and light yellow, beige and grey.
"Sunrise"—vivid yellow and deep rust
Red stripe on beige tweed—deep rust, dark brown, beige on grey
Note: It is difficult to accurately estimate the exact yardage on rugs with such deep pile, as some of the yarn is used double in each knot. It would be wise to knot a 6" square, being careful to note exactly how many yards of yarn were used in completing the square. Measure the total rug and divide by 6"; then multiply the number of squares by the total amount used in a single test square.

GENERAL INSTRUCTIONS:
(See the Latch Hook and Rya section of The Portfolio of Rug Techniques for complete instructions.)

One method of creating a thick pile rug is the rya method in which the yarn is knotted into a backing material. The best backing to use is a material called scrim which is durable and has an open weave which allows room for the yarn to be knotted into it.

When making a rya rug with scrim backing, you can knot the yarn into every third row, or to make it even thicker, you can knot every row or every second row. The last four rows of pile should be knotted as follows: in the fourth row from the end every fourth knot should be knotted backwards by turning the rug around while tying the knot, in the next row every third and fourth knot should be backwards, next the second, third and fourth knots backwards, and in the last row all the knots should be backwards. This hides the last row of knots and allows the pile to fall in the right direction.

One of the most exciting aspects of making a rya rug is experimenting with color. You can change color at any point by just cutting the yarn at the bottom of the gauge and beginning a new color. Two or three different colors can be threaded together, and the combinations can be changed gradually to create interesting shades. It is also fun to experiment with different lengths of pile in different areas of the rug and with clipping the loops unevenly to create a shaggy texture.

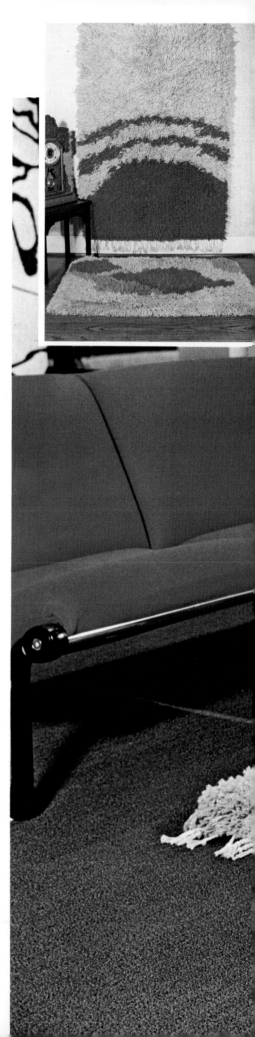

longer center start will create an oval rug.

3. At the deepest part of the first coil tie the cord in a knot, securing it to the rope. This knot will be tucked or pushed to the wrong side of the rug. Anywhere lengths of cord are joined push the knot to the wrong side.

4. Follow figures 1 through 4 to lace the coils of ropes together. Practice the stitch with a scrap of rope or twine.

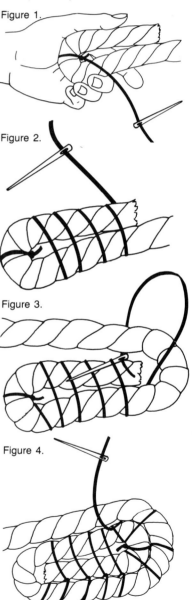

Figure 1.

Figure 2.

Figure 3.

Figure 4.

DOCK-SIDE ROPE RUG

This durable coiled-rope rug will weather several seasons at dock or poolside. Made of heavy-duty rope laced together with vinyl cord, this rug should be considered a stationary item since the weight of the rope will distort the rug if it is picked up. Thirty yards of rope were required to construct this 36" oval.

MATERIALS
30 yards of cotton rope, 1" in diameter
50 yard spool of leather-like cord
White household glue
Large blunt point tapestry needle
Scissors

METHOD
1. Before you begin working with the rope, the cut ends will have to be treated to prevent raveling. Dip each cut end in a mixture of one part white household glue and three parts water. Coat at least 3 or 4 inches of each end and allow at least 24 hours to completely dry.
2. Curl the rope in the palm of your hand to begin coiling. Note that a tighter center start will produce a circular rug and

GALLERY OF HOOKED DESIGNS

The "Alice" rug shown above, and those shown on the succeeding pages, make up our own special gallery of hooked designs. These rug designs range in intricacy from "Alice" and "Violets" through the simple "Black and Grey Geometric" and the "Family Pet" rugs. Refer to the Hooking Section of The Portfolio of Rug Techniques for general instructions. The patterns for "Alice," "Violets," "Stained Glass" and "Poppy" rugs are given in the Patterns Chapter.

"ALICE"

MATERIALS
Collect fabric in several shades of green, white, gold, grey, red, pastel blue, pink and gold, and black. Shaded swatches are also available from various manufacturers.
Handhook
Scissors
Binding tape
Needle and thread
Superior quality burlap or two-ply monks cloth 41" x 52"

METHOD
1. Cut various colored strips and sort according to color.

2. Transfer pattern,(p.157) enlarged to desired size, to right side of top-quality burlap or monks cloth.
3. Stretch fabric on frame.
4. Beginning in the center of the rug, hook the large Alice design, then the smaller figures and finally the background. Remember to always hook towards yourself.
Note: Experience will bring uniformity to the heighth of each loop hooked. The thrust and twist motion of each hooked loop will also develop with practice. If you are relatively new at rug hooking you may prefer to begin hooking in the border or any inconspicuous area.

"VIOLETS"

MATERIALS
Collect wool fabric or wool clothing in at least six shades of blue to purple and similar amounts of light green to dark green. If you feel unsure of your color sense refer to seed catalogues or floral-patterned fabric for assistance. Select an off-white for the background and a medium blue for the border.
Scissors
Superior quality burlap or two-ply monks cloth 4' 4'' by 6' 4''
Handhook
Rug binding

Note: A frame is desired by some rug hookers.

METHOD
The pattern for this rug is given on pages 176-177 in the Pattern section.
1. Flowers
Hook each floral cluster, completing each individual petal before beginning the next petal. Begin with the darkest shade, then the lightest, and fill in with the intermediate colors. Plan the colors in the center flower of each bouquet first, as this is the point of interest. Plan other flowers to compliment the center flower. A good general rule is to have the floral colors stronger toward the center of the rug and softer toward the edge of the rug.
2. Leaves
Veins are important. An effective method of relating the flower to the leaves is to hook the leaf vein in the darkest shade used in the flower next to the leaf. Sometimes when the vein is broad, a second shade of the same color may be worked along the vein before beginning the greens. Leaves may be worked from dark at the base to light at the tips. They are also pretty worked from dark at the vein to light at the edge. In a group of leaves, make some darker than others for variation.

"STAINED GLASS WINDOW"

MATERIALS
Collect wool material or clothing in at least six shades of green, medium gold, white and pink.
Handbook
Scissors
Burlap or two-ply monks cloth—3'4'' x 5'4''
Rug binding
Needle and thread

METHOD
1. Draw the rug design from page 156 on graph paper and enlarge, following the directions given in the Appendix.
2. Transfer the design to the rug backing using black waterproof markers.
3. Hook the central window diamonds and flower-like scrolls, using four to six shades in each scroll. Accomplished hookers usually hook the darkest shade, then the lightest shade and then fill in with the intermediate shades. To make your hooking easy and smooth, it is best to hook

toward yourself, or from right to left.

4. Fill in the central gold background and finish with the outer green background and border.

5. Complete hems or binding either before or after rug is hooked.

6. Lightly size or shellac the back side of the rug.

"CIRCLES AND SQUARES"

MATERIALS

Superior quality burlap 37" x 50½"
Fabric—⅛ to ¼ yard of wool fabric in each color desired.
1 Handhook
Scissors—Note: Always cut with sharp scissors and don't worry if your strips are not perfectly even in width. When an uneven strip is hooked in, it will give the rug a hand-made rather primitive look which compliments this quilt-like design.
Rug binding
Thread

METHOD

1. Draw center circle and four half-circles to create the field of this rug. An easy way to have accurate circles is to use dinner plates or round pizza pans as a guide. Then draw border and corner squares. Within the border you can add other geometric designs, keeping their placement balanced. A good source of simple designs is quilting books that include patterns. Note: this rug included some circles in the border, which will complement the central field.

2. Start hooking in the center circle and complete the center of the rug. Then hook the border designs, being careful to balance the colors in the border.

3. Hem the finished rug and apply a light coat of sizing or shellac to the back side.

Note: Caring for hooked rugs.

The best way to keep your rug clean is by vacuuming it on both sides once or twice weekly. Always clean spots as soon as they appear. Do not attempt to clean a hooked rug by shaking, as its weight could damage the burlap foundation at its bound edge or pull out the loops. Heavy traffic over a period of years may cause the colors to fade and a thorough cleaning will be necessary. The following formula will effectively clean and restore the brightness of the colors.

1. Mix four parts water with one part ammonia, and then add a mild liquid detergent.
2. Vacuum the rug thoroughly.
3. Use a vegetable brush to stir this solution until suds are made. Scoop up the suds with the vegetable brush and brush over rug, a small section at a time. Towel dry each section as you clean, and try to use as little water as possible to avoid weakening the burlap foundation.
4. After scrubbing the rug, spread it on newspapers, right side up, and dry in direct sunlight.

POPPY RUG

MATERIALS
1. Top-quality burlap or monk's cloth back 32" x 35"
2. Wool strips in black and red shades (allow ½ to ⅓ pound per square foot)

METHOD
1. Draw your design (p.156) with a water-proof pen on the right side of the rug backing.
2. Place the wool strip under the design, holding it firmly between two fingers. Push the hook through the burlap on a line of the design, and pull up the end of the strip. Skip a thread or threads and begin pulling up loops. You may find it easier to begin working the center of the rug or a major design area first.
3. Hem your rug by applying rug tape, or as an alternative, hook to within 2 inches of the edge. Fold under and hem the rug; then continue hooking, through the hem to the edge.
4. A light application of sizing or shellac will keep the rug from slipping. Or if you choose, line the rug or use it over a rug pad.

BLACK AND GREY GEOMETRIC

MATERIALS
24" x 40" burlap
3½ yards binding
1 yard red wool
2 yards black wool
2 yards grey-green wool
1½ yards grey wool

METHOD
1. Draw your design on paper in proportion to the size of the rug. When you are satisfied with your design on paper you are ready to go on.
2. Tape or tack your burlap to a hard surface, being careful to get the grain straight and corners square.
3. Draw your design onto the burlap (leaving one or two inches on all sides for hems) using waterproof felt tip markers. Markers of various colors may be used to indicate color on your design. On each area of the design write in the color to be used.
4. Sew rug binding to edges of burlap with a double-stitched seam on the machine.
5. Working from the middle of the rug out, begin hooking. Hold a strip of wool beneath burlap, pulled tight between the fingers of your left hand. Reach through the burlap from above with your hook. Grab the wool strip with the hook and pull a small loop up through the burlap. Re-insert the hook two or three threads over and pull through another small loop. Continue this process, working in swirled patterns rather than straight lines when possible. Keep loops of a consistent length. Tension must be kept on strip of wool being worked.
6. When all hooking is accomplished, fold rug binding under and whip down.

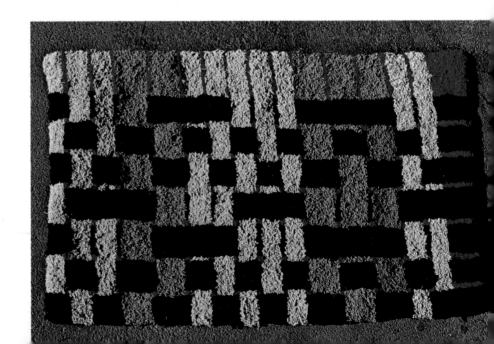

CALICO CAT RUG

MATERIALS

Four or five yards yellow-gold wool for background
One wool skirt in each color or ¼ yard wool for flowers
Several small green garments or ¼ yard wool in shades of green
One garment or odds and ends of several colors or 1 yard wool for cat section
Two black garments or 1½ to 2 yards black wool for scalloped border

METHOD

1. Use a photograph of the family cat and enlarge the design using the graph paper method described in the Appendix.
2. Transfer the design to the burlap rug back, using waterproof felt markers. The scalloped border pattern can be easily accomplished by drawing halfway around a small plate.
3. Sew rug binding around entire outer edge. Stitch by hand or use a sewing machine.
4. Select wool strips of random colors to hook Calico Cat section. Next, hook flowers and leaves; then hook black scalloped border. Hook the background.
5. Lightly size or shellac the rug backing. This will keep the rug firmly in place on the floor and add years to its wearability.

THE FAMILY PET

MATERIALS

Four or five red skirts, or approximately three yards of wool in four or five shades of red for the background. By using different shades of one color, the background of your rug will achieve a feeling of movement.
A wool scarf, one pair of pants or ¼ yard of wool in two shades of grey
One skirt or about ½ yard of solid black wool or a black wool tweed

METHOD

It is a good idea to cut all your wool strips and sort according to color before you begin hooking.
1. Use a photograph of your family pet and enlarge your design using the graph-paper method described in the Appendix. Then trace the design onto the burlap backing.
2. Sew rug binding around the entire rug. This will prevent the burlap from unraveling while you work.
3. Begin hooking the center Family Pet design first. After completing the center design, radiate outward with various shades of red loops.
4. After the rug has been hooked, lightly size or shellac the back of the rug.

KNITTED HEARTS

This charming double heart knitted rug works up quickly in the simple moss stitch and sturdy rug yarn used double throughout. The finished size is 35½'' by 35½''.

MATERIALS

Rug yarn: 19 (1.75 ounces) skeins Light Olive, 11 skeins Dark Green, 2 skeins Scarlet, 4 skeins Cardinal; two number 7 knitting needles.
Size: 36'' square.
Tension: 3 sts. to 2''; 8 rows to 3''.

METHOD

With 1 strand each of Ov. and G. cast on 54 sts. 1st row—(K. 1, p. 1) to end. 2nd row—(P. 1, k. 1) to end. These 2 rows form patt. for m.st. Rep. last 2 rows 15 times. Still working in m.st. work 32 rows in pattern from chart above thus: 1st row—With 2 strands of G. m.st. 17, join on 2 strands of C. and p. 1, with G., m.st. 18, join on 1 strand each of C. and S. and k. 1, join on 2 separate balls of G., and m.st. 17. 2nd row—With G. m.st. 16, with C. and S. m.st. 3, with G. m.st. 16, join on 2 strands of C. and p. 1, with G. k. 1, with C. p. 1, with G. m.st. 16. Beg. with 3rd row (right side), continue working center 44 sts. in m.st. from chart, reading right side rows from right to left and wrong side rows from left to right. With 1 strand each of Ov. and G. work 32 rows m.st. Cast off. Darn in ends neatly on wrong side. Iron non-slip backing to wrong side if required.
Abbreviations: K.—knit; p.—purl; sts.—stitches; m.st.—moss stitch; rep.—repeat; patt.—pattern; Ov.—olive; G.—green; S.—scarlet; C.—cardinal.

APPLIQUÉD FLOORCLOTH

This floorcloth gives the impression of a painted floor, but it is actually done with fabric appliqué, making it easier to accomplish if you trust your cutting skills more than your painting skills. The use of fabric gives you the opportunity to plan a wonderfully coordinated color scheme. Note that the ties of the chair cushions are the same fabric as the leaves on the floor cloth, and that the fabric of the screen is repeated in the chair cushions, tying the room together simply, but with style. The finished size of this piece is 9' by 9' and the patterns are given on page 167.

MATERIALS

Heavy brown wrapping paper
Canvas 9'4'' x 9'4''
Background color or acrylic
Polymer sealer medium
Plastic dropcloth
String
Push pins
Appliqué fabric as desired for your color scheme: 2 yards for leaves, 1 yard for basket background, ½ yard each for basket detail and both flower colors.
Chalk pencil
Heat-sensitive fabric bonding web in strips or yardage
Spray fabric adhesive
Iron
Artist's brush
High gloss polyurethane
Mat knife
Cardboard
Metal ruler or T square
Pencil
Tight space roller

METHOD

1. Enlarge the design from page 167 to full size, transferring one full repeat to a large square of brown wrapping paper. Fold paper in half diagonally, bisecting the corner motif; cut a small hole at the top and at the bottom of the motif, along the diagonal line, to serve as registration points. Using a mat knife, carefully cut out all leaves, stems, flowers and the basket parts. Glue to cardboard and cut out. The re-

(Continued on page 167.)

CROCHETED WATER LILY

This fanciful crocheted water lily rug works up quickly—using heavy, durable, jute yarn—to become the focal point of this poolside hospitality area. The finished size is a four-foot-in-diameter round rug that will enhance any pool setting, season after season.

MATERIALS

Jute tone (Lily Mills)—70 yd. spools:
dark green—9 spools;
radiant rose—3 spools;
canary yellow—2 spools;
willow green—4 spools.
Letter I metal crochet hook
16 yarn needle (blunt point)

METHOD

Large Leaf (36" in diameter) with #59 dark green—(wrong side while working—will be right side when finished)
ch 5—Join to form ring
rnd. 1. ch2, 13DC in ring, sl st in top of ch 2
rnd. 2. ch 2, sc in first sc, 2 sc in each sc around, sl st in top of ch 2
rnd. 3. ch 2, DC in first sc, 2 DC in next sc, 1 DC in next sc, (2 DC in next sc,—2x, 1 DC in next sc) around, ending with 2 DC, 2 DC, sl st in top of ch 2. (You should have 42 DC and ch 2)
rnd 4. ch 2, DC in first DC, (1 DC in next DC, 2 DC in next DC) around sl st in top of ch 2
rnd. 5. ch 2, DC in first DC (DC in each of next 5 DC, 2 DC in next DC) around. sl st in top of ch 2
rnd. 6. repeat rnd. 5.
rnd. 7. ch 2, 1 DC in first DC, 1 DC in each DC around sl st in top of ch 2.
rnd. 8. ch 2, DC in first DC, DC in each of next 3 DC , in 4th DC—(thread over, pull loop thru DC, Pull thread thru 2 loops keeping 2 loops on hook, thread over (in same DC) pull loop thru, then pull thread thru 2 loops, then 3 loops,—(Double Stitch). Double st in every 4th st around. sl st in top of ch 2.
rnd. 9. ch 2, DC in first DC. Dbl. st. in every 3rd st around. sl st in top of ch 2
rnd. 10. ch 2, DC in first DC, (DC in next DC, Dbl st in next DC, DC in next DC, 2 DC in next DC) around, sl st in top of ch 2.
rnd. 11. repeat rnd. 10.
rnd. 12. repeat rnd. 10.
rnd. 13. ch 2. (Dbl st in each 6th DC) around. sl st on top of ch 2.
rnd. 14. ch 2, DC in next 3, DC, (Dbl st, DC in next 5 DC) around. sl st in top of ch 2.
rnd. 15. ch 2 (Dbl st in each 10th DC) around, sl st in top of ch 2.
rnd. 16. ch 2, DC in first 4 DC (Dbl st in next DC, DC in next 4 DC, 2 DC in next DC, DC in next 4 DC) around. sl st in top of ch 2.
rnd. 17. ch 2, DC in first DC, (DC in next 3 DC, Dbl st, DC in next 3 DC, 2 DC in next DC) around. sl st in top of ch 2.
rnd. 18. repeat rnd. 17.
rnd. 19. ch 2 DC in first DC (DC in next 2 DC, Dbl st in next DC, DC in next 2 DC, 2 DC in next DC) around sl st in top of ch 2.
rnd. 20. repeat rnd. 17.
rnd 21. ch 2, DC in each DC around. sl st in top of ch 2.
rnd. 22. (First crochet a chain of dark green—do not have any knots on chain—leave end on spool—to increase chain as needed to go around leaf.) Now—working also with dark green, work 1 sc in each DC around—OVER dark green chain—easing in chain as sc's are worked to give fullness and body and natural texture. End off chain—when rnd. completed and to dark green, join willow green.
With willow green—turn leaf to wrong (now right) side up.
row 1—ch 1, 12 sc, 12 hds, 12 DC, 84 +R, 12 DC, 12 hdc, 12 sc. sl st in next sc.
row 2—(turn work for each row) ch 1, sl st, sc, 12 hdc, 108 DC, 12 DC, 11 sc, sl st.
row 3—ch 1, 2 sl st, 12 sc, 12 hdc, 104 DC, 12 hdc, 12 sc, 2 sl st.
row 4—repeat row 3.
row 5—ch 1, skip sl st, sl st, 12 sc, 12 hdc, 20 DC, 62 +R, 20 DC, 12 hdc, 12 sc, 2 sl st. (Skip next to last sl st.)
row 6—ch 1, skip first sl st, 3

sl st, 12 sc, 12 hdc, 96 DC, 12 hdc, 12 sc, sl st.

row 7—ch 1, skip first sl st, sl st, (2x) 12 sc, 12 hdc, (5 DC, Dbl st) 14 X, 4 DC, 12 hdc, 12 sc, 2 sl st.

row 8—ch 1, skip first sl st, 3 sl st, 12 sc, 12 hdc, 12 DC, 12 +R, 2 +R in next DC, 3 +R, 2 +R in next DC, (6 +R, 2 +R in next DC) 4x, 3 +R, 2 +R together, 12 +R, 12 DC, 12 hdc, 12 sc, 3 sl st.

row 9—skip 1 sl st, 2 sl st, 12 sc, 12 hdc, 90 DC, 12 hdc, 12 sc, sl st.

row 10—ch 1, skip 1 st, 2 sl st, 12 sc, 12 hdc, 86 DC, 12 hdc, 12 sc, sl st.

row 11—ch 1, skip 1 st, 2 sl st, 12 sc, 15 hdc, 76 DC, 15 hdc, 12 sc, sl st, end off.

row 1—with dark green—sc around willow green—end off

row 2—do with edge of large leaf. Work with dark green (sc) around over willow green chain—easing in as before. End off.

Flower—(22" in diameter)

With canary yellow—loosely ch 6, sl st in first ch to form a ring.

rnd 1. ch 2, 23 DC in ring, sl st in top of ch 2.

rnd 2. ch 2, (sc in DC, ch 1) around sl st in top of ch 2. (You should have 24 sc.)

rnd 3. ch 2, (sc in ch 1 space ch 1) around, sl st in top of ch 2.

rnd 4. repeat rnd 3.

rnd 5. End canary yellow. Join radiant rose—ch 2, 3 sc in ch, 1 space (skip 1 ch 1 space, ch 1, 4 sc in next ch 1 space) around (12 groups) ch 1, sl st in top of ch 2.

rnd 6. ch 2 sc in sc, 1 sc in next sc, 2 sc in next sc (ch 1, 2 sc in first sc, 1 sc in next sc, 2 sc in last sc). (You should have 5 sc) around. ch 1, sl st in top of ch 2.

rnd 7. ch 1, 3 sc in 4 sc (ch 2, 4 sc in 5 sc—working between sc) around. ch 2, sl st in top of ch 2.

rnd 8. ch 1, (3 sc in 4 sc, ch 3) around, ch 3, sl st in first sc.

rnd 9. ch 1, (2 sc between 3 sc; ch 2, DC in ch 3, (work DC around ch, not in ch) ch 2,) around sl st in ch 1.

rnd 10. ch 1 (DC between 2 sc, ch 2, 3 sc in 1 DC ch 2) around sl st in ch 1.

rnd 11. ch 1, sl st 2x—to cover ch 2, to reach 3 sc, ch 1, (4 sc in 3 sc, ch 5) around (1 sc in first sc, 2 sc in center sc, 1 sc in last sc) sl st in first ch.

rnd 12. ch 1, (2 sc in first sc, sc in next sc) 2x, 2 sc in last sc—ch 4) around. sl st in first sc.

rnd 13. ch 1, (2 sc in first sc (1 sc in each of next 3 sc, 2 sc in last sc, (7 sc) ch 3) around. sl st in first sc.

rnd 14. ch 1 (2 sc in first sc, 1 sc in each of next 4 sc, 2 sc in last sc—(8 sc) ch 3) around. sl st in first sc.

rnd 15. ch 1 (sc in first 3 sc, skip 1 sc, 4 sc, (7 sc) ch 3) around. sl st in first sc.

rnd 16. ch 1, (sc in first 3 sc, skip 1 sc, sc in last 3 sc (6 sc) ch 2, sl st in ch 3 bar, ch 2) around. sl st in first sc.

rnd 17. ch 1, (sc in first 2 sc, skip 1 sc, sc in last 3 sc (5 sc) (ch 2,) sl st in ch 3 bar)) 2x, ch 2) around. sl st in first sc.

rnd 18. ch 1 (sc in first 2 and last 2 sc, (4 sc) ch 4, sl st in center of ch 2 bar—ch 4) around. st st in first sc.

rnd 19. ch 1 (sc in first sc, skip 1 sc, 2 sc in next 2 sc. (ch 3 sl st in ch 4 bar 2x) ch 3) around sl st in first sc.

rnd 20. ch 1 (sc in first and last sc (2 sc) ((ch 3, st st in ch 3 bar)) 3x, ch 3) around sl

st in first sc.

rnd 21. ch 2 (DC in 2 sc, ((ch 3, sl st in ch 3 bar)) 4x-ch 3) around st st in DC. End off.

With canary yellow—work with spool held under work at base DC of any 'petal'—bring up loop—loosely chain around petal and over top DC. (1 st around each ch bar) keeping spool under work and bring thread up to top for each ch st. Work each petal separately (24 petals).

Edging of flower—1

Work on right side.

rnd 1. With radiant rose—ch 1, 3 sc in each ch 3 around.

rnd 2. With canary yellow make a chain—approx. circumference of flower—with rose—sc in each sc around over canary yellow chain (no knots in chain). Pull chain frequently to ease any frill and to flatten edge.

Edging of flower—2

rnd 1. (Except for ch keep thread in back of work—pulling loops from back to front)—with canary yellow, start on any point of petal—(ch 1—over 2 sts diagonally, ch 1, over top sc, 3 sc in top 3 sc, ch 1, down and diagonally over 2 sc, ch 1, over 2 sc, ch 1 to top of lower petal around (11 sts)—12x. End off.

rnd 2. (Working with thread on top of work as usual)and with canary yellow (sc in top of lower petal, sc in ch—2x, 2 sc in next ch, sc in sc, DC in sc, sc in sc, 2 sc in next ch, sc in ch—2x) around. sl st in first sc.

rnd 3. (Skip center sc) (sc in next 5 sc, in top DC—sc, DC, sc, sc in next 5 sc) around, sl st in first sc—End off.

Continued on page 174.

"PERSIAN FANTASY" AND "FLORAL MOSAIC"

The "Persian Fantasy" rug, at left, and the "Floral Mosaic" rug, at right, exhibit unrivaled excellence of needlepoint design, further enhanced by exquisite use of color. The "Persian Fantasy" highlights its solid white field with a floral scroll motif and exciting roman key border. The "Floral Mosaic" features an unusually beautiful repeat-patterned field that successfully blends with a multitude of different-colored and patterned borders. Either of these two needlepoint rugs will become a treasured heirloom in your room settings. The finished size of the "Persian Fantasy" is 40" by 54", and the "Floral Mosaic" is 54" by 85". The charts for these rugs are given in the Patterns Chapter on pages 158-161.

(Note: Since there is no way to figure yarn exactly, the amounts specified are slightly more than most workers will need. Dye-lots are important, so be sure to purchase enough yarn to finish your rug project.)

"PERSIAN FANTASY" MATERIALS
Canvas: 40" x 54"
Yarn:
2½ lbs. cream
½ lb. of medium light green
¼ lb. of medium green
¼ lb. of light gold
¼ lb. light coral
⅛ lb. of dark coral
⅛ lb. of medium blue
1¼ lbs of medium coral

"FLORAL MOSAIC" MATERIALS
Canvas: 54" x 85"
Yarn:
6 lbs. of cream
1½ lbs. medium light green
1 lb. light coral
1½ lbs. dark coral
1 lb. medium green

METHOD

Needlepoint rugs are priceless, especially after you have finished one. They are, however, time consuming, expensive projects and it is important to weigh all the considerations before beginning. The Basket Weave (diagonal tent) stitch is a superior rug stitch that must be mastered before beginning to work. This stitch insures proper blocking and long-lasting wearability.

These two rugs are worked alike, the designs are outlined with a Continental stitch and then filled in with a Basket Weave stitch. The borders are not outlined, but worked only with a Basket Weave stitch. When working these beautiful designs remember the following suggestions:

Your color selection will be far greater if you choose Persian yarns instead of tapestry yarns. If the rug is worked without a frame, fold back a double one-inch hem on all sides, then machine stitch in place. This excess canvas will be used later for blocking purposes. Begin working an unframed canvas in the upper right hand corner completing both the design and background areas as you proceed. If a frame is used, begin stitching anywhere, carefully counting the graphed design. A frame will assist in handling a large canvas and also free both hands as you work. Choose a number 18 or 20 needle and cut each yarn strand in half, to minimize fraying as you work. Carry each new strand through at least one inch of worked stitches to assure permanent attachment. Bind all of your stitches horizontally or vertically; never follow the diagonal stitch pattern. Work all stitches in the same direction maintaining a natural stitch tension for a consistent finished effect.

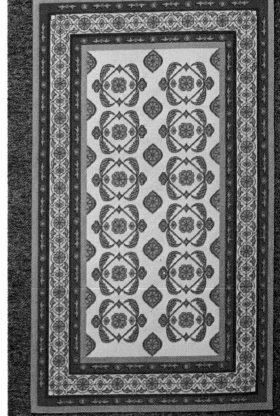

WOOLLY LAMB

This adorable needlepoint rug blends into a nursery setting to complete a collection of baby bunnies, squirrels, and lambs. The background in moss green looks like a grassy meadow, but could be changed to match your own color scheme. The deep, thick-pile lamb will be a real treat to wiggle little toes in; the dense pile is created by a special knotted loop stitch that is quick to work and easily mastered. The finished rug measures 2' by 3' and the pattern is given in the Patterns Chapter on page 169.

MATERIALS

Canvas—Zweigart 5/1 canvas—1 yard
Yarn—DMC Laine á broder (heavy rug yarn) 25 gram skeins:
Light Green 7341: 13 sk. Half cross st., or 18 sk. Basket weave
Medium Grey 7282: 1 sk. Half cross st., or 2 sk. Basket weave
White—Blanc: 20 sk. Half cross st., or 21 sk. Basket weave
Black—Noir: 1 sk. Half cross st., or 2 sk. Basket weave.
Blunt yarn needle
Sewing thread—Light green
Waterproof marking pen
Hard lead pencil
Rust proof tacks and large board

METHOD

1. Mark off canvas in 3 square inch grid with hard lead pencil.
2. With waterproof marking pen transfer design following grid on diagram.
3. Work background in either half cross st., continental or basket weave st.
4. Work knotted loop st. as in diagram but do not work all meshes of canvas, work 3 sts. skip one, work 3, etc., and on row above—have skipped st. over center of worked 3 beneath.
5. Work from bottom of design (knotted loop sts.) to top.
6. Work from left to right.
7. Height of loops varies from ½" to ¾".

Finishing

Turn under hem—using green sewing thread and only catching one thread of mesh—and overcast turned under canvas. Turn raw edge double, selvage singly, and cut excess canvas off corners.

Note: this rug cannot be blocked face down because of loops.
1. Tack down right side up with tacks on board (over large towel) and straighten.
2. If soiled—sponge in a solution of cold water soap, let set, then sponge with clear water.
3. Vacuum as dry as possible (still tacked down) with hose attachment—moving nozzle with line of diagonal sts. and in all directions on loops.
4. Iron (on wool setting) over damp cloth if no cleaning was needed, and over dry cloth if damp.
5. Vacuum again—especially loops—to fluff up, (any fuzz can be snipped off). Leave tacked down to complete drying.

CALICO BOUQUET

Our cover rug is one of the most interesting needlepoint designs we've ever seen—and one of the prettiest. Roses, daisies, morning glories and chrysanthemums in small and large gingham baskets are adapted from a calico and gingham quilt design. The finished size of Calico Bouquet is 31 inches by 57 inches and the charts are given in the Pattern section, pages 170-171.

MATERIALS
DMC Tapestry or Persian type wool in the following colors and quantities:
Color 7900: medium blue—56 skeins (494 yards);
Color White: 96 skeins (864 yards);

Color 7943: medium green—40 skeins (360 yards);
Color 7899: medium blue—12 skeins (108 yards);
Color 7526: brown—10 skeins (90 yards);
Color 7769: medium olive green—8 skeins (72 yards);
Color Black: 8 skeins (72 yards);
Color 7912: medium green—8 skeins (72 yards);
Color 7342: medium green—2 skeins (18 yards)
Color 7107: dark rose—8 skeins (72 yards)
Color 7110: wine red—10 skeins (90 yards)
Color 7554: dark orchid—2 skeins (18 yards)
Color 7655: medium orchid—2 skeins (18 yards)
Color 7435: medium yellow—8 skeins (56 yards)
Color 7316: medium blue—3 skeins (27 yards)
Color 7319: dark blue—4 skeins (36 yards)

Color 7437: medium orange—6 skeins (54 yards)
Color 7104: medium coral—2 skeins (18 yards)
Color 7434: light yellow—1 skein (9 yards)
Color 7106: deep coral—5 skeins (45 yards)
Tapestry needle
Scissors
10 mesh canvas
1¾ yards upholstery-weight velveteen for lining
Sewing needle and thread

Note: Refer to the Needlepoint section of the Portfolio of Rug Techniques for diagrams of the brick, basket weave, and straight gobelin stitches. The baskets, flowers and blue triangles were worked in the basket weave or continental stitch. The brick stitch was used in the white and dark green background areas. The blue and green borders were worked in a straight gobelin stitch. A final row of the binding stitch was used to turn the canvas.

METHOD:
The charts for the Calico Bouquet rug are given in the Patterns Chapter, pages 170-171. Transfer the design, using waterproof markers, to the rug canvas. The flowers and baskets were worked first, and the green center squares were completed next. Work the white background areas and finally the blue outer triangles, then the borders.

THREE WOVEN RUGS

These beautiful rugs, shown above and at right, are all easily woven on a simple frame loom with basic weaving patterns. The bold abstract patterns are right at home in contemporary room settings. Refer to the Weaving section of The Portfolio Rug Techniques for general weaving instructions. The finished size of each rug is as follows: White Stripe on Red, 41 inches by 84 inches; White Woven, 42 inches by 87 inches; Animal Farm, 29 inches by 37 inches.

RED AND WHITE

MATERIALS
Warp—1333 yards of cotton yarn
Weft—300 yards of white yarn
1700 yards of yarn dyed in various shades of red

METHOD
1. A modified frame loom 6 feet by 10 feet was used. The loom was warped up to 50" at eight ends per inch. The ends were picked up in the following sequence.
a. Alternate ends were picked up on a shed stick to form shed 2.
b. Shed 1 consists of alternate ends behind the shed stick and were picked up on string heddles.
c. The remaining ends were picked up on string heddles and form shed 3. The threading sequence of 1,2,3,2,1,2, etc., provides short floats on the surface of the rug with the odd sheds while the even shed provides a solid backing. The end result is a firm rug.
Note: This rug was made from white thick and thin wool, some of which has been dyed with cocchineal. This effect could be duplicated with purchased yarn by selecting closely related shades of red to oranges and dark pinks.

WHITE WOVEN

MATERIALS
Choose a rug wool that gives
the appearance of raw fleece.
Warp—1409 yards of nylon
fishing line
Weft—1330 yards of white
wool
115 yards of walnut brown
wool
345 yards of black wool

METHOD
1. A simple frame loom 6 feet
wide by 10 feet tall was constructed of 2 x 4's bolted together. An adjustable upper
beam was used to allow for
the increase in tension during
weaving.
2. The frame was warped up
to 54" (45" for finished width
plus 10% for draw-in, and 10%
for shrinkage) at 8 ends per
inch.
3. Alternate ends were picked
up with a shed sword and the
remaining ends were picked
up with string heddles.
4. The standard tapestry
weave was used on all sections except the black area,
where a modified loop soumak
was used. See Appendix.

"ANIMAL FARM"
The Animal Farm, shown at right,
derives its name from the use
of real horse hair in the highly
colored deep-pile areas.

MATERIALS

Estimating Warp Yardage
The number of warp ends
equals 245 times the total
length of 44 inches, which
equals 10,780—divided by 36"
which equals approximately
280 yards of 4-4 linen carpet
warp.
To the above figure allow 1½
to 2" take up per woven foot.
A safer estimate would be 300
yards.

Estimating Weft Yardage
The number of weft rows per
inch, (6)—multiply by total
length of rug, (44"), which
equals 264. Then multiply by
width, (27) to get 7,128, divide
by 36" to get 198 yards.

Since the majority of this
rug has a deep pile surface,
the safest estimate for pile
yardage requirements is to
multiply the weft estimate by 4.
For this rug you will need approximately 800 yards of red-
orange, red, black and beige
tweed rug wool. It is very difficult to accurately estimate the
exact yardage. To check your

estimations it would be to wise
to weave a small 12 inch
square using the warp and
weft materials of your choice.

METHOD
1. This rug is woven on a simple frame loom using 8 ends
per inch. It is part rya knotted
pile, and part flat weave. The
knotted areas use the Rya
Knot illustrated in the Rya section of the Rug Techniques
chapter. Depending on the desired thickness of pile from

one to three strands of yarn
can be used in each knot.
2. A two-row binder is between each rya row and forms
the plain weave in the non-pile
area.
3. Close shading may be ob-
tained by mixing colors of yarn
within a single knot. Knot 1—4
strands red; Knot 2—3 strands
red, 1 strand red orange; Knot
3—2 strands red, 2 strands
red orange; Knot 4—1 strand
red, 3 strands red orange.
4. The rug can be finished
with several rows of twining or
chaining. Or it may be cut off
the loom, allowing warp space
to create a tied fringe. Another
possibility would be to tuck
under the warp and hem the
ends.

CHECKERBOARD-BACKGAMMON GAME CANVAS

The unfailing popularity of checkers and backgammon will assure this rug's position as a focal point in any game room. Add large, hard-to-lose checkers and plump floor cushions for the total story.

MATERIALS
Canvas 51" x 52½" (Note: no hem has been allowed as this is a reversible rug.)
Acrylic paint: red, gold and black
Gesso primer
Acrylic paint brushes
Enlarged pattern
Standard checkerboard: this is an accurate guide for your pattern design.
Heavy brown paper
Pencil
Ruler or T-square

METHOD
1. Using a ruler or T-square, make sure that the corners of the game canvas are a true square.
2. Apply an even coat of gesso primer to top (whichever game will be played most) side of the game canvas. Note: gesso is not painted on both sides of canvas because it would make the game rug too stiff to roll up for storage. Allow to dry thoroughly.
3. Draw the checkerboard and the backgammon on 1" graph paper. Enlarge and draw each gameboard on a large sheet of heavy brown paper. Color-key each pattern.
4. Divide the game canvas into four large squares. Lightly mark with a pencil. Using dressmaker's tracing paper under each pattern, transfer the gameboards to each side of the game canvas. Note: you may prefer measuring your enlarged pattern and (using a pencil and ruler) transfering the gameboards in this manner.
5. Draw a small border on all sides of the checkerboard and backgammon fields. The remaining canvas will be a large black border.
6. Checkerboard: Refering to your color keyed paper pattern, paint all red and black checkerboard squares. You should have 32 red and 32 black squares. Allow to dry thoroughly. Paint gold divider strips between all squares. Paint gold border surrounding checkerboard. Allow to dry and then paint remaining large black border.
7. Backgammon: Paint 12 red and 12 black elongated triangles and red center divider strip. Allow to dry thoroughly. Paint gold center field and red border surrounding the game. Paint large black border.

SEED PACKET CANVAS

The Seed-Packet rug delights the eye with the colorful border surrounding a spring green central field. (Note: You will continue to enjoy the finished effect of the colorful acrylic paints, because they do not fade or crack. If you desire more protection for the painted surface, apply several coats of clear polymer medium.)

MATERIALS

Canvas—9'4" by 6'10" (including 2" hem allowances). It is better to allow extra canvas yardage as sometimes the cut edges are uneven.
Acrylic paint
Gesso
Glue for hem
Enlarged designs from 20 seed packets (See pp. 162-166.)
Pencil
Scissors
Paint brushes

METHOD

1. Straighten the edges of the canvas using a T-square.
2. Enlarge to size and draw each seed packet around the edge of the rug. Remember to turn half the designs in one direction and half the designs in the opposite direction.
3. Turn under the hem allowances. Steam press with an iron. Glue the hems with commercial fabric adhesive following the manufacturer's instructions.
4. Size the top side of the rug with gesso, applying one or two coats.
5. Paint each individual seed packet design.
6. Paint the printed matter for each seed packet.

AREA RUGS FROM CARPETING

The area rugs at left and the rugs shown on page 147 are made from carpet remnants. The techniques for making these rugs are the same no matter what design you choose. The large peach remnant shown above left was divided to become the central field of both the large and small area rugs shown at bottom left. Additional small pieces of pale gray, brown, and peach were cut to form the double border on the large rug and the triple border on the small rug. The dark brown border defines the two conversation areas and relates the floor areas to the brown leather rocker and the wicker settee.

The owner's love of quilt designs led to the designing of this positive-negative traditional Churn-Dash pair. Reexamine your quilting books and add these delightful designs to your floors. For the rugs on page 147, you will need two 10 foot pieces of acrylic carpeting, one in rust color and one cream-colored, and the pattern on page 178, enlarged to 10' x 10'. (Note: carpeting is sold in 12-foot widths.)

MATERIALS
Carpet seaming tape or Hot Tape—2 rolls
Carpet seaming iron (Call a general rental store to obtain, or use a home iron you don't mind sacrificing.)
Ruler and T-square
Carpet thread and needle
Utility or carpet knife
Bent-handled scissors
Rug binding and all purpose rug glue
Chalk, pencil or waterproof markers (Photo A)

GENERAL INSTRUCTIONS
1. Carefully measure the area where the rug will be placed to determine a satisfactory size. Consider the placement of furniture, traffic paths and the decorative effect of a large design.
2. Draw the entire design on graph paper and enlarge to scale as directed in the Appendix. If you desire, make heavy brown paper pattern pieces.
3. Label each piece as you would sections of a quilt block. Mark the top of each piece so the nap direction will be maintained for the entire rug.
4. Assemble all materials and prepare a large work area. A garage or basement floor, covered with newspapers, would

Photo A

Photo B

Photo C

Photo D

Photo E

Photo F

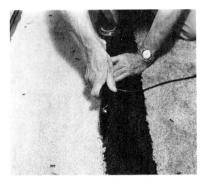

Photo G

Photo H

Photo I

be ideal. If the rug must be assembled on existing interior floors, protect the surface with several layers of newspaper. Use a long scrap of linoleum or vinyl flooring under the rug seams and carpet iron.

5. Turn the carpeting to the wrong side, using a ruler or a T-square. Make sure the carpet corners are true 90° angles. (Photo B)

6. Using a pencil or waterproof marker, mark *all pattern pieces* on the carpet back before cutting. Make sure the top of each piece is towards the top of each carpet piece. (Photo C)

7. Using a utility knife, cut carpeting on design lines. Place a ruler edge along the cutting line to serve as a cutting guide. Practice cutting straight lines on carpet scraps to become familiar with this material. Carpet backing cuts quite easily if pressure is exerted on the knife. Replace the utility knife blade as it becomes dull. (Photo D)

8. Lay out carpet pieces, right side up, and check to see that all pieces fit in place. (Photo E)

9. Cut a piece of carpet seaming tape the length of your first seam. Place the cut edge of

the rug piece to the center line of the carpet seaming tape. Butt the adjoining carpet piece up to the first piece, completely covering the seaming tape. Preheat the carpet seaming iron. (Photo F)

10. Place the heated iron plate (set rayon, or lowest, setting on a home iron) over the tape and under the carpet pieces, (the handle will be above the carpet pieces). Slowly move the iron the entire length of the seam. Note: the iron melts the web of glue on the tape. The cut edges of the rug pieces are pulled together behind the iron, over the melted glue. Allow each seam to cool and completely bond before beginning a new seam. (Photo G)

11. Turn the seamed rug to the right side (Photo H). Overcast rug binding to the rug, right sides together, using a double strand of carpet thread (Photos I and J). Turn the free edge of the rug binding to the wrong side and secure with fabric adhesive or hand stitching (Photos K and L).

Photo J

Photo K

Photo L

DEERSKIN RUG

This deerskin rug has as interesting story to tell. A young couple, both wildlife conservationists, built their dream home in a rural area heavily populated with deer. Finding one of their special animals fatally wounded one day, they decided to remember it by incorporating the beautiful hide into a dramatic fire-side rug.

For *your* deerskin rug, curing the hide can be easily accomplished by following the manufacturers' instructions in a do-it-yourself tanning kit. The finished size of the deerskin rug is 50 inches by 70 inches and the pattern is given in the Pattern section, page 168.

MATERIALS

21 skeins 100% wool 4 ply yarn in ecru, tan and chocolate brown
3 skeins jumbo acrylic in white—3 ply
2 skeins 3 ply white knit yarn—acrylic
10 yards 4 ply soft macramé twine
3 yards 60" burlap backing
7 yards 2" bias rug binding
1 spool heavy-duty rug thread (to secure bias binding)
1 spool heavy-duty twine (such as parcel cord) to secure hide to backing
1 heavy duty tapestry needle

METHOD

1. After the hide has been properly tanned and cured following one of the hair retaining methods, the skin is carefully trimmed to remove any extra-hard, curled or excessively irregular area from the edges.

2. The burlap backing is prepared by attaching 2" bias rug binding around all edges.

3. Position the hide on the burlap so that a margin of fabric extends on all sides. The skin is then attached with a tapestry needle and heavy-duty twine. Secure the hide first down the center, using overlapping or crossed stitches. Whip tightly and completely around the entire skin close to the edges.

4. So that the natural beauty of the hide will be enhanced, the colors and textures should be carefully placed so they best relate to the natural coloration; light yarns against light furs, accent fringing against longest fur, etc.

5. Once all hooking has been completed, fold the bias rug binding over, mitering the corners and whipping binding securely into place all around.

PUFF-QUILTED BATH MAT

Combine terry cloth towels and fiberfill with basic plain machine seams and create this sinfully soft puff-quilted bath mat. This bath mat measures 22 inches by 30 inches but could easily be made larger or smaller, to fit your bathroom floor perfectly.

MATERIALS

1 yard towelling for puffs
1⅝ yard of second-color towelling for border and backing
1 yard unbleached muslin
One package polyester fiberfill

METHOD

1. Cut 24 5½" squares of the towelling for the puffs.
2. Cut 24 4½" squares of muslin to use as backing.
3. Follow the Basic Method instructions, making the quilting 4 puffs wide and 6 puffs long. The finished border is 2½" wide.
4. For the edging and lining, cut the contrasting-color towelling into a 28" by 36" rectangle and finish, referring to Basic Method instructions.

BASIC METHOD FOR PUFF QUILTING

You'll Need: Fabric to cover the puff tops; backing fabric for the puff squares; fabric for edging and lining the quilting once the squares are sewn together; stuffing for puffs (we used washable polyester fiberfill); scissors; pins; thread.
How to make: Start by cutting out the required number of puff squares in your top fabric (for size of squares, see instructions for individual items). Then cut same number of squares out of backing material. These squares are about three quarters the size of top fabric squares. (Again check exact size.) Wrong sides together, pin one puff square on to a backing square at each corner (Diagram 1). Then pin a tuck in the middle of three sides, taking up the excess material on each side (Diagram 2). Seam, ¼" from edge, around the three sides, leaving the fourth side open to insert stuffing (Diagram 3). Next pin a tuck in the middle of the open side as before and seam, so completing a puffed square. Make up all puffs in this way. Now with right sides of fabric facing, seam side edges of two puffs together, allowing ¼" seam (Diagram 4). Continue joining puffs until required width is reached. Make up the number of strips you need for your specific item. With right sides of strips facing, seam them together, allowing a ¼" seam. With wrong sides facing, lay puff quilting centrally on your lining and edging fabric. Our edgings varied in width, but for a narrow ¾" edging, you'll need to make the lining 2" larger than quilting all round. Turn in a ⅜" hem, then fold shorter sides of the lining fabric over so it covers the raw edges of quilting (Diagram 5). Tack down and slipstitch along the line of the quilting seam. Finally fold over longer edges and finish in same way. Press edges.

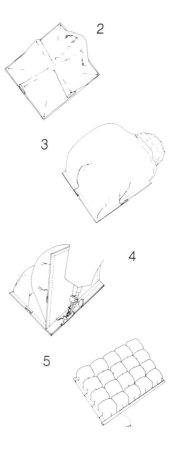

Wood stain
Tape
Steel wool
Push pins
String
Polyurethane sealer
Pencil
1" masking tape
Cardboard
Newspapers

METHOD

Preparing stencils

1. Enlarge each motif to proper size.

2. Make a separate copy of each motif on heavy paper. Mark a 1" border for each motif, and indicate guidelines and registration marks. Color key each copy and save copies for future use as your master templates in making duplicate stencils. Using tracing paper, trace all shapes to be stenciled in color "A" onto one sheet, all shapes to be stenciled in color "B" onto another sheet, etc.

3. Make a color separation as just described for each motif. Include guidelines and registration marks on each copy.

4. Cut a piece of 6 mil. thick acetate the size of the area bounded by the border of each motif template and copy registration marks onto acetate. Tape each template over its piece of acetate.

5. Place a piece of scrap acetate over a pane of glass and practice cutting sample designs out of the acetate until you can control the path of the blade well enough to follow a traced line. Score completely through tracing paper and acetate, using a small craft knife with a replaceable, sharply pointed blade.

6. Carefully cut along the traced outlines of each shape,

(Continued on page 173.)

WOOD STAIN STENCIL

The beauty of this wood-stain stenciled floor is rivaled only by the hand-fashioned wood inlays found in fine antique furniture. The stencil design was inspired by the delicate blossoms and foliage in the floral wallcovering. The dark central field is diagonally divided by delicate bamboo stems and leaves with a small bloom at each intersection. The contrasting light border area shows more of the original floor color and repeats the floral patterns, using dark stain as the stencil color. Congratulations are definitely in order for the young couple remodeling this older kitchen with such imagination. The patterns are given in the Pattern section, page 172.

MATERIALS
1" graph paper
Heavy brown paper
6 mil. thick acetate
Piece of window glass
Small craft knife with extra blades
Tracing paper
Mineral spirits

TWO BRAIDED RUGS

The braided rugs shown at right were constructed at little or no cost by using various colored polyester double knit sewing scraps. All the features (durability, resistance to fading, quick drying), so appreciated in polyester double knit garments are equally valuable when used for a rug that receives a lot of hard wear. These braided round rugs are both approximately 4 feet in diameter and each requires from 7 to 8 yards of polyester double knit fabric to construct. See the Portfolio of Rug Techniques for complete instructions for Braiding.

Notice the difference in color plans between the two rugs. The one in the top photograph has a tweedy, overall random pattern. The one in the lower photograph has definite rings of bold color. If you like a less eclectic use of color, plan your rug colors in advance and save or purchase fabric in shades of one color to produce a monochromatic rug.

MATERIALS

1. Heavy weight stencil paper, one sheet for each color used in the design. Each sheet should be at least 3" larger on all sides to allow for over-spraying and to prevent tearing.
2. Paint:
Epoxy paint—for concrete floors
Enamel paint—for wood floors
(These can be either spray paints or liquid paints applied with a stiff brush.)
3. Mat knife for cutting stencil.

METHOD

1. When considering a stencil design, remember that every area of color is separated by a band of non-color. Keep this in mind and you can adopt any design to work as a stencil.
2. Draw the selected design full scale on tracing paper. Color in or color key each section of the design. Use this colored design as a guide when you begin painting the floor. Make registration marks on the design, then the stencil.
3. Place the tracing paper over one sheet of stencil paper and trace around all areas of one color. Repeat this step for each individual color. You will then have a separate stencil for each color.

PAINTED FLOORS

Painting will quickly and inexpensively camouflage cracked and marred cement floors and drab, worn-out linoleum flooring. The Tole-style painted floor, shown above, enhances the early-American style furnishings and bears handsomely the heavy traffic a large family creates. The design itself covers the blemishes and seams of the cement floor. This three-color design can be retouched indefinitely, because the owner chose spray-paint colors normally used for retouching major appliances. See page 175 for pattern.

4. Use a sharp mat knife and cut out those areas to be stenciled.

5. The floor should be clean and completely dry before painting begins.

6. Lay stencil in the desired area and lightly mark the floor with a pencil at the proper registration marks.

7. Begin painting in a corner and work your way across the floor using only one color at a time. Allow sufficient time for this colored area to dry completely before applying the next color.

Note: If you are using spray paints, be especially careful of overspraying, thus marring areas to be left unpainted. You may choose to mask, with newspaper, the outer edges of your stencils to prevent this accident from occuring. Keep each stencil as flat as possible to prevent paint from flowing under the stencil paper.

8. When each color section is completely dry, the floor is ready to use. You may choose to protect the painted floor with varnish or a coat of polymer.

RAMBLING ROSE

You'll have to look very closely at the Rambling Rose kitchen floor, shown at right, to realize that the brick pattern is really a sponge stencil repeated to simulate bricks. The two different-sized roses were inspired by the rose blooms in the wallpaper, and placed at

random spots over the brick pattern. Painting was the perfect solution to this problem kitchen floor in a rented apartment, as it required very little investment of money and not too much labor. The biggest investment was time, and that was in the waiting periods between each application of paint so that it would dry thoroughly.

MATERIALS
Printing sponge
Mineral spirits or wax stripper
Tack cloth
Heavy floor sanding paper
Oil-base enamel primer-sealer
2½" china bristle brush
Tight-space roller
Roller pan
Light green high-gloss enamel
Polyurethane finish coat
Chalk
String
Large cardboard square
Newspaper
Masking tape
Red spray paint
Dark green spray paint

METHOD
The patterns for the Roses are given in the Patterns section, page 175.
1. Clean floor thoroughly with mineral spirits or commercial-strength wax stripper to remove all dirt and oily stains. Allow to dry overnight.
2. Sand with heavy floor paper to rough up the surface so the paint will adhere. Sweep, vaccum and wipe with a tack cloth.
3. Thin oil-base enamel primer-sealer with mineral spirits if necessary, and apply a base coat to floor. "Cut in" next to base boards and appliances with a 2½" china bristle brush. Use a low-nap, tight-space (cigar) roller to paint the rest of the floor. Allow to dry 24 hours or longer. Clean brush, roller and roller pan thoroughly.
4. Apply an even background coat of light green high-gloss paint, using a brush and roller. Clean tools and allow to dry overnight.
5. Divide your floor space into quadrants, as described on page 133 (marking guidelines on the stenciling surface). Mark by snapping a chalkline primed with white chalk along the guidelines. Make a cardboard template the size of a square containing 8 adjacent bricks plus their mortar lines. Use this template to mark large squares along the guidelines in all directions until you have filled the floor with a grid pattern.
6. Moisten your "printing sponge" in water and squeeze out excess. Trim sponge edges with a mat knife if necessary to fit within template. Pour medium green high gloss enamel into roller tray, dip sponge in paint, pounce off extra paint on pad of newspaper. Carefully print "bricks" in their proper positions within the template outline. Wrap sponge in plastic wrap when finished. Clean roller pan. Leave "half-bricks" at edges and around appliances until the following day. Allow to dry overnight.
Note: At first you may wish to use additional markings to "register" the bricks but with practice you will be able to judge their proper location. Try to achieve some variety in your prints. Slight irregularities will add charm to the finished floor.
7. Print half-bricks by masking unmarked portions with news-paper or masking tape. Discard sponge when all units are printed. Clean roller pan. Let dry overnight. While you are waiting, cut rose stencils and stencil masks. Select and try out spray colors for roses and leaves. Spray back of stencil with spray adhesive and let dry. Use this to affix stencil to floor so that it can resist "underspray." Cut an 18" wide newspaper mask to go around the stencil to protect surrounding floor area from overspray.
8. When floor is dry, selectively mask and spray stems, leaves and blossoms of rose stencils. Place roses in random positions around the floor, changing size and orientation of the stencils to achieve variety. Allow to dry overnight or 24 hours.
Note: If a mistake is made, blot paint with dry toweling, then blot remaining stains with paper towels moistened with mineral spirits. Leave overspray until after all the enamel paint has dried, then rub off or remove with solvent.
9. Using a tight-space or cigar roller, apply a good, even coat of high-gloss polyurethane to the floor. Select a polyurethane that will "age" to a yellow or green tint, which will complement the green floor. Your local paint supplier will assist you with this selection. Allow to cure 24 hours before walking on the floor.
10. When polyurethane begins to show wear, lightly sand glossy areas and apply a second coat.

**PATTERNS FOR
THE PROJECTS**

Pattern for Poppy, page 130

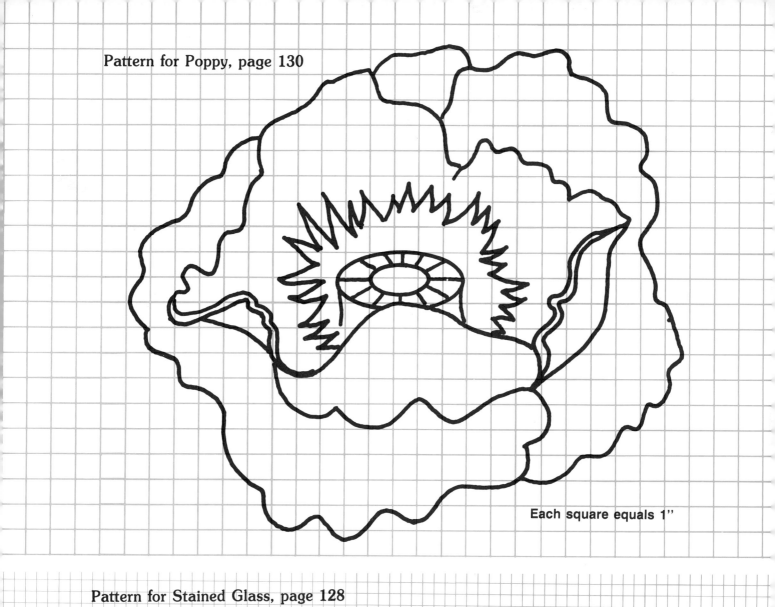

Each square equals 1"

Pattern for Stained Glass, page 128

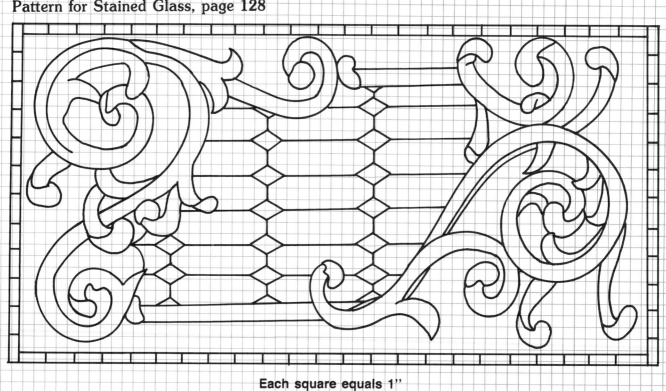

Each square equals 1"

Each square equals 1"

Graph for Persian Fantasy

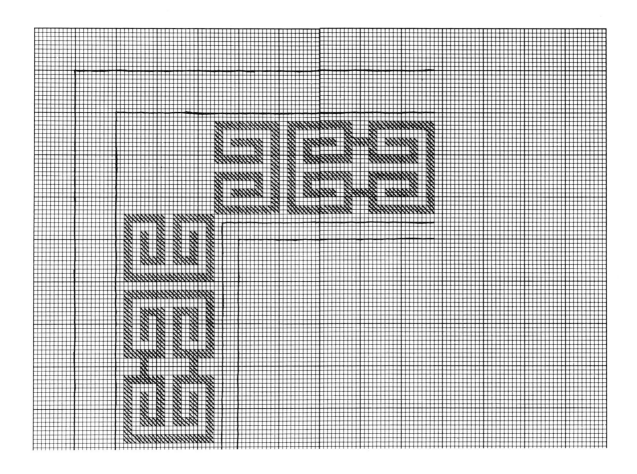

Graph for Floral Mosaic

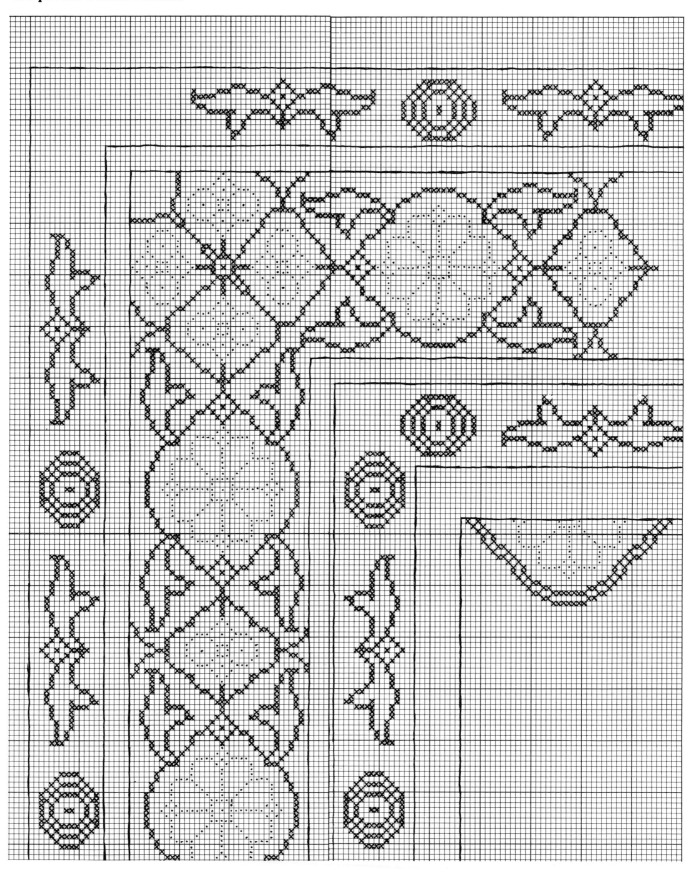

ZINNIA
GIANT DOUBLE
39¢
NET WT.
600 mg

NORTHRUP KING SEEDS

MINNEAPOLIS, MINN. 55413 - FRESNO, CALIF. 93776

BEANS, GARDEN
Tennessee Green Pod
FERRY-MORSE SEEDS
NET WT. 1.5 OZ.

TOMATO
HYBRID
BURPEE'S BIG BOY®
59¢
NET WT.
106 MG

FERRY-MORSE SEEDS

MORNING GLORY
HEAVENLY BLUE
NET WT. 1.50 G
45¢

AMERICAN SEED CO.
LANCASTER, PA. 17604

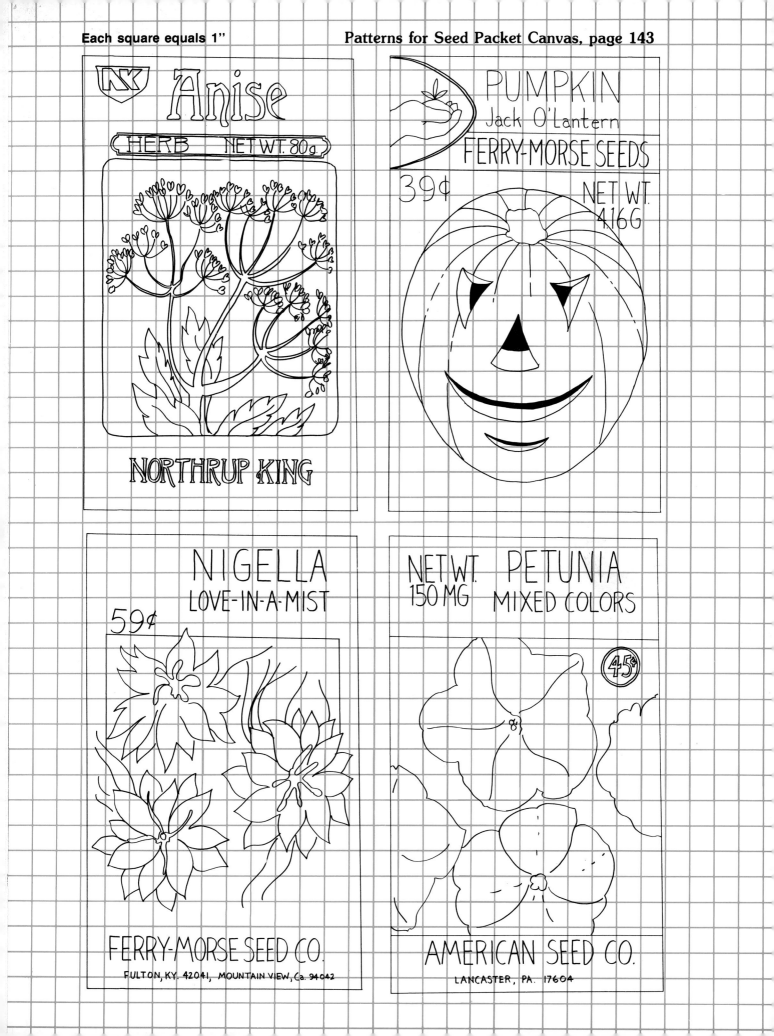

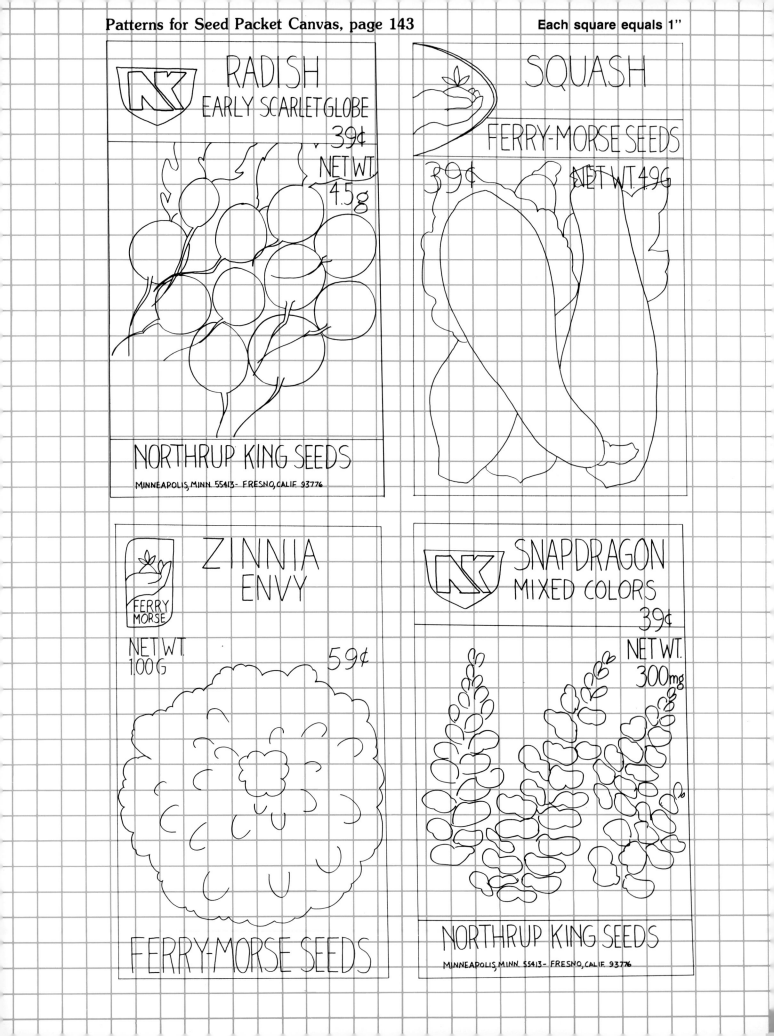

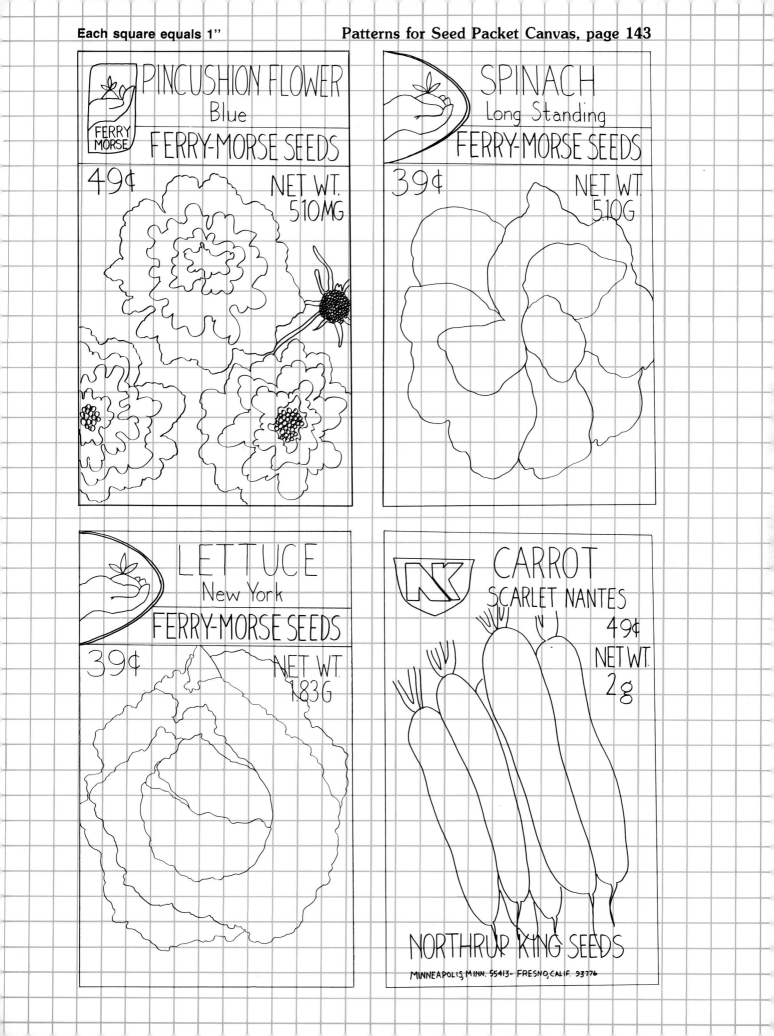

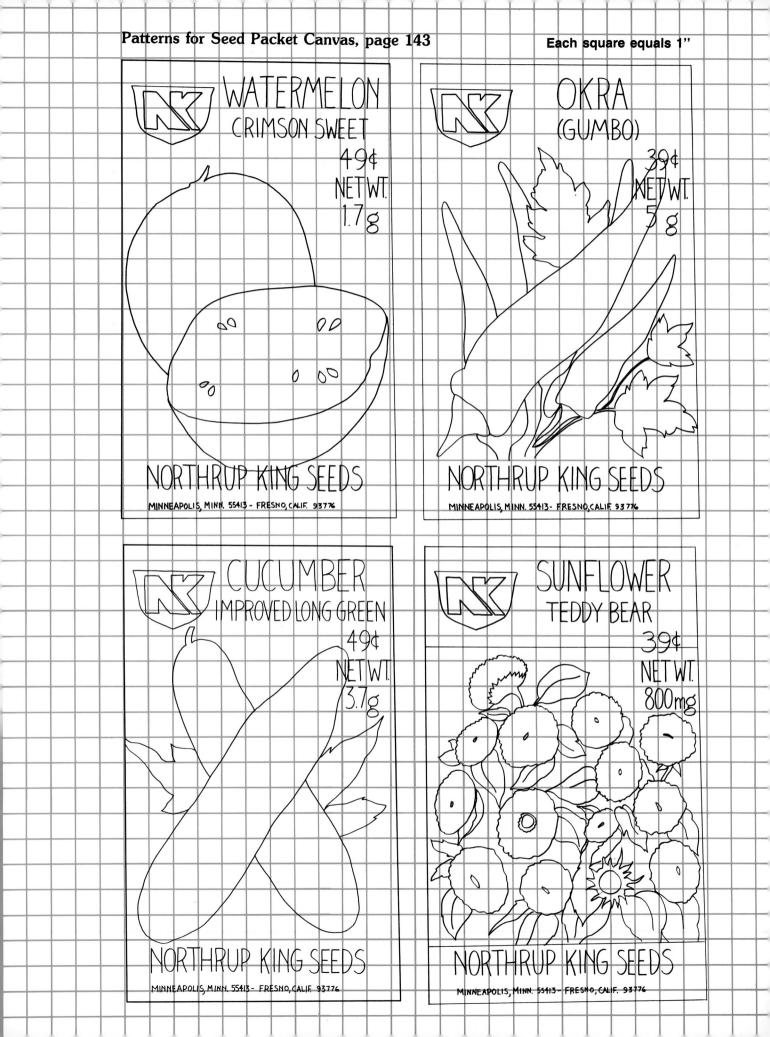

maining brown paper square, with its holes, will serve as a giant template to assure correct pattern placement.

2. Clean and iron your canvas, if necessary.

3. Fold hems on canvas to wrong side and bond in place with strips of fabric adhesive. If canvas must be painted a background color, or sealed with a clear finish, do this now (two coats of acrylic polymer medium will retain the look of a natural canvas background).

4. Protect the floor with a plastic dropcloth, and anchor the edge of the canvas to the floor with push pins.

5. Stretch a string between two diagonally opposite corners of the canvas, anchoring the string with push pins inserted into the floor just beyond the canvas. Mark the remaining pair of corners in the same way. Now locate the midpoint on each edge of the canvas, and stretch a string between each pair of opposite points.

6. Select appliqué fabrics, and lightly coat the back side of each fabric with spray adhesive. Gently position the heat-sensitive fabric-bonding web over the adhesive-coated side of the fabric. Do not bond. The applique shapes can now be traced onto the fabric and the bonding agent at the same time, using marking templates and a chalk pencil.

Note: Flop pattern pieces to get right and left leaves and buds.

When all pieces are marked, cut them out carefully, using sharp scissors.

7. Place your brown paper template in position on one corner of the canvas, making sure the diagonally stretched string is passed directly under the two registration holes, and that the bottom of the basket is the correct distance from the corner point. Place appliqué piece in position according to template and anchor by iron-basting directly to the canvas at a point near the center of each appliqué piece.

8. Carefully remove brown paper template. Permanently bond appliqué pieces in place, following manufacturer's directions for temperature setting on iron. Experiment with scrap fabric on a scrap of canvas. When a satisfactory permanent bond is achieved write down the exact setting from your iron.

9. Apply appliqué pieces to remaining three corners.

10. With an artist's brush, carefully paint appliqué pieces only with one coat of clear acrylic polymer sealer. Let dry overnight.

11. With a brush or tight-space roller, coat entire floor cloth with an even coat of high gloss polyurethane. Allow to dry 24 hours.

Note: Although the top of the layer of polyurethane will "skin over" quickly and feel quite dry, the bottom of the layer may cure much more slowly. Only when cured is the poly-

urethane fully abrasion resistant, and until fully cured, the bottom of the layer may not be tightly bonded to the surface to which it was applied. Once fully cured, the tougher, high-gloss finish provides a poor surface upon which to apply a second layer. To achieve a clear surface of optimum strength and durability, it is therefore best to allow an interval of a week or more between successive coats, lightly sanding the first coat to improve bonding before applying the second coat. It is also possible to wait until the first coat begins to show signs of wear before sanding and applying the second coat.

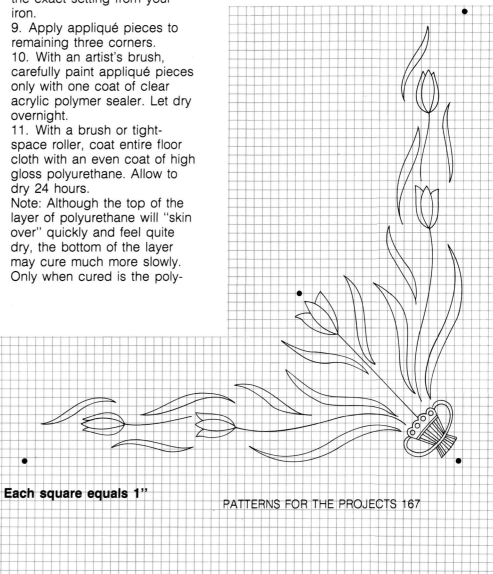

Each square equals 1"

Diagram for Deerskin and Latch Hook Rug, page 168

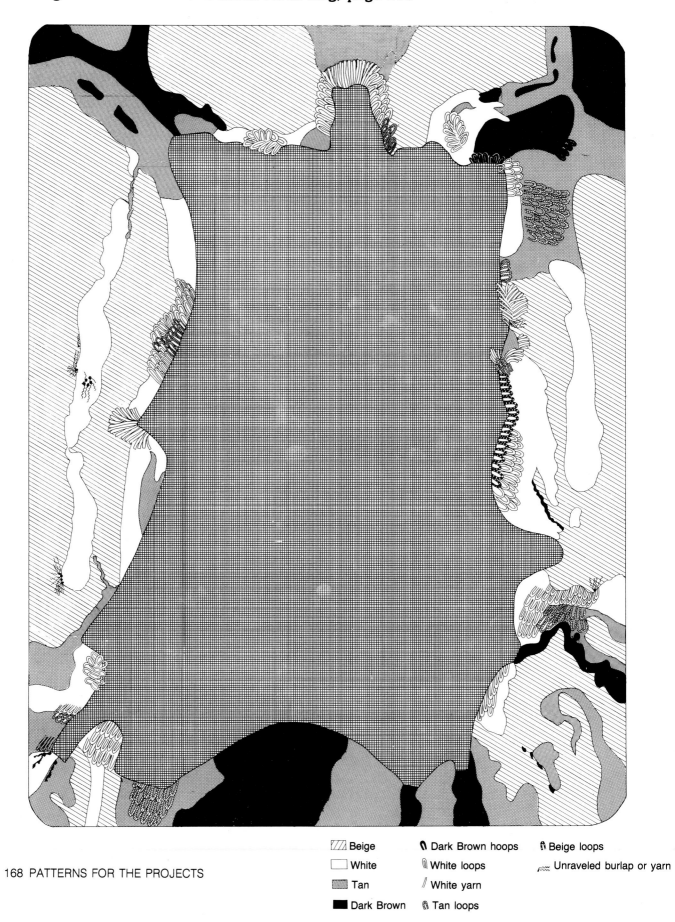

Beige

White

Tan

Dark Brown

Dark Brown hoops

White loops

White yarn

Tan loops

Beige loops

Unraveled burlap or yarn

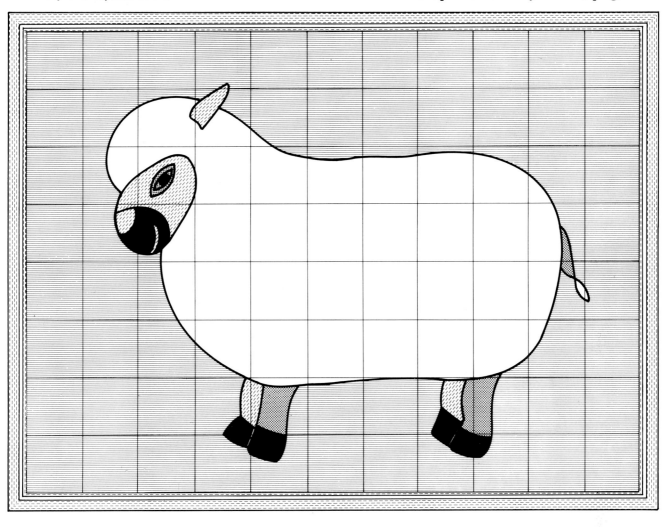

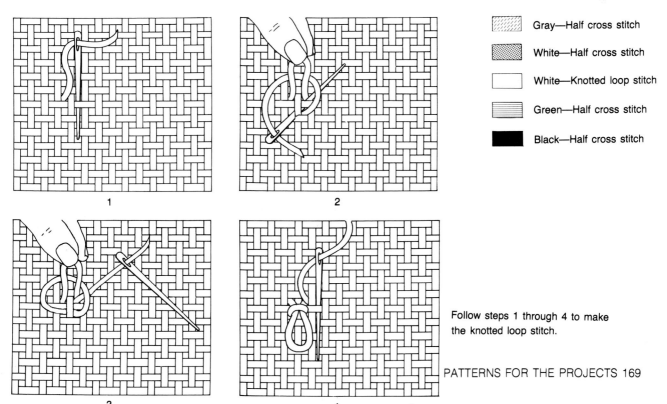

Gray—Half cross stitch

White—Half cross stitch

White—Knotted loop stitch

Green—Half cross stitch

Black—Half cross stitch

1

2

3

4

Follow steps 1 through 4 to make
the knotted loop stitch.

Charts for Calico Bouquet, page 139:

Note: Examine cover photograph carefully if you want to copy our rug exactly. Bouquets may be placed in triangles and diamonds as you desire. We elected to alternate brown-and-white and red-and-white large baskets on either side of the center. The small baskets in the center diamonds are all blue-and-white and the ones in the outer triangles are all green-and-white. Because there are four different bouquets in each of the baskets, infinite variety can be achieved. You may make the rug as large as you wish by adding rows of diamonds and triangles. The diamonds are exactly twice the size of the triangles. Size of canvas and yarn selection will determine the finished size of your rug.

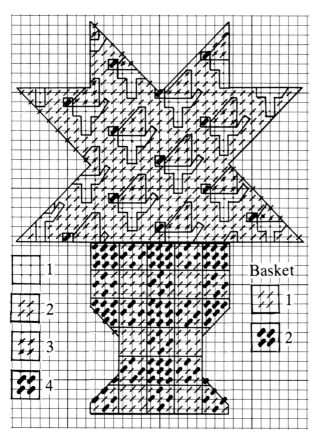

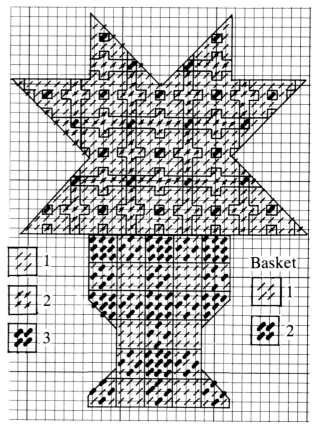

Color scheme A
1. light green wool
2. brown wool
3. white pearl cotton
4. black pearl cotton
Basket—1. white 2. green

Color scheme B
1. light green wool
2. brown wool
3. dark rose wool
4. black pearl cotton
Basket—1. white 2. green

Color scheme C
Top bouquet (rose)
1. light green wool
2. bright yellow pearl cotton
3. pale lilac wool
4. black pearl cotton
Basket—1. white 2. blue

Color scheme D
1. light green wool
2. bright yellow pearl cotton
3. deep coral wool
4. black pearl cotton
Basket—1. white 2. blue

Color scheme A
1. gray blue wool
2. brown wool
3. black pearl cotton
Basket—1. white 2. green

Color scheme C
1. bright yellow pearl cotton
2. brown wool
3. black pearl cotton
Basket—1. white 2. green

Color scheme B
1. deep coral wool
2. bright yellow pearl cotton
3. black pearl cotton
Basket—1. white 2. blue

Color scheme D
1. orange pearl cotton
2. bright yellow pearl cotton
3. black pearl cotton
Basket—1. white 2. blue

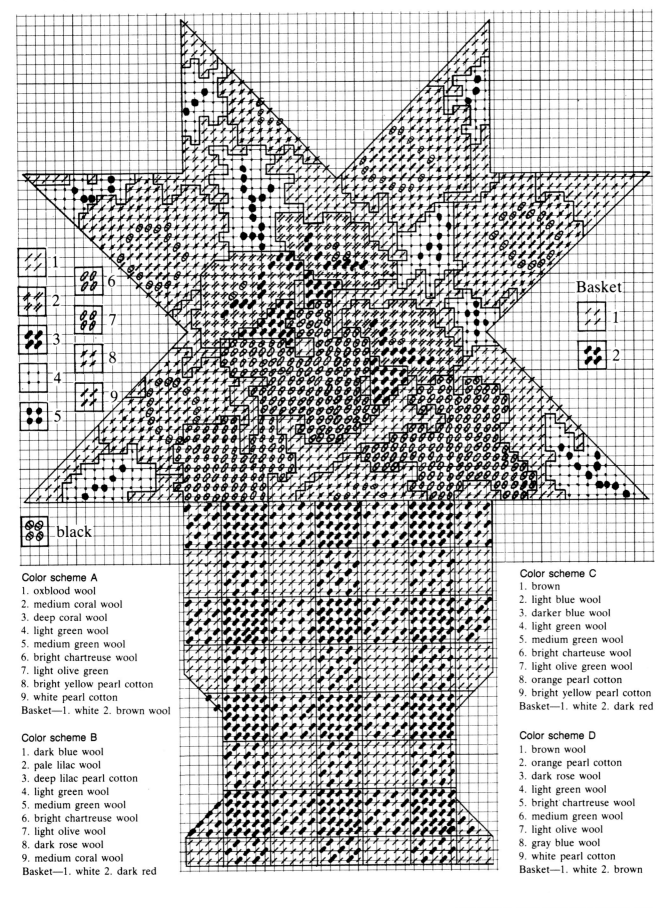

1

6

2

7

3

8

4

9

5

Basket

1

2

black

Color scheme A
1. oxblood wool
2. medium coral wool
3. deep coral wool
4. light green wool
5. medium green wool
6. bright chartreuse wool
7. light olive green
8. bright yellow pearl cotton
9. white pearl cotton
Basket—1. white 2. brown wool

Color scheme B
1. dark blue wool
2. pale lilac wool
3. deep lilac pearl cotton
4. light green wool
5. medium green wool
6. bright chartreuse wool
7. light olive wool
8. dark rose wool
9. medium coral wool
Basket—1. white 2. dark red

Color scheme C
1. brown
2. light blue wool
3. darker blue wool
4. light green wool
5. medium green wool
6. bright chartreuse wool
7. light olive green wool
8. orange pearl cotton
9. bright yellow pearl cotton
Basket—1. white 2. dark red

Color scheme D
1. brown wool
2. orange pearl cotton
3. dark rose wool
4. light green wool
5. bright chartreuse wool
6. medium green wool
7. light olive wool
8. gray blue wool
9. white pearl cotton
Basket—1. white 2. brown

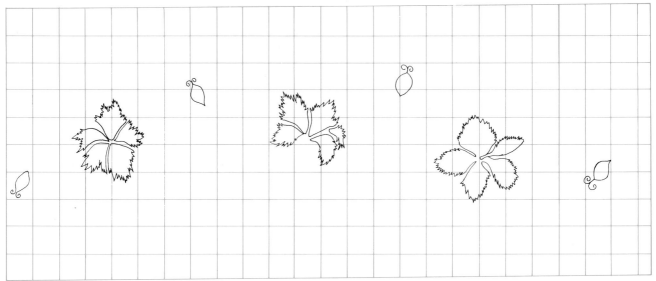

Border: Blossom stencil

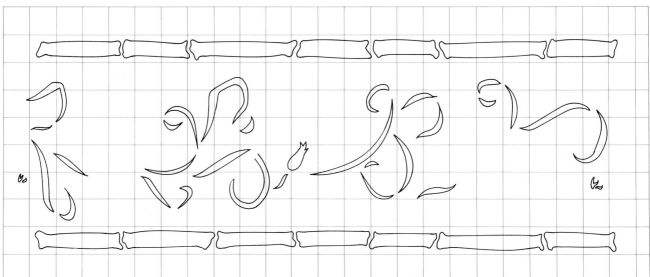

Border: Leaf and Stem stencil

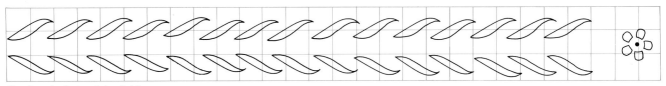

Bamboo leaf stencil for field

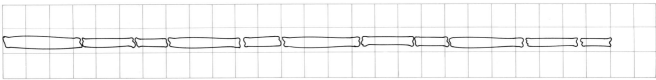

Bamboo stem stencil for field

and gently lift out and discard the pieces of tracing paper and acetate as you cut them free.

7. Sheets of acetate and prepared stencil motifs should be stored lying flat to prevent warping and curling.

Preparing floor surface and testing stencils

1. Have floor professionally sanded, then sweep and vaccum surface.

2. Test stencils and stenciling process in an inconspicuous area, such as the floor beneath the stove, or test on a separate piece of wood, similar in quality and finish to the floor.

3. If using an airbursh, strain stain through a piece of nylon hose to remove refuse. Fill the airbrush with stain, mixed with mineral spirits in a ratio of 5 to 1. Tape stencil in place to secure it, and mask the area around the stencil with newspaper to protect from overspray.

4. Hold the airbursh nozzle directly above the stencil and

spray downward at a right angle to the stencil. Begin by discharging the first burst of spray onto the newspaper mask, then move on to the open areas of the stencil, applying a light coat of stain to the entire area, then building up depth of color with repeated light applications of stain. This procedure should minimize the problem of stain being forced under the stencil. Test each color of stain and allow to dry.

5. Inspect stain samples for signs of color bleeding outside the crisp outline of the stenciled motif. If bleeding occurs, stain has been loaded on too quickly, or the wood is too porous, and should receive a second buffing with steel wool to produce a less absorbent surface, or should be partially sealed with thinned shellac.

6. Clean airbrush with mineral spirits, and reload with polyurethane sealer, which has been strained and mixed with mineral spirits in a ratio of 3 to 1.

7. Spray stencil with polyurethane, and allow wood to dry overnight. Brush on stain and wipe off excess to test resist. If the wood underneath the polyurethane has taken the stain, then additional layers of polyurethane are needed to resist the color. Evaluate the effect of polyurethane on color of stained areas.

8. Carefully clean stencils with mineral spirits after each use, and whenever a buildup of color seriously diminishes transparency. Allow to dry thoroughly before re-using.

9. As soon as you get a satisfactory result with the stain, proceed to lay out guidelines for stenciling the floor.

Laying out guidelines for stenciling

1. Place the upper edge of the bamboo border stencil against the shoe molding along the wall and mark a light pencil dot on the floor at the end opposite the wall, marking a dot every 18", until you have circled the room. An imaginary line connecting this series of dots will form the imaginary border line for the inside edge of the "leaves and flowers" stencil motif. Place 1" wide masking tape against this line and within the border area, following the procedure indicated in False Rugs.

2. Locate the position of the "flowers" spot stencil of the inside filling pattern. Cut a cardboard template 1" x 26" long. Divide your space into quadrants as indicated in "marking guidelines" in False Rugs. With push pins and strings mark additional lines, 26" apart and parallel to the two lines dividing the original quadrants using push pins every 26" in each direction.

3. Place a light pencil dot at each intersection of two strings.

4. Locate position of flower filling "motif." You will stencil a flower over odd numbered dots on odd numbered rows, and over even numbered dots on even numbered rows.

Stenciling Filling Pattern

1. Fill airbursh with polyurethane, and test spray on paper. Take care to avoid spilling polyurethane on floor by accident, and use as much masking as necessary to prevent any possibility of overspray. Such mistakes will not be visible until stain is applied. (By this time, polyurethane will be completely dry, and no solvent will successfully remove it.) If polyurethane is spilled

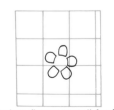

Bamboo flower stencil for field

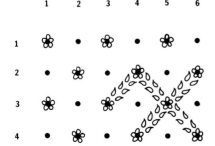

How to place flower centers

and you can remove it while wet, gently blot with a dry paper towel, then blot with a paper towel moistened in mineral spirits. Now flush the area with mineral spirits to remove any traces.

2. Stencil all flower spot motifs. Note: Pencil marks are made very lightly, and are not normally to be erased when working over a bare or lightly sealed surface which will later be stained; erasing may affect penetration of stain and produce spots on the finished floor.

3. When all flower spot motifs are sprayed and dry, align "stem and leaf" stencil so it connects two flower centers on the diagonal. Spray, then connect two more centers, and spray them. Continue until all centers are connected and "stem and leaf" motif outlines diagonally oriented "squares." As you approach the masking tape, shield all areas outside the taped border with newspaper before spraying. Spray up to, but not beyond, the taped line. Allow polyurethane to dry overnight.

4. Sweep and vacuum entire floor. Brush on stain, completing one "square" at a time and wiping off excess before proceeding to next square. Apply stain up to, but not beyond, the taped line.

5. Let dry overnight. Sweep, vaccum, and brush on a coat of polyurethane which has been thinned with mineral spirits in a ratio of 3 to 1. Let dry completely.

Stenciling border pattern

1. Carefully mask the working area with a drop cloth and place newspaper under stenciling supplies. Refer to "Borders" section in "order of work" for order of stenciling motifs. Position the upper edge of the Bamboo border stencil directly against the wall. Lightly tape in position or have partner secure stencil while you spray. Apply stain to open areas until desired depth of color has been achieved. Remove stencil and allow motif to dry to the touch.

2. Position second repeat directly to the right of the first, if possible, aligning the ends of the bamboo borders and allowing a small space between them equal to the small space between bamboo units within the motif. Stencil should be roughly parallel to imaginary border line. Continue spraying adjacent units until you approach a corner.

3. Mask off any portions of the design which will not be needed to turn the corner, by sliding newspaper under unwanted portions. Pay attention to the way in which the bamboo borders will meet at the corners, and to how the "flowers" will turn the corner once they are stenciled.

4. Once you have turned the corner, continue stenciling adjacent repeats as before.

5. Once you have completed the "leaf" portion of the border, clean stencil and airbrush, then position "flower stencil over "leaf" repeat, using registration marks. Change stain colors, and spray all "flower" repeats.

6. Allow stain colors to dry overnight. Sweep and vacuum floor surface to remove debris, and thin polyurethane with mineral spirits 3 to 1.

7. Remove taped border and coat entire area between imaginary borderline and wall with polyurethane, thinned with 25% mineral spirits and allow to dry thoroughly.

Crocheted Water Lily, continued from page 135

Edge—over chain of willow green—sc around (3 sc in each top sc) with radiant rose. End off.

Buds—Make 2

With green (one in dark green and one in willow green) ch 31, 30 sc in chain. End off green—join canary yellow.
row 1—ch 1, 3 sc in top sc of stem.
row 2—ch 1, 2 sc in each sc.
row 3—ch 1, sc, 2 sc together—sc in nest 3 sc, 2 sc together 1 sc.
row 5—ch 1. sc, 2 sc together sc in next 7 sc, 2 sc together 1 sc.
row 6—ch 1, 13 sc across.
row 7—ch 1, sc, 2 sc together, sc in next 9 sc, 2 sc together 1 sc.
rows 8 to 14—15 sc across.
row 15—End off canary yellow—join radiant rose ch 1, skip first and next to last sc, sc across—decrease 2 sc.
row 16—repeat row 15.
row 17 and 18—ch 1, 11 sc across.
row 19—ch 1, skip first and last sc, 9 sc across.
row 20—ch 1, 9 sc across.
rows 21-28—Repeat rows 19 and 20 until 1 st left. End off.
Edge of buds
(On dark green—work with dark green and on willow green work with willow green)—work sc around each bud and stem—over chain. with 2 sc in each top and bottom sts.

Veins—Holding thread underneath—chains—(as in flower—pulling loops from back to front as working) make rows from center of leaf to last DC row—chain loosely.

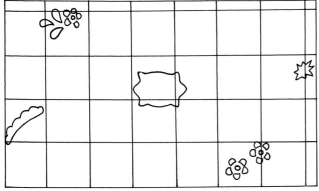

Red stencil

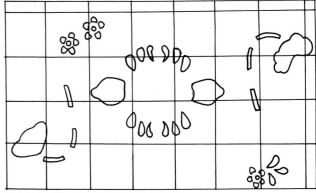

Gold stencil

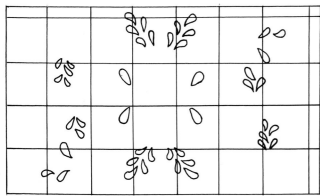

Brown stencil

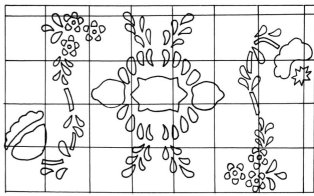

Complete design

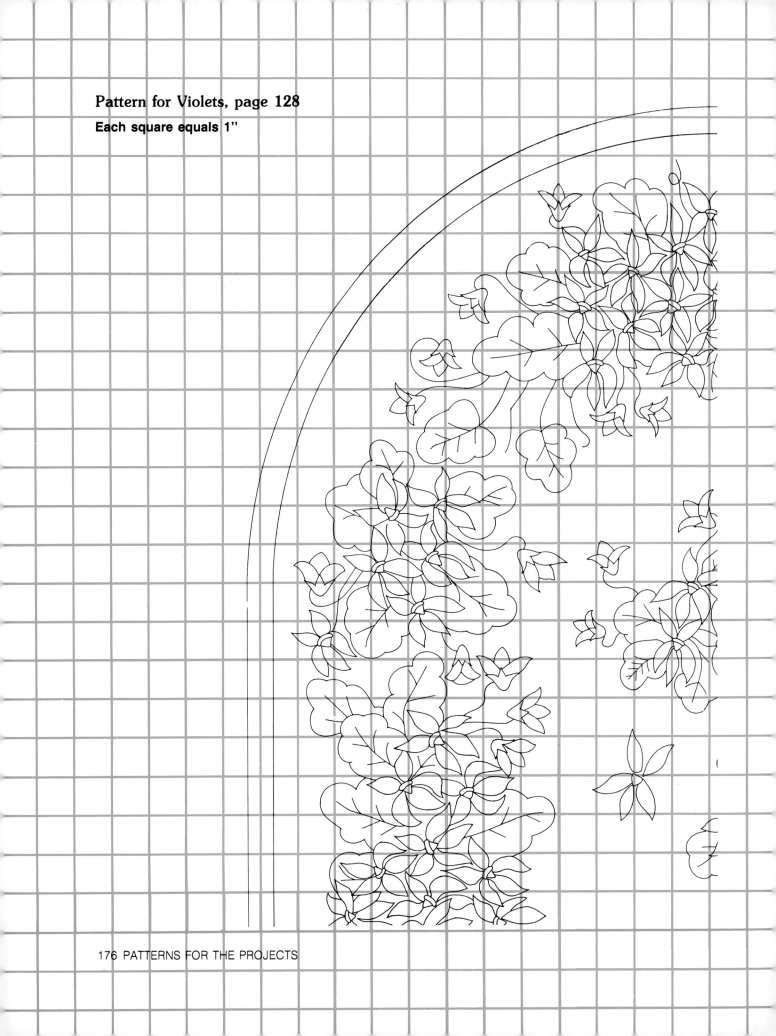

Pattern for Violets, page 128

Each square equals 1"

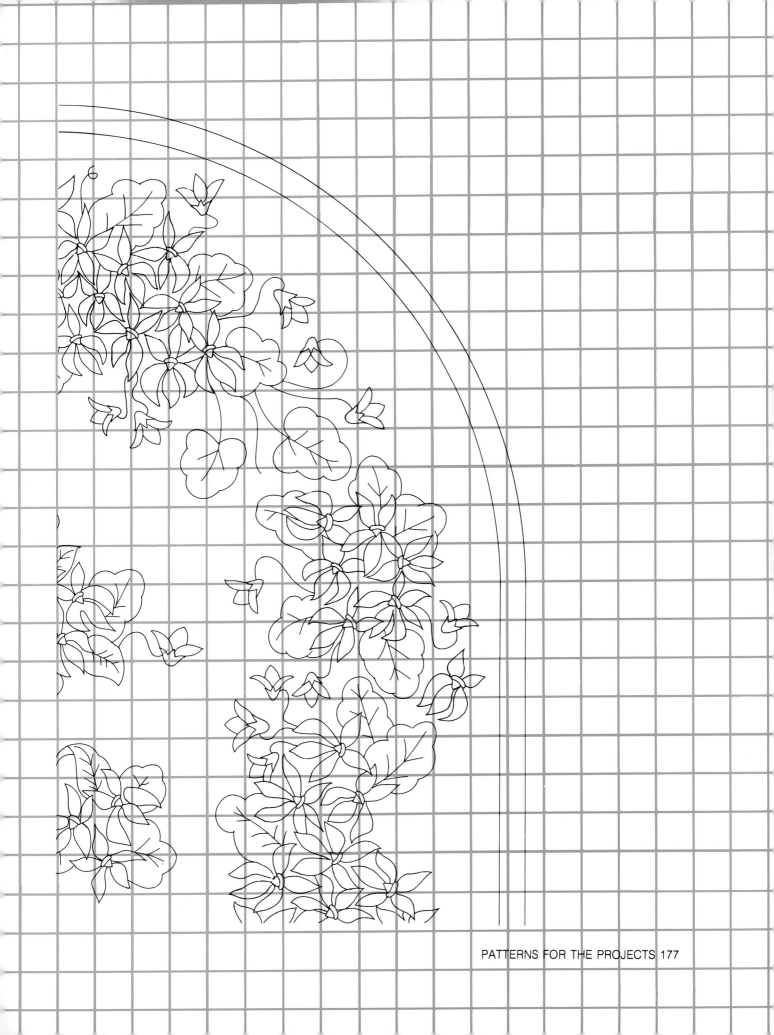

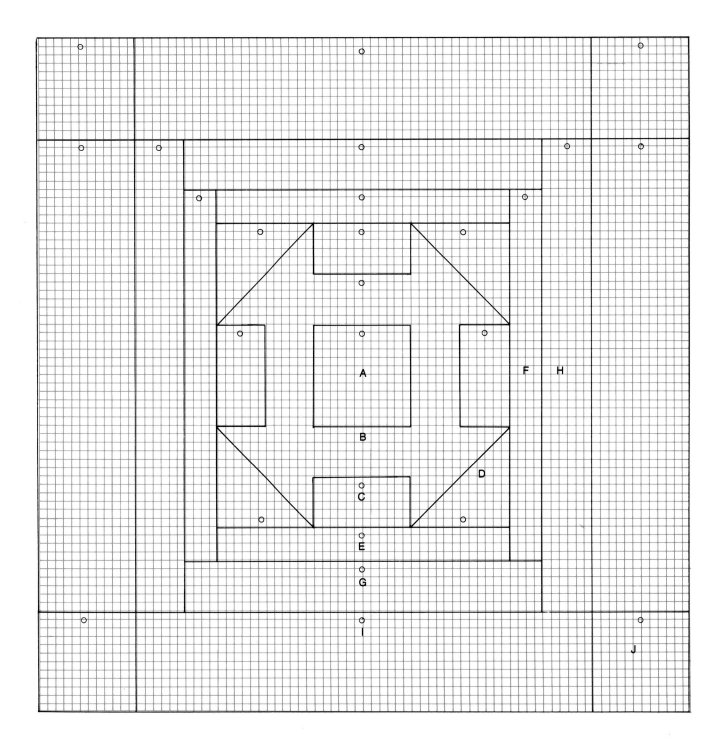

APPENDIX

Afgan Stitch

Afghan hooks are a variation of the standard crochet hook. They look something like a combination crochet hook and knitting needle. Afghan hooks come in lengths from 9 to 14 inches and have straight, uniform shafts, with a cap or knob at one end and the traditional hook at the other. They are available in numbered sizes from No. 1 to No. 10, and lettered sizes from Size F to Size K.

Make a foundation chain of the desired number of stitches.

Row One, First Half: Insert the hook under the top strand of the second chain from the hook, wrap the yarn over the hook and draw hook and yarn through the chain stitch. There will now be two loops on the hook (Figure 1). Repeat the

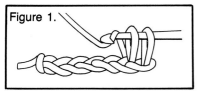
Figure 1.

procedure in the top strand of each chain stitch, keeping on the hook each loop that you draw up. At the end of the row you will have the same number of loops on the hook as there were stitches in the foundation chain (Figure 2). Do not turn the work.

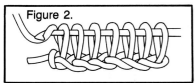
Figure 2.

Row One, Second Half: Wrap the yarn over the hook and draw hook and yarn through the first loop on the hook. Then wrap the yarn over the hook and draw hook and yarn through the next two loops on the hook (Figure 3).

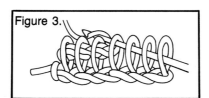
Figure 3.

Continue wrapping the yarn over the hook and drawing both hook and yarn through two loops on the hook until you have worked all the stitches off the hook except for the last one.

Row Two, First Half: Keeping all loops that you pick up on the hook as you work across the row, insert the hook from right to left under the second vertical bar of the row just worked (Figure 4). Wrap

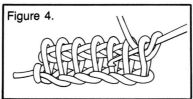
Figure 4.

the yarn over the hook and draw a loop through. Repeat to draw a loop through under each vertical bar in the row until you reach the last vertical bar.

Row Two, Second Half: Work the loops off the hook as in the second half of Row One.

Continue the pattern by repeating Row Two as many times as desired. If you wish the top edge to be very firm, after working the last row of stitches off the hook, make a slip stitch in each vertical bar across the row.

INCREASING AFGHAN STITCH. This is always done on the first half of a row. Insert the hook under the top strand of a chain stitch between two vertical bars, wrap the yarn over the hook and draw a loop through. Then insert the hook under the next vertical bar and draw a loop through in the usual way (Figure 6).

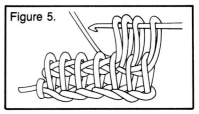
Figure 5.

DECREASING AFGHAN STITCH. Always decrease on the first half of a row. Insert the hook under two vertical bars, wrap the yarn over the hook and draw a loop through (Figure 7).

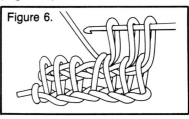
Figure 6.

Modified Loop Soumak Stitch
(from page 141)

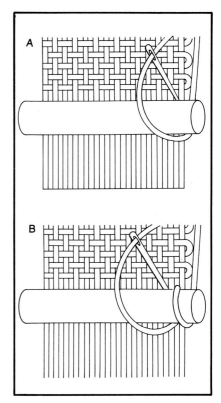

Enlarging Patterns

It is seldom that you find a pattern that is exactly the size you need. Do not let this inhibit your creativity; enlarging or reducing a pattern is quite simple.

The very easiest way to size up a pattern is to have it photostatically enlarged. Simply instruct the photostat company as to what size you want the pattern pieces to be. The cost will vary and this service is usually found only in larger towns and cities.

You can easily enlarge or reduce a pattern yourself by using ¼" (6mm) graph paper. You should be able to tell in advance whether or not the piece you want to enlarge will fit on one sheet of paper, or whether you must tape several pieces together to get the area you need.

First trace the design you wish to enlarge onto graph paper. If the design is to be twice as large, use two blocks for every one block on the original. Copy carefully, transferring what is in each square to the larger scale. It is helpful sometimes to outline the design with a series of dots, then connect the dots using your straight edge and French curve to make the lines smooth. Study the following examples carefully.

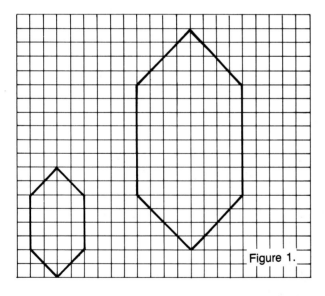
Figure 1.

In Figure 1, we want to enlarge a "church window" from a quilt pattern. The original scale is that each block equals ¼" (6mm). To make it twice as large, each space which is presently contained in one block must be stretched to two. The length of the church window from end to end is eight squares; the width is four squares. When enlarged, the length should be sixteen squares and the width

eight. Count off sixteen in length and eight in width on graph paper as shown. Draw the lengthwise and crosswise lines every two blocks to give yourself a larger scale. Draw the church window onto the new scale, transferring exactly to the larger squares what is in each of the smaller squares.

Irregular shapes are just as easily enlarged. Draw your new scale onto your graph paper, then copy exactly what is in each of the smaller squares. In Figure 2, you see how easy it is.

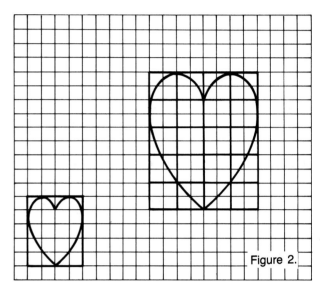
Figure 2.

A regular shape such as a diamond or a square can be enlarged by merely extending the sides with a straight edge to the desired length, as shown in Figure 3.

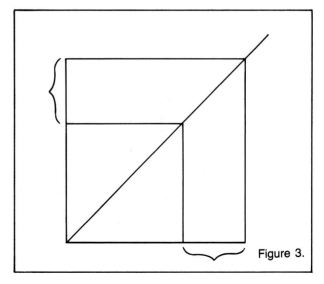
Figure 3.

Transferring Designs

Once the pattern has been enlarged to the desired size it is ready to transfer to the rug canvas or backing. On needlepoint canvas allow a 2 inch (5.1 cm) margin on all sides, then center the design beneath the canvas. Make sure that any definite vertical and horizontal lines in the design line up with the vertical and horizontal lines of the canvas; then tape the canvas over the pattern. To outline and paint the design on the canvas, use either needlepoint markers or acrylic paints. (Note: Ideally, the canvas should be painted a tint lighter than the yarn color you plan to use.) Acrylic paints allow you to mix colors in exact shades. Thin the paints to a creamy consistency with water; they will dry quickly and be waterproof.

To spread the paints without blocking the holes in the canvas, use a stiff, flat acrylic brush and a small amount of paint. If a few holes are blocked, just blow the paint out of the holes.

If you are not comfortable with paint and brush, you may find markers easier to handle. Be sure to use the waterproof markers that are specifically for needlepoint; otherwise, the ink will run when the finished needlepoint is blocked.

If your rug backing is a burlap or monks cloth fabric, you will place the enlarged design above, not beneath, the rug backing. Pin the design securely in place so that it will not shift during the transferring process. (Note: If your design is very large, you may choose to divide the pattern in quadrants and transfer each section separately.) Use dark shades of dressmakers tracing paper between the burlap and enlarged pattern, and a tracing wheel to transfer all design lines. If the design is not clearly visible, remove the pattern and trace over the design lines with waterproof marking pens. (Note: Hooking, rya and latch hooking are marked on the right side of the canvas; punch hooking is marked on the wrong side of the canvas.)

STENCIL MATERIALS

	DESCRIPTION	PREPARATION	CUTTING	MARKING	DURABILITY	CLEANING	STORAGE
ACETATE	Transparent, comes in various thicknesses. Sheets or rolls .005 to .0075 gauge	If purchased from a roll, acetate will curl slightly. Place concave side down when cutting, test your pigment & its solvent to see if either softens or dissolves the film.	Ease of cutting depends on thickness. More difficult than papers. Knife tends to "track" along the cut already made instead of turning in a new direction—use knife or punch.	Place template under film, mark directly on acetate with China marker.	Strong but brittle; may crack or break if edges become bent during cleaning. May reuse indefinitely. Use adhesive cautiously-bridges may crack or break when pulling stencil up after use.	Wipe clean as needed to retain transparency for registration. Clean thoroughly between uses, or whenever you notice build-up on edges or staining of underside. Allow to dry completely before re-using.	Store flat, with heavy paper or cardboard between individual stencils.
MYLAR	(Same as acetate)	(Same as acetate)	(Same as acetate)	(Same as acetate)	(Same as acetate)	(Same as acetate)	Same
HEAVY PAPER	Any heavy paper to survive repeated use & cleaning	Before cutting, coat paper with boiled linseed oil thinned with mineral spirits or turpentine. Allow to dry. Repeat process until paper is saturated with oil mixture.	Easy to cut. Use knife, punch, or awl	Dressmaker's carbon between drawing and heavy paper. Trace outline of drawing to transfer markings to paper	Good. Not affected by polyurethane or common solvents.	Clean after using, whenever back side becomes stained, or when pigment build-up begins to distort edges of stencil.	Same
OILED STENCIL BOARD	Lightweight oiled cardboard, yellow, comes in sheets, opaque	After cutting, coat stencil with varnish or polyurethane to seal cut edges & strengthen. (Make sure your coating won't be dissolved by the solvent for the pigment you intend to use. Allow to dry.)	Fairly east to cut. Use knife, punch, or awl	Same as heavy paper	Good. Not affected by polyurethane or common solvents.	Same as heavy paper.	Same
STENCIL PAPER	.005 to .0075 gauge heavy, white, oiled paper, comes in sheets, Slightly translucent	Same as oiled stencil board.	Easy to cut. Use knife, punch, or awl	Same as heavy paper	Fair. Good where only a few repeats are required. Ease of cutting makes use of paper worthwhile even on larger projects.		Same
ARCHITECT'S LINEN	A sized water proof fabric		Use Embroidery scissors		Durable		

Suppliers of Rug Materials

Manufacturers

Belding Lily Company
Handweaving Department
P.O. Box 88
Shelby, North Carolina 28150
704-482-0641
All Yarns and Fibers, Textures,
Cotton Warps, Fillings, Linens,
Wools, Macrame & Threads.

Frederick J. Fawcett, Inc.
129 South Street
Boston, Massachusetts 02111
617-542-2370
Flax, Linen, Embroidery, Wool.
Have new samples.

Emile Bernat & Sons
Depot & Mendon Sts.
Uxbridge, Massachusetts
01569
Tabriz Rug Yarn, Craftsman
Rug Yarn

D.M.C. Corporation
107 Trumbull Street
Elizabeth, New Jersey 07206
Persian and tapestry yarns as
well as other types; embroidery threads

Bucilla
30-20 Thompson Avenue
Long Island City, New York
11101
Needlework and Weaving
Supplies

Boye Needle Company
916 Arcade
Freeport, Illinois 61032
Needlework and Weaving
Supplies

Columbia-Minerva
295 5th Avenue
New York, New York 10016
Needlework Supplies

Paragon Needlecraft
230 Fifth Avenue
New York, New York 10001
Needlework Supplies

Bartlettyarns, Inc.
Harmony, Maine 04942
207-683-2341
Rug Punch-Hooking Yarns,
Wools, Heavy 4 ply, Complete
line samples available for 50¢.

Ulltex, Inc.
P.O. Box 918
59 Demond Avenue
North Adams, Massachusetts
01247
413-664-4301
Imported Wool, Weaving
Looms.

Briggs and Little's Woolen Mill
LTD
York Mills, Harvey Station, York
Co.
N.B., Canada
506-366-5438
100% Pure Wool Yarn

William Condon and Sons
Limited Woolen Mills
P.O. Box 129
Charlottetown, P.E.I., Canada
902-894-8712
Weaving Wool, Blankets

Northern Yarns
1648 Grand Avenue
St. Paul, Minnesota 55105
612-222-7005
Mop Cotton (4 and 8 ply),
Wool, Acrylic, Cotton Carpet
Warp in Natural Color and 10
Colors. Will send samples on
request.

Scotts' Woolen Mill
Hecla Street
Uxbridge, Massachusetts
01569
617-278-6060
Wool, Linen, Llama, Alpaca,
Mohair, Novelty Yarns, Wool
Carpet Yarns, Silk and Cotton.

Yarn Loft International, Inc.
1329 Stratford Court
Del Mar, California 92014
Needlework and Weaving
Supplies

Retailers

Contessa Yarns
P.O. Box 37
Lebanon, Connecticut 06249
203-642-7630
Blends, very good special of-
ferings, Rayon, Orlon, Cotton,
Wool, novelty yarn.

Cooper-Kenworthy, Inc.
564 Eddy Street
Providence, Rhode Island
02903
401-351-6300
Good Acrylic and Wool Rug
Yarn, Mohair, Orlon, Rayon,
Odd Lots, Mink and Lambs
Wool, Cashmere, Synthetics
and Silk yarn. Send sample
and will match.

Davidson's Old Mill Yarn
109 Elizabeth Street
Eaton Rapids, Michigan 48827
517-663-2711
Mohair, Natural Wool, Chenille,
Cotton, Boucle, and New
Samples.

Fort Crailo Yarns Company
2 Green Street
Rensselaer, NY 12144
518-465-2371
Color Coordinated Wools,
Linen, Rayon, Wool, Cotton,
Rug Yarn. Samples 50¢.

Greentree Ranch Wools and
Countryside Handweavers
163 North Carter Lake Road
Loveland, Colorado 80537
303-667-6183
Spinning Supplies, Yarns,
Fibers, Looms, Accessories,
Wools, Fleece (Catalogue 25¢).

Ironstone Warehouse
P.O. Box 196
Uxbridge, Massachusetts
01569
617-278-6092
Wools, Cotton, Dyed yarns.
144 yards to pound, 3 ply
480-single ply. English spun,
soft muted dyed colors, mixture of English and New Zea-
land Wools.

The Mannings Creative Crafts
Rural Delivery 2
East Berlin, Pennsylvania
17316
717-624-2223
Weaving Supplies, Rug Weaving, Cotton and Linen Combinations, Wool, Silk, Goats Hair,
Camel Hair, Mohair, Jute, Chenille, Samples 50¢.

North Central Wool Marketing
Corporation
101 27th Avenue, S.E.
Minneapolis, Minnesota 55414
612-331-1813, Ext. 40
Wool, Mohair, Camel, Yak,
Tops, Flax, Silk, Cotton,
Greece Fleece (raw stage).

Paternayan Brothers, Inc.
312 East 95th Street
New York, NY 10028
212-876-9600
Wool and Worsted Yarns

The Plymouth Yarn Company
P.O. Box 28, 500 Lafayette
Street
Bristol, Pennsylvania 19007
215-788-0459
Job lots, cotton, dyed wools,
and acrylics.

Robin and Russ Handweavers
533 North Adams Street
McMinnville, Oregon 97128
503-472-5760
Wools, Spun Silk, Macrame,
Odd Lots, Looms accessories.

Rumplestiltskins
710 Northwest 14th Avenue
Portland, Oregon 97209
503-222-1865
Eggbeater hooks and rug
supplies.

Straw Into Gold
5509 College Street
P.O. Box 2904
Oakland, California 94618
415-652-7746
Fibers, equipment, odd lots,
yarns, books.

Textile Crafts
P.O. Box 3216
Los Angeles, California 90028
213-660-4887
Retail company, carry all
yarns.

Village Wools
401 Romero, N.W.
Albuquerque, New Mexico
87107
505-344-3184
Retail and discounts, catalogue and sample card 75¢.

LOOMS AND LOOM ACCESSORIES

First Fibre
351 Moraine Road
Highland Park, Illinois 60035
312-432-0440
Looms, Shuttles, Reeds, Bobbins, Linen

Leclerc
Highway 9 North
P.O. Box 491
Plattsburg, NY 12901
518-561-7900
Counter-balanced looms, spin-
ning wheels, loom parts, and
weaving books.

Looms 'N Yarn
A Division of Spangle Supply
Company
3700 Brookpark Road
Wilcox Transfer Complex
Cleveland, Ohio 44134
216-398-5255
Floor and Tapestry looms and
accessories, good assortment
of yarns.

Mr. Robert Norris
52 Willowbrook Road
Stones, Connecticut
203-429-2986
Looms and Equipment

Schacht Spindle Company,
Inc.
P.O. Box 2057
Boulder, Colorado 80306
303-442-3212
Tapestry looms, Floor Looms,
Table Looms, Accessories,
rigid heddle inkle looms, weav-
ing accessories.

Tools of the Trade
RFD
Benson, Vermont 05743
802-537-3183
Looms, and accessories, Floor
and Table Looms and
Benches.

Circadian Woodworks
120 Main Street
Colusa, California 95932
916-no listing
Finely crafted maple floor
looms and four and eight harness matching benches.

Good Karma Looms
440 West Fourth
Chadron, Nebraska 69337
402-no listing

	DESCRIPTIONS	SOLVENTS	TRANS-PARENCY	BONDING CHARACTERISTICS	APPLICATION	DRYING & CURING TIME
SHELLAC	A soft, easy to sand sealer, used as underbody. Not resistant to water, alcohol, or abrasion.	Denatured alcohol	Clear, transparent orange or opaque white; highgloss, soft finish.	Used on raw wood as an underbody—most finishes will bond to it once it has been deglossed.	Brush, roller, or paint pad—(All are difficult to clean afterwards.)	Temperature and humidity effect drying time.
OIL-BASE VARNISH	Hard, transparent finish, resists water, alcohol, abrasion	Mineral spirits, turpentine, naptha, paint thinner, mineral spirits when wet-none effective when dry.	Transparent, clear to yellow brown in color, satin finish to high gloss—the higher the gloss, the tougher the varnish	Should bond to most clean, dry de-glossed, except latex. *Most finishes will bond to it once it has been de-glossed.	China bristle brush, brush, roller, paint pad	
POLYURE-THANE	Tough, transparent finish, water & alcohol resistant. Darkens the surface to which it is applied	When wet, use mineral spirits, paint thinner, or turpentine as a solvent. When dry surface cannot be altered.	Transparent, yellow to green tint with aging. Satin to high gloss—both de-glossing & pigmenting agents will make the finish less abrasion-resistant	Should bond to most clean, dry, de-glossed surfaces except latex. *Most finishes should bond to it once it has been de-glossed.	China bristle brush, brush, roller, paint pad.	Odorous when drying
ALKYD OIL ENAMELS	Opaque, tinted paints which are scrubbable, abrasion resistant.	Mineral spirits, turpentine, naptha, paint thinner	Opaque; satin to high-gloss; premixed in many colors or custom-tint with "Universal Tinting Colors" in tubes, the higher the gloss, the tougher the finish	Will bond to most clean, dry, deglossed surfaces except latex.*	China bristle brush, brush, roller or paint pad.	Odorous when drying
LATEX ENAMELS	Soft, fairly flexible, opaque finish. Resistant to water & alcohol.	Water for thinning, soapy water for cleaning.	Opaque, available in many pre-mixed colors, or custom-tint with universal tinting colors in tubes, medium hard finish. Soft-finish-protect with polyurethane or varnish.	Bonds well to any clean, dry de-glossed surface. Bonds well to latex with no surface preparation.	Polyester or nylon brush.	
PENETRATING STAINS	Oil-base stains capable of penetrating into the wood	Mineral spirits, turpentine, naptha for spray gun	Transparent, impart no sheen. Available premixed in wood tones or hues. May custom-mix these stock colors to obtain desired hue	Applied to freshly sanded or partially sealed wood. All finishes should bond to it.	Rags, brush, roller, or pads, depending on effect desired. Wipe all excess, or repeat application to control amount of color change.	24 hrs. under prime conditions—more if humid or cold
GESSO	Shiny, white primer for wood, fabric	Water to thin, soap & water to remove when wet	Opaque, glossy, white—or tint with acrylic artists colors	Bonds well to any clean, dry, de-glossed surface. Most finishes should bond well to it once it has been de-glossed	Nylon or polyester brush, roller or paint pad	
ACRYLIC POLYMER MEDIUM	Clear, flexible, medium-hard finish	Water to thin, soap & water to remove while wet-no solvent once dry	Transparent, glossy, clear (but may be tinted with acrylic artists colors)	Bonds well to any clean, dry, de-glossed surface. Most finishes should bond well to it once it has been de-glossed.	Nylon or polyester brush, roller or paint pad	
SANDING	Mechanical abrasion with sandpaper or chemical de-glossing to rough up smooth hard surface			Sanding or chemical de-glossing usually improves bonding of any hard, slick surface with a compatable finish		
WAX	Soft, finish that can be buffed to a high gloss—scratches easily, resists water. Penetrates & seals wood	Mineral spirits, wax stripper, ammonia	Transparent, shiny colorless. May dull & cloud with age & repeated coats.	Applied to base or finished wood, linoleum, etc. Must be removed from floor before other finishes are applied.		

*To de-gloss a high-gloss finish, wipe with a "Liquid Sander", or sand to roughen surface.

INDEX